THE MARKET OF VIRTUE

Law and Philosophy Library

VOLUME 60

The titles published in this series are listed at the end of this volume.

THE MARKET OF VIRTUE

Morality and Commitment in a Liberal Society

by

MICHAEL BAURMANN

University of Düsseldorf

KLUWER LAW INTERNATIONAL

THE HAGUE / LONDON / NEW YORK

A C.I.P. Catalogue record for this book is available from the Library of Congress.

ISBN 90-411-1874-8

Published by Kluwer Law International,
P.O. Box 85889, 2508 CN The Hague, The Netherlands.

Sold and distributed in North, Central and South America
by Kluwer Law International,
101 Philip Drive, Norwell, MA 02061, U.S.A.
kluwerlaw@wkap.com

In all other countries, sold and distributed
by Kluwer Law International, Distribution Centre,
P.O. Box 322, 3300 AH Dordrecht, The Netherlands.

Printed on acid-free paper

translated from the German by Ruth Zimmerling
Kluwer Law International incorporates
the imprint of Martinus Nijhoff Publishers.

Printed in the Netherlands.

For Margaret, Jan and Katjuscha

TABLE OF CONTENTS

ACKNOWLEDGMENTS

In preparing the present volume, I have accumulated large debts of gratitude. I am especially indebted to Norbert Hoerster and Hartmut Kliemt who greatly contributed to the shaping of this book and to the fundamental ideas and insights developed in the following pages. Over the years, I have engaged in innumerable fruitful discussions with them and benefited enormously from the suggestions and stimuli they offered. The present investigation is an attempt to examine one particular question, employing a theoretical programme and a way of thinking which we share. But I have benefited from them not only in their general capacities as authors and interlocutors. They also read several drafts of the text and pointed out errors, inconsistencies and weaknesses, thus enabling me to eliminate a number of mistakes and shortcomings. But, of course, they had no influence on, and therefore share no responsibility for, the final use I have made of their valuable suggestions. For the errors and misinterpretations which, I fear, remain, I alone am responsible.

I also wish to thank my friend Ernesto Garzón Valdés for his tireless encouragement and the support he gave me for the publication of the book in the *Law and Philosophy Library* of Kluwer Academic Publishers. I further wish to express my gratitude to Ruth Zimmerling who employed her expertise in the subject matter in the translation of the book. And my thanks also go to Sonja Vogt for her tireless research to find the original English quotations.

Last, but not least, I wish to thank my extraordinary wife, Margaret Birbeck, who bore with me while I was writing this book, and who gave me invaluable help in proof-reading the English translation.

Frankfurt a. M., July 2001 — Michael Baurmann

A VISION OF LIBERALISM

I. Enlightenment, Prosperity, Freedom, and Morality

In the seventeenth and eighteenth centuries, especially in Scotland, England and France, eminent philosophers – pioneers and precursors of modern Political Economy – developed an optimistic vision of a secular social order in which enlightened individuals, in "pragmatic acceptance of the world this side of the grave "[1], pursue their personal goals and interests, free from religious indoctrination and political repression. Such an order of free and enlightened people, they thought, would not only further the economic prosperity of society; it would also have a positive effect on the morality of citizens and political rulers alike. The work of David Hume presents probably the most profound integration of the different aspects of this vision. But that intellectual current came to an end, at least temporarily, with Adam Smith who, with the metaphor of the 'invisible hand', graphically expressed its fundamental idea – only that it was now restricted to the realm of economics, and he was much less optimistic about the moral and political dimensions of such a social order. With Smith and the foundation of modern economics, the original vision not only reached a point of culmination, but having been reduced to a conception of an efficient economic order, it also already began to lose some of its splendour.[2]

It is interesting to note that the optimistic vision of harmony between ideological enlightenment, economic prosperity, political freedom and individual morality is based on a model of man that appears to be far from optimistic. On the contrary, man is conceived as a being who is naturally driven by potentially destructive passions and vices, with one single dominating motive and goal above all others: the increase of his own utility and the satisfaction of his egoistic desires. As such, a pessimistic conception of the nature of man was, of course, neither new nor surprising. Given the background of Christian doctrine and tradition, it was a perfectly familiar view. What was new, however, was that in the wake of the Renaissance, this view developed into the even stronger conviction that the nature of man must be *accepted* 'as it is' without illusions and as a

[1] To use a phrase from Schumpeter 1942 (1947, 127).

[2] In this same context, one can also mention Adam Ferguson, Bernard Mandeville, John Millar, Charles de Montesquieu, Thomas Reid, James Steuart or Dugald Stewart. On the development and the history of the vision of liberalism, cf. above all Hirschman 1977, 70 ff., 1982; Myers 1983, 37 ff., as well as the collections of writings by British and Scottish moral philosophers in Schneider 1967 and Raphael 1969. From a somewhat different perspective, Wilhelm von Humboldt (1792) and John Stuart Mill (1859) also held that individual liberty in a liberal society promotes the morality of citizens. Of course, not all representatives of classical and modern liberalism have adopted *this* idea of liberalism. Especially the assumption that the free interplay of purely interest-directed actions will *generally*, i. e. not only in the economic sphere, lead to desirable outcomes has often been rejected. John Rawls, the most prominent of all contemporary liberals, for instance, expressly emphasizes that a liberal social order must *presuppose* that citizens have a sense of justice. Cf. Rawls 1985.

matter of fact. The belief in the possibility that, through moral and religious instruction or the appeal to abstract reason, man's destructive propensities and egoistic dispositions can be tamed and transformed sufficiently to convert him into a peaceful and social being came to be regarded as a delusion. It was now believed that the nature of man makes it impossible to divert his actions and aspirations fundamentally and permanently from pursuing his own well-being: "these passions and principles are inalterable".[3]

On the basis of such an 'empiristic' model of man and in view of the historical experience of political turbulences, civil and religious wars, tyranny and revolution in sixteenth- and seventeenth-century Europe, an optimistic picture of human society, let alone a utopia of people living peacefully together, certainly cannot have been the first thing which sprang to mind. It must have seemed much more obvious to think that human egoism and selfishness leads people to fight for power and predominance and, thus, to permanent conflict and battle.

And, indeed, two radical thinkers who made no concessions to convention and consistently stuck to that model of man – Niccolò Machiavelli and Thomas Hobbes – came to hold a rather sombre view. While Machiavelli confined himself to the formulation of strategic maxims and advice for prudent – and that meant above all: ruthless and insidious – power politics of the prince, Hobbes extended his theoretical interest to comprise the state and society as a whole. In his analysis of the consequences of human nature for life in society, he comes to a conclusion which, at first glance, can hardly be considered optimistic. According to Hobbes, man's natural selfishness, if left uncurbed, must necessarily lead to a "warre [...] of every man, against every man". Natural propensities dissociate men and drive them "to invade, and destroy one another". Hence, in the "state of nature" of unrestricted freedom there is "continuall feare, and danger of violent death; And the life of man, solitary, poore, nasty, brutish, and short".[4] But if it is impossible to improve man with the help of moral appeals and religious commandments, then the only solution is to oppose his dangerous impulses with coercion and repression. Man's dangerous nature must be contained by the strong hand of an absolute authority which – since man as such cannot be changed – imposes, through the power of the state, at least external constraints on his actions. Thus, according to Hobbes, we must choose between two evils: life-threatening anarchy, on the one hand, or total political submission, on the other. And since for man death is the worst of all evils, he will rather choose to live under the *Leviathan* than to face constant conflict and war.

Although on the basis of his premises – and especially his firm conception of the 'selfishness' of human nature – Hobbes's conclusions appear to be cogent, his own reasoning already contains elements which seem to make a more optimistic solution to the 'problem of social order' possible. This possibility, together with the psychological incentive of refuting Hobbes's rather unpleasant ideas, motivated subsequent generations of philosophers to develop a very different view of human society – a view, however, which was based precisely on the impressive foundation laid by Hobbes.

This is so because Hobbes did not content himself with merely spelling out the harmful consequences of human egoism. He assumed that through a 'social contract'

[3] Hume 1739, 573.
[4] Hobbes 1651, 96.

and the establishment of an authoritative state men can, in principle, solve the problems resulting from their nature *themselves*, with their own powers and insights. They are not dependent on the intervention of some superhuman external entity who imposes the necessary institutions on 'sinful man' from the outside, as the traditional, Augustinian solution to the problem of social order had proposed. However, for a solution to the problem of social order in the sense of a social contract to become feasible, Hobbes needed to make at least two other assumptions besides the fundamental premise of the selfish nature of man: *first*, the assumption that even for selfish, egoistic persons peaceful life in society and cooperation are more advantageous than permanent battle and conflict; and, *second*, the assumption that because of their reason and their intellectual capacities men are able to recognize these fundamental advantages of peaceful cooperation and take the necessary measures to make such cooperation possible and protect it against the dangers emanating from human selfishness.

Seen in this light, the step from the pessimistic opinions of Hobbes, the 'realist', to the optimistic versions of his successors is not as large as it may at first seem. Hobbes focussed primarily on the dilemma that can arise for self-interested individuals, from their desire for peaceful cooperation, on the one hand, and the temptation to resort to violence and deception, on the other. The founders of the vision of liberalism, in turn, primarily pointed out ways of attenuating and overcoming the dilemma without necessarily relying on state power. In contrast to Hobbes, they came to be convinced not only that rational reflection and calculation would induce people to transform their impetuous passions and inclinations into 'reasonable self-love' and enlightened interests,[5] but that, in addition, foresight and the prudent balancing of reasons would enable them to realize the advantages of peaceful cooperation *directly*, i. e. *voluntarily*, without the threat of repression and sanctions by the state. A rational egoist, they thought, would recognize that in the long run he would be able to reap greater gains by treating his fellowmen well than by attacking, deceiving and cheating them, thus making further cooperation impossible: "Hence I learn to do a service to another, without bearing him any real kindness; because I forsee, that he will return my service, in expectation of another of the same kind, and in order to maintain the same correspondence of good offices with me or with others."[6]

Therefore, the free interplay of forces between self-interested individuals in the 'state of nature', without a state, must not necessarily lead to a war of everyone against everyone else. On the contrary, it can induce individuals who rationally pursue their own personal interests to indulge in permanent cooperation and peaceful exchange. Anarchy without a central regulating power is not necessarily inferior to the organization of society in a state.[7] That does not mean, however, that the state is therefore totally superfluous. The *limits* of human rationality and prudence must be taken into account too. Especially the human "propension to prefer contiguous to remote" produces "fatal

[5] Hirschman 1977, 46 ff.

[6] Hume 1739, 573.

[7] "Though government be an invention very advantageous, and even in some circumstances absolutely necessary to mankind; it is not necessary in all circumstances [...] And so far am I from thinking with some philosophers, that men are utterly incapable of society without government [...] society without government is one of the most natural states of men" (Hume 1739, 591 f.).

errors"[8] which are "the reason why men so often act in contradiction to their known interest"[9] and time and again endanger their peaceful and harmonious coexistence. Even from this new perspective, it does not seem advisable to do completely without the framework and the coercive means of a state – but the state is now given a more subsidiary role. We can trust that 'social' forces of cooperation will be effective without absolute state power.

The hope that human nature may be compatible with the prerequisites of social cooperation was considerably strengthened by an epoch-making discovery, namely that even *without the insight or conscious effort* of those involved, the pursuit of self-interest and the concentration on private well-being can have highly beneficial consequences. In his famous fable of the bees, using the example of the pursuit of material goods, Bernard Mandeville explained the workings of such a miraculous transformation of 'private vices' into 'public benefits'.[10] In later times too, the attention of theorists interested in the mechanism of the beneficial, though unintended side effects of self-interested action usually focussed on the provision of society with economic goods and services. But the idea of an 'invisible hand' bringing about a positive overall result, as if by 'magic', without systematic planning or conscious effort, came to be used increasingly also as a *general* principle for the reconciliation of individual and collective interests. Confidence in the workings of such an invisible hand was thus to become one of the main incentives for the development of a view which – although likewise based on a 'realistic' conception of human nature – presented an alternative to Hobbes's pessimism.

Out of the elements of self-interest, rationality and the desire for peaceful cooperation, together with the strong catalyst of the 'invisible hand', could thus emerge the vision of a society in which peaceful coexistence and cooperation was to be possible *without* the need to suppress or transform people's natural dispositions through systematic external or internal interventions. According to this vision, we need neither to establish a public system of dominion with extensive means of coercion, the permanent threat of sanctions and absolute power over citizens, nor to suppress human nature through moral indoctrination or the threat of eternal damnation. Of course, there must be a social order imposing certain constraints on individuals in the pursuit of their personal ends and helping them to compensate for their limited rationality and lacking long-term vision. But within the framework of such an order, individuals can then also enjoy a large sphere of material and intellectual liberty – a sphere, that is, in which they are not only largely able to pursue their own material interests, but also free from metaphysical fears and pangs of conscience because of the alleged 'sinfulness' of their nature.

The development of a counter-position to Hobbes *and* the Christian conception of the depravity of human nature thus led to a surprising conclusion: the solution to the problem of the 'evil' nature of man was not to be found in the suppression of that nature, nor in the imposition of impediments to prevent men from giving in to their natural instincts. On the contrary: what was to be done was to create the social conditions that would allow them to follow their nature without narrow ideological or material restric-

[8] Hume 1739, 590.

[9] Ibid., 586.

[10] Mandeville 1714.

tions. If such conditions are satisfied, the message said, then not only will an excessive manifestation of human impulses and passions be prevented; their potentially destructive forces can also be turned to work for the benefit of individuals and collectivity alike.

More specifically, the vision of liberalism contains three promising prophecies: economic efficiency, the taming of political dominion, and individual morality.

1. THE MIRACLE OF THE MARKET

The proof that the unrestricted pursuit of individual interests can promote the common good was especially convincing with respect to the economic effects of such behaviour. The 'miracle of the market' lies in the fact that people acting exclusively with a view towards their own material interests are induced to employ their economic resources precisely in the way that is most beneficial to society as a whole. Neither do the individuals themselves need to plan that result consciously nor does it require the purposeful intervention of the law or of political forces. The mechanisms of the market and price system lead to an adequate division of labour, the efficient use of available resources and the effective co-ordination of economic activities even when the participants direct their economic decisions solely towards their respective individual benefit.

2. THE TAMING OF DOMINION

In the realm of politics, the rational pursuit of individual interests on the part of citizens and political rulers is thought to prevent arbitrary power and despotism. Two reasons support this belief: on the one hand, the fact that an efficient economic order does not tolerate unrestricted and unforeseeable interferences. A ruler's greed is more likely to be satisfied when he practices political moderation and good governance which, by protecting the freedom of commerce and industry, assures that the economy can flourish, than through a policy of unrestrained exploitation. Despotism and tyranny would be follies which reduce rather than increase a ruler's wealth. On the other hand, political rulers must also take into account that the *bourgeoisie* as the main beneficiary of a free economy has come to constitute a significant power factor and has learned to hold its own against the 'princes'. The rise of a middle class of increasingly independent property holders whose members are permanently interconnected through a dense network of economic relations, increases the risk of a ruler facing effective resistance should he abuse his position. A society which gives its members the liberty to pursue their own economic interests also encourages them to recognize and realize their political interests.

3. THE *DOUX COMMERCE*

From the perspective of later times, the most surprising aspect of the vision of liberalism is that the free interplay of the forces of self-interest was also expected to have a positive *moral* effect. Thus, the idea was not that in a liberal, interest-directed society people will be merely unscrupulous opportunists who, undeservedly, are lucky enough to live in a world in which their vices miraculously combine to produce a public benefit.

But the assumption that in such a society morality and virtues too will be promoted seems paradoxical: How could it possibly be that the free pursuit of self-interest leads to moral behaviour when what moral behaviour requires is precisely the constraint of selfishness? The paradox dissolves if one takes into account the central assumption of liberalism, namely that the rational pursuit of self-interest prescribes the choice of a cooperative conduct which is advantageous for all sides involved and thus implies that the interests of all participants are taken into consideration. In that sense, the fact that people are allowed freely to pursue their own personal ends does not lead to the unrestrained pursuit of those ends to the disadvantage of others. Quite to the contrary, they will realize that it is to their own advantage in the pursuit of those ends also to respect the interests of their fellowmen, and thus to comply with the basic commands of morality. The circumstance that in order to attain their goals and satisfy their desires people are unavoidably dependent on each other is thought to induce automatically the coincidence of moral and virtuous with self-interested behaviour.

According to this line of reasoning, especially the market with its infinite chain of cooperative exchange transactions not only provides a cost-free mechanism of coordination; it also gently coerces participants to become peaceful citizens who satisfy their aspirations to accumulate gains in a morally acceptable way. The rational pursuit of personal ends within the market is thought to be practically *synonymous* with certain moral conducts and attitudes: Peacefulness, honesty, credibility, reliability, loyalty, sincerity or the willingness to compromise appear to be indispensable virtues for a successful participation in the market. In this view, trade becomes the 'doux commerce', a powerful instrument for the civilisation and refinement of barbaric customs, associated with properties such as gentleness, calmness, and friendliness – the free economic market is seen not only as a source of economic prosperity, but of individual morality and virtue as well.[11]

II. Moral Crisis and Self-Destruction: a Verdict on Liberalism

As already mentioned, it was, curiously enough, the work of Adam Smith that initiated the decline of the liberal vision of an interest-directed society of enlightened and free citizens. Smith was already much more sceptical than his predecessors about the political and moral consequences of self-interested behaviour. In his view, the advantages of the pursuit of self-interest accrued only to the economic sector – and even there he assumed that it needed to be tamed by 'moral sentiments'. With this restriction Smith laid the foundations of economics as an independent discipline. But together with the advantages of specialization this also meant a narrowing down of the field of investigation. The approach of analysing *social* phenomena in general from the perspective of interest-directed behaviour was thus reduced to the study of *economic* phenomena and interests. It was to take more than two-hundred years until that approach, with its more encompassing original claim, reappeared – and then, ironically, it was labelled the 'economic' approach, although the attempt to explain the ordering of human society and the indi-

[11] Cf. Hirschman 1977.

vidual behaviour of its members on the basis of individual interests is older than economics itself. Adam Smith's 'economization' of that approach had, in fact, led to the renunciation of its universal applicability.

But also in a more general sense, towards the end of the eighteenth century the idea that the self-interested behaviour of individuals can have socially and morally beneficial consequences lost much of its appeal. It soon seemed especially absurd to think that a social order that unleashes the forces of selfishness and 'materialism' can contribute not only to economic efficiency, but also to the promotion of the individual virtue of citizens and the political morality of the rulers. Instead, public attention turned to a sceptical assessment of the developmental possibilities of liberal capitalist societies in general and to a severe critique of the social relations engendered by capitalism. This dramatic change in the assessment of a society dominated by interests affected all three aspects of the hitherto positive view. Instead of seeing human interests as beneficial forces, the capitalist market was henceforth regarded as the source of social and moral evils. The 'miracle of the market' gave way to the 'Moloch of the market':

1. THE 'BLINDNESS' OF THE INVISIBLE HAND

The thesis of the economic productivity and efficiency of a market-oriented society was confronted with a crisis theory, inspired first by generally socialist, later primarily by Marxist ideas. According to this theory, already from a purely economic point of view the capitalist mode of production sets free destructive and, above all, self-destructive energies. The invisible hand of the market, in this view, does not lead to the continuous increase of economic prosperity; on the contrary, it is a pernicious mechanism which 'behind people's back' must inevitably end in economic catastrophe. According to Karl Marx, the concentration of capital, monopolization, declining rates of return and periodical overproduction impose inherent constraints on any economic system that is not based on systematic planning and the conscious direction of economic processes. Such prophecies seemed to be corroborated by the experiences of the Industrial Revolution in the nineteenth and beginning twentieth century. Millions of uprooted lives, economic depression with widespread unemployment and social misery as well as the imminent collapse of the international economic system clearly offered no reason for placing much confidence in the beneficial economic workings of the 'invisible hand'. It now appeared rather as a 'blind' force, with coincidental and arbitrary consequences.

2. "CAPITALISM BREEDS FASCISM"[12]

No less negative was the assessment concerning the hopes for a superior political quality of interest-directed societies. True, after the French Revolution and the imperialist politics of the Napoleonic era the expectation of the 'taming' of political dominion was basically confirmed by the moderate political situation during the nineteenth century. But in the twentieth century it was to be disappointed all the more radically. It now seemed that, on the contrary, instead of being able to stabilize a liberal political order, a

[12] Slogan of the German student movement of the Sixties.

liberal society based on trade and industry would all too easily – and not the least because of economic necessities – slip into despotism and dictatorship.[13] The retreat into private economic activities, the fear of the rich of losing their wealth, and the dependency of trade on 'law and order' came to be regarded as potential causes of, instead of antidotes against, the establishment of autocratic political regimes. The fact that the institution of the market needs stable protection, it was now thought, not only constitutes a barrier to the whims and desires of rulers, but also a strong incentive for the expansion of state power.

3. THE DESTRUCTION OF MORALITY

Even more devastating was the verdict on the 'doux commerce' thesis. The critics of so-called 'bourgeois morality' claimed that the ideology produced in the context of trade and industry is diagonally opposed to a moral attitude towards other people. Under the dictates of the drive to amass benefits and profits, other human beings are put on the same level with tools, land and cattle, as mere means toward economic ends. From this perspective, the pursuit of economic prosperity and wealth no longer appeared to be 'gentle' and 'innocent'. Rather, it was revealed to be a subversive force which leads to the collapse of social communities and personal ties and, instead of traditional values such as love, family and honour, permits as the only cohesive bonds between people the unsentimental and 'alienated' relations of an economic kind. The 'enlightened' and 'pragmatically secular' individual who, unconcerned about metaphysical rewards and punishments, about traditional social barriers, status, rank, or descent, soberly concentrates on pursuing his or her personal ends and interests was now regarded as a creature of capitalism causing destructive effects by penetrating the old, morality-conducive social relations of precapitalist societies. The critics conceded that incentives for cooperation and exchange are created by the division of labour, by trade, commerce and industry. But against the expectation of the defenders of the 'doux commerce' thesis that those forces will evolve into strong and reliable constraints on egoism and make morality and self-interest coincide harmoniously, the critics regarded them merely as a veneer thinly concealing naked egoism and discord which would break through at the slightest scratch.

Émile Durkheim presented this view paradigmatically. According to Durkheim, if the bond of common interests can bring people closer together "never for more than some few moments", it remains external and superficial, and merely conceals the potential conflict which can erupt any time.[14] It is wrong, he says, that trade and industry produce civilised behaviour and moral virtues; on the contrary, trade and industry can function reliably only where a certain measure of morality and virtue already exists. A beneficial exchange between people with no personal interest in each other, in the anonymous situation of the market, can only come about where reliability, honesty, and a sense of duty are already present.

[13] The fear that self-oriented 'individualism' may breed despotism had already been formulated by Alexis de Tocqueville: "no vice of the human heart is so acceptable to it as selfishness: a despot easily forgives his subjects for not loving him, provided they do not love one another." (Tocqueville 1835, 102).

[14] Cf. Durkheim 1893, 203.

Just as the thesis about the evils of the market and the dangerous political consequences of egoism, the thesis about the destruction of morality seemed to be undeniably confirmed by empirical data. Vices like avarice, meanness or unscrupulousness could be linked directly to the citizens' pursuit of profits and benefits in their capacity as participants in the market. In the eyes of its adversaries, the unjust distribution of social wealth, the "exploitation of man by his fellowmen" (Marx), reached historical heights with capitalism, which was supported by a tacit agreement between the economically dominating class and political rulers. The majority of the members of society were doomed to pauperization, illness, social insecurity and an early death unless they resorted to collective violence. The prognosis for the case of a triumph of capitalism seemed to be moral devastation instead of 'doux commerce'.

These three counter-theses to the optimistic view that a liberal, capitalist and secular society will develop self-preserving economic, political and moral forces can be aggregated into a *negative* "self-destruction-thesis"[15] in the sense that such a society, by unchaining egoistic motivations, subverts its own foundations and will consequently be defeated in an economic, political and moral crisis. On the individual level, the continuously progressing expansion of the 'Moloch of the market' undermines the moral orientation of behaviour and consumes the 'capital of virtue' needed for functioning market relations. Citizens interested exclusively in their private well-being will eventually abandon the field of politics to despots and autocrats whose reign will in the end also destroy the necessary political framework for a stable market institution.

III. A New Vision?

For a long period of time, the supporters of a politically and economically liberal social order were in the defensive. Following the course already indicated by Adam Smith, they retreated to their innermost bastion: the sphere of pure economics. At least the miracle of the market had to be rescued, even if that miracle now required a bit of a helping hand, for instance in the form of an 'anti-cyclical' economic policy. That retreat was, inevitably, accompanied by a substantial reduction in the scope of theoretical considerations. The original intention of developing a general theory of society on the basis of the conception of man as a being driven by self-interest was, for the time being, abandoned.

This development could not but cause intellectual resignation. As a mere instrument of rational economic activities, liberal capitalist society did not seem to be able to withstand the ideological critique. Thus, the critics' thesis that such a society will lead, if not to economic collapse, then at least to a moral and political crisis, was left basically uncontested. It was adopted not only by socialists and communists. Even a thinker as sober as Max Weber, certainly no enemy of a liberal economic order, regarded the destruction of individual morality and the expansion of a freedom-constraining public bureaucracy as the inevitable consequences of a capitalist market.[16] The corresponding

[15] Cf. Hirschman 1982, 1466.

[16] Cf., e. g., Weber 1921, Vol. 2, 635 ff.; 1920a, 36, 202 ff., 544; 1920b, 330 ff.

mindset is typically represented in Joseph A. Schumpeter's belief that despite its economic success capitalism will be unable to survive because of a lack of ideological and intellectual support.[17]

But the disastrous prophecies of the adversaries of capitalism and liberalism proved just as false as their early supporters' optimistic utopia of the harmonious interplay between enlightenment, prosperity, freedom and morality. Since the middle of the twentieth century, another situation has emerged. The so-called Western world was enjoying a period of economic growth and relative political stability. The problems of a liberal economic and social order came to appear, at least in principle, resolvable. The historic changes of the past decade provided an enormous additional boost. Suddenly it seemed as if market societies not only refuted the negative prophecies from an *economic* point of view, but that, surprisingly, they could also look forward to their rehabilitation from the *political* and *moral* perspective. A veritable ideological renaissance occurred. The capitalist way of handling the economy and the underlying social constitution were now defended even from the point of view of social ethics. The ideological adversaries who had been so strong that Schumpeter considered them practically invincible suddenly seemed to abandon the field.

Besides, the temporary retreat to the area of 'pure' economics had provided an opportunity for the concentration and realignment of forces. The external fortifications had been abandoned to the opponent only to reconstruct the inner core of the castle relatively undisturbed and to equip the troups with better weapons. And when the defenders had reorganized their formation, they (again) sallied forth, in order to win back the territory the founding-fathers of modern economics had once successfully, but only transitionally occupied. This new 'economic imperialism' first captured the outer 'walls' of the economic fortress: the social institutions of politics and law came to be analysed again from the 'classical' point of view according to which in all kinds of situations human beings – whether politicians, lawyers, criminals, or policemen – behave as self-interested actors trying to make the best of the scarce means at their disposal. These attempts at expansion were supported by the powerful new tools of modern decision theory and game theory. They facilitated the application of the model of the 'rational utility maximizer' to all spheres of life. As already mentioned, this renewed 'classical' approach is now commonly called the 'economic' approach, even though historically it had been precisely the focus on economic phenomena which was initially responsible for the distortion of the classical approach.

Is this, then, a belated full-scale victory? Can we now also expect the resurrection of that old vision of harmony between ideological enlightenment, economic prosperity, political freedom, and individual morality? It would be a deception to think that the scientific success of the economic approach and the improved reputation of market economies will necessarily be accompanied by the revival of the optimistic vision of the classics according to which the all-round consideration of individual interests has beneficial consequences for the public as well as for its individual members. Instead, what we have today is a situation in which from a normative point of view the core institutions of liberal society – and therefore also the idea that, at least in the economic sphere

[17] Schumpeter 1942, ch. XIII.

of the market, people are guided by their interests – certainly are openly endorsed; but at the same time there is doubt, often voiced by the very same persons, whether the stable existence of those institutions is compatible with individual interest-orientation in *all* areas of social interaction.

IV. Society Without Community: the External Critique

What, then, are the impediments to a revival of the old vision of liberalism? One of the greatest challenges the theory of liberalism actually faces, despite the *prima facie* impressive success of liberal societies, are the modern versions of so-called 'communitarianism'. The reproach supporters of communitarianism voice against the liberal *theory* of society as well as against the *reality* of liberal societies is their alleged excessive emphasis on 'individualism' and the corresponding disregard of 'community'.[18] The objection is that the priority of individual rights over the collective good proclaimed by liberalism underestimates the need for a substantial collective identity, enabling the individual to feel as a member of a unique social community rather than merely of an instrumentally expedient alliance. The liberal conception of society is said to forget that the sphere of freedom it concedes to the individual and its pursuit of personal interests needs to be counterbalanced by a commitment to shared values and forms of life; only on the basis of such commitments, they say, could the egoism of purely private interests be transcended in favour of an orientation towards the common interest.

To some extent, modern communitarianism merely continues the traditional critique of liberalism. But this critique is now embedded into the framework of modern philosophical, ethical and sociological theory building. Hence, the current debate between liberalism and communitarianism takes place in the context of philosophical theories of the self and of personality, of the controversies between utilitarian and contractarian positions in moral philosophy, as well as between deontological and teleological approaches in metaethics, and the alternative between individualistic and holistic conceptions in sociology. While the different communitarian positions present a multitude of aspects, three main arguments against the theory and practice of liberalism can be found:

1. THE PHILOSOPHICAL ARGUMENT

According to the philosophical argument, liberalism is based on the wrong model of man and a mistaken conception of the relationship between individual and community. Liberal theory is thought to presuppose an 'atomized' and 'isolated' self who, detached from predefined social roles and commitments, can voluntarily choose his ends, values and social relationships. In the communitarian view, such a conception overlooks the elementary fact that without being 'embedded' in social relationships, without an awareness of being part of a community with a collective conception of the good life and a

18 Representatives of modern communitarianism are, among others, Amitai Etzioni (1988), Alasdair MacIntyre (1985, 1988, 1990), Michael J. Sandel (1982), Charles Taylor (1979; 1985; 1989), Michael Walzer (1992), and the group of authors around Robert N. Bellah (Bellah et al. 1985; 1991).

common tradition, human beings cannot develop an authentic personal identity.[19] Communal life not only has an instrumental value as a means of pursuing one's personal interests more effectively, they say, it also offers "internal goods" linked to the participation in a common practice as such.[20] The individual who is 'deprived' of all social attachments and the values incorporated in them is a chimera: "we cannot regard ourselves as independent in this way".[21] The only adequate conception of man is a social one according to which "an essential constitutive condition of seeking the human good is bound up with being in society".[22] It is impossible for human beings to distance themselves from all social attachments: "the individual self finds its fulfilment in relationships with others."[23]

2. The ethical argument

In the opinion of communitarian critics, the 'atomized' and 'deprived' individual of liberalism suffers not only from a lack of personal identity and the loss of a continued history of life; he is also incapable of reaching reasoned and binding decisions about moral values and norms on the basis of his subjective interests alone. Thus, it is believed to be no mere coincidence that in modern liberal societies the search for answers to fundamental moral questions is characterized by permanent controversy and interminable disagreement.[24] Without "constitutive attachments", moral attitudes will be characterized by arbitrariness and a loss of orientation: "some relative fixity of character appears essential to prevent the lapse into arbitrariness".[25] Someone who is completely detached from the tradition and values of a community is said to lose the ability to lead a morally coherent life. When the values and norms that guide our actions become a question of personal preferences and are regarded as a matter of subjective choice, "separated from family, religion, and calling as sources of authority, duty, and moral example",[26] they remain "precarious" and rest on "a fragile foundation".[27] "It is the moral content of relationships that allows marriages, families, and communities to persist with some certainty that there are agreed-upon standards of right and wrong that one can count on and that are not subject to incessant renegotiation."[28] For a communitarian, the rational foundation of and rationally motivated compliance with moral norms, based on the 'abstract' interests of a socially unencumbered individual, is impossible. The principles of *as well as* the motives for moral behaviour can, in his view, derive only from life in the respective community: "detached from my community, I will be apt to lose my hold upon

[19] Cf. above all MacIntyre 1985, 218 ff.; Sandel 1982.

[20] Such "internal goods [...] can only be identified and recognized by the experience of participating in the practice in question" (MacIntyre 1985, 188 f.).

[21] Sandel 1982, 179.

[22] Ch. Taylor 1985, 292.

[23] Bellah et al. 1985, 218.

[24] Cf. MacIntyre 1985, 6 ff.

[25] Sandel 1982, 180.

[26] Bellah et al. 1985, 79.

[27] Ibid., 8.

[28] Ibid., 139 f..

all genuine standards of judgment [...] without life in this community I would have no reason to be moral."[29]

3. THE SOCIOLOGICAL ARGUMENT

According to communitarian judgment, individuals in a liberal society cannot develop a moral character and can only assume binding social commitments with difficulty. This is seen as running counter to their 'real' interests and as problematical from a moral point of view. But it is also seen as a confirmation of the traditional critique of liberalism that a liberal, interest-dominated society necessarily tends to undermine its own foundations. In the long run, such a society is believed to be doomed because – due to the lack of common values, the propagation of an egocentric individualism and the dissolution of all particular communities – it will be unable to elicit from its citizens the measure of moral motivation, altruism and public commitment that is necessary for the preservation of the political, legal and economic institutions of society.[30] A vicious circle threatens to emerge: The promotion of an individualistic ethos of utility, the dynamics of uncontrolled growth and unlimited social and geographical mobility contribute to the progressive destruction of historically grown communities and their social ties. The collapse and dissolution of those shared ways of life and their traditions, in turn, reinforce the process of privatistic atomization and the propensity for 'utilitarian' individualism. There are no forces that could counter the decline of communal relations and thus detain the destruction of the social foundations of civic virtues.[31] But without such virtues, by means of which elementary common interests such as an effective military defense[32] or the protection against despotism and dictatorship[33] are asserted against individual interests, no liberal society could survive. It is the great illusion of liberalism that only the rational recognition of their own long-term interests can induce individuals to comply with their duties as responsible citizens of a commonwealth.[34]

If we look at all the philosophical, ethical and sociological arguments of modern communitarianism taken together, they brush up with new colours the old picture of liberal society with its alleged inherent tendency towards disintegration, moral crisis and self-destruction. In this view, such a society neglects man's fundamental need for participa-

[29] MacIntyre 1984, 11/10.

[30] "The citizen has been swallowed up in 'economic man'." (Bellah et al. 1985, 271).

[31] "The growth of large-scale, highly interdependent, bureaucratically run, big-city societies is exercising the destructive, alienating effect on our republican life which the writers of the tradition always predicted." (Ch. Taylor 1985, 315)

[32] Cf. MacIntyre 1984.

[33] "Pure enlightened self-interest will never move enough people strongly enough to constitute a real threat to potential despots and putschists" (Ch. Taylor 1989b, 175). Cf. also Tocqueville 1835, 271.

[34] The sociological theses of communitarianism are at odds with the sociological theory of modernization, as developed, for instance, in the work of Émile Durkheim, Max Weber, or Talcott Parsons. While communitarians agree with modernization theorists that even modern societies must be integrated through the collective commitment to values, the former are sceptical about the ability of modern societies actually to achieve such value integration. According to the sociological theory of modernization, however, the transition from 'community' to 'society' does not raise any basically insoluble problems in this respect.

tion in authentic social relationships in the context of shared practices, it promotes social anomy and moral nihilism, and undermines the very bases of civil liberties.

In the present context, especially the sociological argument of communitarianism presents a challenge. However, the following investigation will show that the discussion of the sociological argument also contributes to the assessment of the philosophical and ethical arguments of communitarianism. Special attention will be given to a variant of the sociological argument which seems to be particularly cogent and dangerous for the vision of liberalism. It borrows insights precisely from that scientific tradition out of which the vision of liberalism itself had emerged. Thus, it constitutes a kind of *internal* critique.

V. The Gulf Between Individual and Collective Rationality: the Immanent Critique

One of the great discoveries in classical economics was the working of the invisible hand, the 'miracle' that the rational pursuit of private interests can promote the common good without any intention to that end. In contrast, modern social theory – partly as a consequence of the application of the new tools provided by decision theory and game theory – has given more attention to a phenomenon whose recognition had already been the basis of Hobbes's theory, but which had been neglected by his optimistic successors. This phenomenon is, so to speak, the counterpart to the workings of the invisible hand: it is the dilemma that under certain circumstances the rational orientation towards individual self-interest leads to outcomes which are totally opposed to the self-interest of each and every participant. In such situations, the 'logic of self-interest' leads to an unbridgeable gulf between what rational actors want and what, by their own actions and decisions, they are in fact able to bring about. Since situations with such a dilemmatic structure involve the strategic interaction of several participants, we can here speak of a gulf between *individual* and *collective* rationality.[35]

Thus, it was precisely the 'technical' development of modern economics which led to the discovery that besides the invisible hand there is also an invisible *barrier*. While the invisible hand ensures that desires are satisfied without any effort by the individuals, the 'invisible barrier' prevents the satisfaction of desires even when the individuals rationally attempt to realize them and conditions at first sight seem particularly favourable. Instead of diverging desires and intentions, the parties have an identifiable *common* interest and there is no conflict between them. The dilemma can arise between several individuals as well as in the context of a collectivity. It can prevent mutually advantageous cooperation between the two sides of a potential exchange as well as the provision of a public good urgently wanted by all members of a group. The insight that an invisible hand can produce harmony between private vices and public benefits 'free of charge' was a pleasant surprise. The discovery that the realization of common – 'collectively rational' – ends may be impossible even when all participants have a funda-

[35] The pioneering description of this dilemma with modern game-theoretical tools can be found in Luce/Raiffa 1957. Concerning specifically the provision of public goods, cf. Olson 1965 for a by now classical analysis.

mental interest in it and choose their actions on the basis of prudent – 'individually rational' – deliberation was certainly disillusioning.

This is not to say, of course, that classical economists had a naïve belief in the capacities of human rationality. They admitted that the combination of 'self-love plus rationality' would bring about desirable results only if one presupposed *perfect* decision-makers with *perfect* rationality. Since human rationality and intelligence are always bounded, serious difficulties resulting from *irrational* action would have to be expected. They saw, for instance, that people do not always comply with rules which are in their common interest. As already mentioned, for Hume this was the main reason for the fundamental insecurity of anarchy and the necessity for the state.

But the problem is much more serious than Hume had recognized, because it is not a *lack* of rationality that impedes the conflict-free and efficient cooperation of self-interested actors. Rather, the cause must be seen to lie in a defect which is inherent in the rationality and decision-making capacity of human beings and remains effective even when all participants act perfectly rationally. Precisely if they *do* always make optimal, perfectly rational choices it will be impossible for them to satisfy their interests. A bounded rationality preventing the parties from continuously adapting to actual circumstances would help them out of the dilemma.[36] In that sense, then, human rationality is not 'too weak' but rather 'too strong'.

Now, this insight into the profound gulf between individual and collective rationality raises doubts about all three elements of the vision of liberalism, much like the 'external' critique presented above. Only that this time they arise from the central premises of the economic approach itself and are not due to an external perspective:

1. MARKET EVASION

Market competition, as the basis of economic growth, is in the common interest of economic actors, i. e. it is 'collectively rational'. However, from the perspective of each single actor it is, at the same time, 'individually rational' to try to evade competition and economic rivalry as much as possible and profit only from the fact that *others* are subjected to the market mechanism. From the point of view of individual interests, everyone will struggle for privileges that will protect *themselves* from competition. Monopolies, cartels, associations and unions will organize and attempt to satisfy their particular interests without consideration of the common good. When such interest groups obtain privileges and prerogatives, they undermine competition, endanger the directive function of the market and delay economic adaptation processes. The distributional struggle by political means becomes more important for them than success in the economic market. The emergence of 'distributional coalitions' attempting to reap benefits from the evasion of competition is a dangerous tendency of all markets. In this respect, the invisible hand of 'laissez faire' does not redirect the pursuit of individual interests to work for the benefit of all. Therefore, because of its internal incentive structure – that is, because of the gulf between individual and collective rationality – the capitalist economic system has a

[36] Cf. the arguments and examples in chs. 1 and 2.

propensity towards the 'sclerotic' paralysis of market mechanisms. The consequence is economic stagnation.[37]

2. THE EROSION OF DEMOCRACY

The tendencies inherent in the market which endanger the efficiency of a capitalist economic order produce a demand for institutional devices to counteract those tendencies – for instance, a 'good' government that protects competition by curbing special-interest activities.[38] But instead of providing a remedy, the state threatens to become part of the problem, especially in liberal democracies where the gulf between individual and collective rationality jeopardizes the functioning of democratic institutions as well. Two problems seem to be particularly difficult to solve in a democratic market society:

(1) In order to secure the conditions for an efficient market economy operating in the general interest, a government would need to take measures against all distributional coalitions, cartels, monopolies – against all groups, that is, which try to avoid competition. At the same time, however, in order to stay in power and thus pursue their own interests, the members of government themselves depend on approval, particularly from the more influential parts of the population. But in an interest-directed society they can expect to get that approval only in exchange for political concessions and material benefits. Hence, interest groups can effectively pressure the government into adopting political measures in their favour. This leads to a further expansion of state activities, with the consequence of still higher incentives to pursue economic ends through participation in the political distributional struggle instead of exposure to competition in the market. The upshot of this is that democratic governments will not use their political instruments for the protection of competition. On the contrary: they will continually reduce competition through political measures. Government activity will primarily consist in *creating* prerogatives, privileges and subsidies, rather than in dismantling them in the public interest.[39]

(2) In a democracy, political leaders are made to feel obliged to act in the interest of the public in general – instead of the special interests of resourceful pressure groups – only if otherwise they risk being deposed in the next elections. But this potential power of the voters will produce such a beneficial pressure only under two conditions. On the one hand, voters must actually vote. On the other, they must be well-informed about government policies. The 'collectively rational' fulfillment of these conditions, however, is threatened by each voter's individual calculus.[40] This is so because from the point of view of a self-interested individual it is not rational to bear the costs of going to the polls in order to cast a vote which, in a large country, will certainly make no notable difference to the final result; and because of this lack of influence, it is not relevant either for the individual to acquire any information at all about government policies. In summary,

[37] Cf. Olson 1982, 33 ff.; Buchanan et al. 1980.

[38] Olson 1982, 179 f.

[39] For a concise summary of these self-destructive tendencies of capitalist democracy, cf. esp. Weede 1990, 129 ff.

[40] Cf. Downs 1957.

"individual rationality tends to drive democracy to collapse – through indifference and abstention".[41]

Hence, especially for a liberal democracy, the assumption seems to be wrong that the interest of the political ruling class in the advantages of a well-functioning economy will, together with the interest of citizens in a good government, bring about the general good. Since positions of power are conceded only for a short period of time, rulers are forced to pursue short-term strategies; at the same time, citizens are unable to bridge the gap between individual and collective rationality in order to realize their common interests against the administrators of the state.

3. FREE-RIDERS AND CHEATS

The analyses of some contemporary authors concerning the emergence of morality and virtue in a market society look like an impressive belated confirmation of Durkheim's theses.[42] They maintain that the cooperative forces of the market are too weak to ensure moral behaviour. The complex network of reciprocal exchange relations and personal dependencies in a market society is, they say, not sufficiently dense to make cooperative behaviour always coincide with the participants' self-interest. On the other hand, there are destructive incentives motivating self-interested persons to behave non-cooperatively and without consideration for the interests of others.[43] 'Golden opportunities' for shirking one's contribution to communal tasks or for taking advantage of others at a relatively low risk arise regularly. The market, understood as a sequence of transactions between more or less isolated individuals, cannot 'produce' morality or virtue. Rather, it is itself dependent on their existence. This confirms the thesis, which is opposed to that of the 'doux commerce', that „the amounts of benevolence and morality required for the functioning of the market turn out to be quite impressive".[44] Honesty, truthfulness, trustworthiness or reliability seem to be *prerequisites* of secure market exchanges rather than their result.[45]

If one accepts this 'immanent' criticism of liberalism, the question of the 'moral productivity' of liberal societies, rather than being merely one problem among others, becomes *the key question*. This is so because if in political and economic life the gulf between individual and collective rationality prevents an individual's interests and the interests of other individuals, as well as of society as 'a whole', from coinciding, then there is a fundamental need for morality in these spheres too. In other words, there is a need for individuals who make the common good and the interests of others an *imme-*

41 Weede 1990, 117.

42 A good example in many aspects is Hirsch 1976, 117 ff.

43 In German economics, this idea has been advocated since 1920 in the theory of 'marginal morality' which holds that under conditions of market competition participants of the economic process will be forced to the gradual assimilation of their moral behaviour on a low level. Cf. Briefs 1920; for an informative and critical presentation of this theory, see Willgerodt 1968.

44 Hirschman 1981, 301.

45 Thus, Durkheim's view is repeated almost literally by Kenneth J. Arrow: "A close look reveals that a great deal of economic life depends for its viability on a certain limited degree of ethical commitment. Purely selfish behavior of individuals is really incompatible with any kind of settled economic life. There is almost invariably some element of trust and confidence." (Arrow 1985, 140).

diate end of their own. At the same time the gulf between individual and collective rationality also prevents this need from being met in an interest-dominated society. When there is no harmony between individual and public interests, the predominance of individualism with its orientation towards subjective interests will necessarily lead to behaviour that is harmful to the common good and to the interests of others.

Of course, just how wide that alleged gulf between individual and collective rationality will actually turn out to be and to what extent the dangers implied by it will become effective, depends mainly on social background conditions. But in modern societies those background conditions seem to be especially unfavourable: the gulf between individual and collective rationality widens when social interaction takes place within large anonymous groups not strictly delimited from the surrounding world, with changing partners, and without close personal contacts. For reasons of economic efficiency, the capitalist way of production requires large markets with as much and as perfect competition as possible on the demand as well as on the supply side, a high level of division of labour, and the formation of economic relations depending on the requirements of the market. The market and price system requires participants to be geographically and socially mobile and their mutual relationships to be based on objective, functional reasons rather than on subjective, personal bonds within fixed borders and groups. The triumph of capitalism is accompanied by the destruction of the delimitations and barriers of the traditional estate society which had ensured the transparency and personal intimacy in small social units. Hence, precisely the same conditions which are detrimental from the point of view of the conflict between individual and collective interests are conducive to an efficient and highly productive market economy. The more anonymous and impersonal a society, the more effective its division of labour, competition and price system, but also the wider the gulf between individual and collective rationality.[46]

This seems to confirm once and for all the verdict on the vision of liberalism: according to the preceding analysis, a society which under the conditions of modernity generally permits the unrestricted pursuit of individual interests starts a process that must necessarily undermine the foundations of any society – including its own. It rewards the pursuit of individual interests under conditions where they are not aggregated by an invisible hand to everyone's advantage, but rather lead to collective bads. The invisible hand, it seems, can itself become effective only if it is part of an organism containing other organs too, such as a brain capable of planning purposeful action, and a moral sense which at least now and then overrules self-interest and egoism.

Thus, new fronts have opened, and the vision of the enlightened 'worldliness' of a secular and liberal society has gained new adversaries. Their weapons are the same as those which initially brought victory to the visionaries. Only that this time adversity is not expressed by way of a social critique aiming at the abolition of capitalism as an economic system. However, a sweeping critique of modern Western society is involved here too. The anonymity and mobility of this society, its secularism, its veneration for indi-

[46] Olson 1991, 183 (cf. also 129 ff.): "In any case, it should [...] be clear that, precisely because of the high degree of social and geographic mobility and the basic lack of stable group relations, a society which enjoys the advantages of the economic ideal will also be a society in which individuals will increasingly lose their roots and in which there will likely exist a high degree of alienation."

vidualism and subjectivism, the absence of shared world views and the lacking belief in collectively binding values are the preferred targets of these critics.

VI. The Moral and Religious Legacy

The essence of the external as well as the immanent critique of the vision of liberalism is that even a society wishing to take advantage of the forces of self-interest in one sector depends for its survival, just like any other society, on the existence of individuals who in certain areas give priority to something other than their personal self-interest: "the principle of self-interest is incomplete as a social organizing device. It operates effectively only in tandem with some supporting social principle."[47] Thus, it is contended that it was a serious mistake of the classics to have thought that "morality of the minimum order necessary for the functioning of a market system" was a "kind of permanent free good, a natural resource of a nondepleting kind".[48]

But if a secular society dominated by interests were unable to provide the 'ethos' needed for its own subsistence, if on the contrary it undermined it, then how could it be possible that such societies exist in reality? The answer of the critics is: because in fact the existing liberal societies of the West have *not yet* come to be entirely secularized and completely interest-dominated. Actually, they live off a capital that is not their own, namely the moral "legacy of the precapitalist and preindustrial past"[49] – above all that of religion which has implanted in people the motives for behaving morally and whose roots, though loosened, have not completely dried up yet. But to the extent that the "general behavioural norm of acting on the criterion of selfinterest has won ever-widening acceptance",[50] these remains of individual and collective morality have been destroyed and the legacy has thus been wasted once and for all: "this legacy has diminished with time and with the corrosive contact of the active capitalist values – and more generally with the greater anonymity and greater mobility of industrial society. [...] As individual behavior has been increasingly directed to individual advantage, habits and instincts based on communal attitudes and objectives have lost out."[51]

What can be done to stop this self-destruction of modern Western society? In any case, passivity and confidence in the uncontrolled forces of rational self-interested adaptation is not a feasible remedy if the critics' diagnosis is correct: "we may be near the limit of explicit social organization possible without a supporting social morality." The lack of "moral obligations", they say, has by now become a serious danger to the system's ability to function.[52] Therefore, morality should no longer be left to chance and the spontaneous interaction of human interests. It must be intentionally produced and distributed.

[47] Hirsch 1976, 12

[48] Ibid., 134.

[49] Ibid., 117.

[50] Ibid., 12.

[51] Ibid., 117 f.

[52] Ibid., 196/157.

The prescription thus is a *moral and ideological rearmament*. At issue is the conscious reconstruction of institutions that will eliminate the materialism of the "pragmatic acceptance of the world" and bring morality (back) to society. Especially for some of those who derive their critical diagnoses from the theoretical approach of modern economics, the moral reformation of society is, above all, a task for *religion* and *religious* institutions. This is due to the belief that important social virtues such as "truth, trust, acceptance, restraint, obligation" which "play a central role in the functioning of an individualistic, contractual economy" must be "adopted" in religious faith.[53] Thus, Fred Hirsch, in his influential book on the *Social Limits to Growth*, begins his chapter on "The Moral Re-entry" by striving "to bring out the functional economic role for religious belief". He asserts that in order to fill the moral vacuum "religious obligation [...] performed a secular function that, with the development of modern society, became more rather than less important".[54] The anonymous social system of a modern market society, he contends, is "more dependent on religious binding than the feudal system, having abandoned direct social ties maintained by the obligations of custom and status".[55] In the same vein, the German philosopher Peter Koslowski declares without further argument that for a "socio-economic order" religion is simply "irrenouncable".[56] The only alternative he sees is that moral behaviour is either secured through religion or "through the total external control of people".[57]

If one looks at it more closely, it ceases to be surprising that some authors who argue in line with the tradition of economic theory tend to see the adequate strategy for the recovery of morality primarily as a strategy of strengthening religious institutions.[58] Because if, on the one hand, they think that modern liberal and capitalist societies have irrevocably unleashed the pursuit of self-interest and yet, on the other, they do not want to rely on the expectation that this will automatically lead to morally acceptable outcomes, then indeed the only solution seems to be the possibility to modify people's *ideas* in such a way that they *believe* the compliance with moral norms to be in their personal interest. Thus, from an economic point of view it is perfectly consistent that Hirsch interprets the "role of God-cum-Satan as the deus ex machina for the 'prisoner's dilemma'".[59] A religious faith motivating to compliance with moral norms, whether for

[53] Ibid., 141 f.

[54] Ibid., 138/142.

[55] Ibid., 143.

[56] Koslowski 1988, 47 and 49.

[57] Ibid., 47.

[58] This also applies to 'non-economist' communitarians; cf. Bellah et al. 1985, 187. And even Tocqueville already argued that 'individualism' can only be contained through religion: "liberty cannot be established without morality, nor morality without faith." (Tocqueville 1835, 12) Of course, 'non-economist' communitarians also offer other proposals for the reformation of morality, from the strengthening of local communities and the idea of corporatism, the resuscitation of shared traditions and world views, a 'politics of the common good' and the establishing of a new ethics of community, all the way to the idea that "perhaps a common worship, in which we express our gratitude and wonder in the face of the mystery of being itself, is the most important thing of all" (Bellah et al. 1985, 295). What 'non-economist' communitarians say little about, however, is the chance that their proposals could be effectively implemented in the social reality of twentieth-century Western societies.

[59] Hirsch 1976, 138.

fear of metaphysical punishment or in the hope of rewards of the same kind, reduces the implementation costs of a social order: "the religious belief, once adopted, operates conveniently as a private sanction, being seen to provide rewards and penalties directly in accordance with the individual's performance of his social obligations. A more effective inducement for cooperative action could hardly be devised deliberately."[60] In the same vein, Koslowski comes to the conclusion "that without metaphysics economics and ethics is possible, but not very effective".[61] He argues that only a religiously transmitted "basic ontological trust"[62] gives the subjects the "assurance" that "in the long run morality and happiness converge"[63] and thereby a motive for respecting moral rules: "because of the transcendental compensation of divine justice, moral behaviour, beyond the limits of death, is always the advantageous long-term [...] strategy too".[64]

The old liberal vision of a legal order which gives people the internal and external freedom to pursue their individual interests is thus replaced by the demand for a religious and ideological restoration. In an important aspect the historical process of the Enlightenment is to be reversed, namely, insofar as it contributes to the fact that people let their actions be guided by their knowledge about the empirical world, including their own nature and their given interests, instead of by metaphysical speculation or religious belief. What is to be fought against are the"dis-enchantment of the world" (Max Weber) and the "destruction of ideologies" (Joseph A. Schumpeter) – processes which, according to Weber's and Schumpeter's analyses, typically accompany capitalist societies: "the capitalist process rationalizes behaviour and ideas and by so doing chases from our minds, along with metaphysical belief, mystic and romantic ideas of all sorts. [...] 'Free thinking' in the sense of materialistic monism, laicism, and pragmatic acceptance of the world this side of the grave follow from this not indeed by logical necessity but nevertheless very naturally."[65] Today, for many this vision has become a nightmare.

VII. The Purpose of This Investigation

Is it possible to safeguard the vision of liberalism against those demands for a moral rearmament and the restoration of a community-oriented society? Safeguard it, that is, in view of the dangers to internal and external freedom which accompany all the attempts at an intentional improvement of people's morality, through ideology, religion, indoctrination, or the conscious interference with social institutions?

Or are the critics of this vision right? Is it true that it is a consequence of modern economic theory itself that the classical vision of harmony between enlightened secularism, economic prosperity, political freedom and individual morality was an unrealistic

[60] Ibid., 142.

[61] Koslowski 1988, 15; similarly, Richard B. McKenzie 1977, 217: "in the context of some critical group size and structure, ethics, because of the externalities, may have no force in the absence of a conceptualised God." Cf. also id. 1987, 31 ff.

[62] Koslowski 1983, 40.

[63] Ibid., 38.

[64] Ibid., 37 f., 39 f.

[65] Schumpeter 1942 (1947, 127).

utopia? Must we succumb to the insight that human nature, in as far as it is characterized by self-love and the desire for personal advantage, is inimical to virtue and must be contained with the help of ideology and religion? Should we try to go against human nature in order to transform man into a social being rather than take people as they are? Is contemporary Western society in need of fundamental political, social and moral reformation because its structures and institutions foster materialism and self-interest?

If we want to safeguard the vision of liberalism, we must plausibly show that, in contradiction to the views of its critics, a liberal and secular society can produce and conserve morality and a sense of social commitment in its citizens 'from its own sources' and not only by wasting its inheritance. We must show that in the classical sense of the vision of liberalism virtue has a chance even in societies where rational, enlightened individuals, in 'pragmatic acceptance of the world', free from ideological indoctrination, religious tutelage and political oppression, pursue their personal ends and interests. If we succeed in showing this, then we have reason to hope that a secular social order in which there are morally virtuous citizens, economic efficiency and 'tamed' political power is compatible with the rational pursuit of individual interests by all members of society – and that it may even be promoted by such a general orientation towards self-interest.

The purpose of the following investigation is to show just that. In this endeavour, however, one basic premise will be shared with the critics of liberal society. The 'moral productivity' of a liberal society is indeed a key problem, and the realization of the ends of such a society, and consequently its long-term chances of survival, depend essentially on the solution of that problem. Morality and a sense of social commitment are necessary prerequisites for the stability of a liberal society. Its political and economic institutions cannot function properly if the gulf between individual and collective rationality is not sufficiently bridged by the virtuousness of its citizens. This fundamental 'need for morality' cannot be substituted entirely by the 'artificial' incentives of social institutions such as a legal system. Morality and a sense of social commitment are cohesives which even a society with formal sanctioning institutions and mechanisms of mutual control cannot do without. On the contrary, the more complex the social structure – with its many positions and roles, its numerous rights and duties, its equally numerous opportunities for unnoticed violations of norms and rules to one's own personal benefit – the greater the need of such a fragile construction for the 'moral' loyalty with the constitution and the norms and institutions endorsed by it. Even in a politically and legally organized society, many more informally effective mechanisms of conduct must be at work than it would seem at first sight. For the citizens of such a society, other motives for norm-compliance must be relevant than merely the expectation of sanction or reward.

The legal philosopher H. L. A. Hart has underlined the need for such a moral motivation specifically for the legal order of a society. In his view, a stable legal order is possible only if there is a sufficient number of people who adopt an 'internal point of view' towards the norms of such an order and especially towards its basic constitutional norms.[66] For Hart, to adopt an internal point of view towards a norm means to *accept*

[66] Cf. Hart 1961, 77 ff., 97 ff. A very similar view has been defended by Max Weber when he asserts that without the "belief in the legitimacy" of a social order there can be no social stability: if the members of a society are not guided in their actions "by the belief in the existence of a legitimate order" any order necessarily remains "instable" (Weber 1921, 31).

that norm as a personally binding standard of behaviour, that is, to conform voluntarily to that norm without calculating the advantages and disadvantages to be expected from compliance or non-compliance in each case.[67] In contrast, a legal order would not be viable for Hart if all norm-addressees saw the norms of that order only from an *external* point of view, i. e. if they complied with them only on condition that this is their most advantageous option in a given situation.

The thesis that a social (legal) order is viable only if a sufficient number of individuals act morally in the sense that they adopt an internal point of view towards the norms of that order is a challenge to the vision of liberalism. This is because the assumption that individuals adopt an internal point of view towards certain norms means that the reason for complying with those norms is not simply identical with a calculation of individual benefit or harm. And that assumption, in turn, is hardly compatible with an interest-dominated society in which individuals know no other motive than their personal ends and interests. In such a society, there seems to be room only for what Hart has called the external point of view towards norms, i. e. for a point of view in which the only reason for obeying a norm is the expectation of negative consequences in case of non-compliance or of positive consequences in case of compliance.

Hence, in our investigation a central place must be given to the question whether the adoption of an internal point of view towards norms is compatible with the premise that we are dealing with persons who in 'pragmatic acceptance of the world', pursue their individual interests in a rational manner. Can it be in the *interest* of a person to adopt certain norms as 'personal' norms in the sense that they are accepted as binding standards of action and complied with voluntarily? Only if the answer to this question is affirmative, will it at least be possible that acting morally can coincide with acting according to one's individual interest.

VIII. The Model of *Homo Oeconomicus*

If social phenomena are to be explained on the basis of the assumption that in their decisions and actions people attempt to pursue their individual interests in a rational way, it seems natural to take recourse to the methods and results of that social-theoretical tradition on which the vision of liberalism is grounded. Theories belonging to that tradition explain social facts as consequences of the behaviour of rational, self-interested individuals. As has been explained above, this theoretical tradition goes all the way back to Thomas Hobbes, Bernard Mandeville and the classics of the Scottish school of moral philosophy: David Hume, Adam Smith, and Adam Ferguson. In this century, it has been taken up and further developed by writers such as Max Weber, Ludwig von Mises, Carl Menger, Friedrich von Hayek, Karl Popper, Hans Albert or James M. Buchanan, in the hope that it may provide the foundation for social-scientific theory building in general.[68] This modern 'economic' approach is characterized by four features:

[67] The different aspects of an 'internal point of view' are discussed in detail in MacCormick 1981, 33 ff.

[68] For an overview and a systematic presentation of this process, cf., e. g. Bohnen 1975; Kirchgässner 1991; Raub/Voss 1981; Vanberg 1975.

1. Explanatory purpose: the aim is the empirical explanation of social facts.
2. Methodological individualism: social facts are to be explained by referring them to individual action.
3. Rational model of action: individual action is to be explained as the result of rational decisions based on the assessment of expected consequences.
4. Utility maximization: the assessment of expected consequences of action is to be explained with the help of the principle of subjective utility maximization.

Thus, the economic approach is based on the behavioural model of *homo oeconomicus*, i. e. the model of a 'rational utility maximizer', as it was first elaborated in economics for the purpose of explaining economic phenomena. For a *homo oeconomicus* all that counts is the consequences an action will have for his interests and desires on each particular occasion. He is flexible and responsive and adapts to the specific 'constraints' of every new situation.[69] Above all, *homo oeconomicus* decides in a consistently 'opportunistic' manner. He does not voluntarily subordinate his own personal interest to the interests of others or the norms of morality or law.[70]

Meanwhile, the model of *homo oeconomicus* is being propagated as a basic model of behaviour for all social sciences. Hans Albert has called the development that economically-minded scientists have ventured beyond the strictly economic disciplines and are increasingly exploring subjects sometimes very distant from traditional economic theory the *institutionalist revolution*.[71] The expansion has led to, among other things, a 'New Political Economy',[72] an 'Economic Analysis of Law',[73] a 'Theory of Property Rights',[74] and an economic analysis of collective decisions known as 'Public Choice' or 'Constitutional Political Economy'.[75] Economic approaches can be found in ethics[76] and sociology.[77] This 'imperialist' expansion of the 'new institutional economics' into a general social-scientific research programme, competing openly with other approaches in the social sciences, is carried out as a conscious continuation of classical Political Economy, where the institutional framework of individual action – above all

69 For characterizations of *homo oeconomicus*, cf., e. g. Becker 1976, 1 ff.; Elster 1986, 1 ff.; Kirchgässner 1991; Kliemt 1984, 1991; Kliemt/Zimmerling 1993; Schoemaker 1982.

70 "Acting according to self-interest means never telling the truth or keeping one's promise unless it pays to do so; stealing and cheating if one can get away with it or, more generally, if the expected value of doing so is larger than the expected value of the alternative; treating punishment merely as the price of crime, and other people merely as means to one's own satisfaction. We may use the term *opportunism* for this relentless pursuit of self-interest" (Elster 1989, 263 f.), Cf. also Williamson 1985, 64.

71 Albert 1977, 203; more generally, on this development cf. also Becker 1976; Frey 1980; Kirchgässner 1991; McKenzie/Tullock 1984; Opp 1979; Weede 1989.

72 E. g. Breyer/Bernholz 1993/94; Buchanan/Tullock 1962; Downs 1957; Olson 1965.

73 E. g. Behrens 1986; Coase 1960; Posner 1977.

74 E. g. Furubotn/Pejovich 1974.

75 E. g. Brennan/Buchanan 1985; Buchanan 1975; Mueller 1979, 1991; Tullock 1970.

76 E. g. Kliemt 1980, 1985; Hoerster 1977, 1981, 1983; Mackie 1977.

77 E. g. Blau 1967; Coleman 1990; Opp 1979; Vanberg 1975; Weede 1990.

the economic and legal order of society – had from the start been at the centre of attention.[78]

The 'institutionalist revolution' replaced a conception of economic theory building which had regarded the social and legal framework of economic activities as 'exogenous data' and therefore essentially as a subject matter of other disciplines. Social norms and institutions were treated merely as 'constraints', as restrictions of individual actors' options which they must take into account in their choices. With the expansion of the economic approach, however, the institutional framework itself became a primary subject of theoretical analysis and explanation. It is now considered to be a phenomenon of social reality which comes into existence through utility-maximizing actions of individual actors. The model of *homo oeconomicus* is thought to be applicable not only to actions *under* the norms and rules of a social order; but also to the genesis and maintenance of social order *itself.*

For our present purpose, the economic approach with its behavioural model of *homo oeconomicus* thus appears rather attractive at first sight. With its theoretical premises it seems to postulate exactly what is our basic empirical assumption: that individuals as enlightened and pragmatic actors rationally pursue their interests and personal benefit. But despite this coincidence and despite the impressive 'triumphal march' of *homo oeconomicus* we cannot simply rely on that model without further consideration.

On the one hand, we must keep in mind the explanatory limits of the *homo oeconomicus* model. The optimistic and self-confident expansion of the economic approach itself has been accompanied by increasing doubts about the universal applicability of its behavioural model. With good reason it has been called into question whether the model of *homo oeconomicus*, when adopted as the only foundation of a *general* social-scientific research programme, satisfies the minimum requirements of empirical adequacy which must be demanded even of the 'hard core' of an empirical theory. The more attempts there have been to apply the economic model of behaviour to all kinds of human action, the more empirical counter-evidence has been found. That evidence suggests that rational utility maximization as postulated by the model is „more the exception than the rule".[79]

Reactions to these difficulties oscillate between the conscious 'immunization' of the model and more or less drastic modifications of its core assumptions. A typical example of the latter is the concept of 'bounded rationality'.[80] Another option has been the elaboration of several variants of the economic model of behaviour, each of which is thought to apply to specific empirical conditions. Some of these variants, however, are notoriously close to the 'rival' model of *homo sociologicus.*[81] Other revisions of the

[78] "Constitutional political economy is best interpreted as a re-emphasis, a revival, a re-discovery, of basic elements of earlier intellectual traditions that have been set aside, neglected, and sometimes forgotten in the social sciences and social philosophy" (Buchanan 1990, 10).

[79] Schoemaker 1982, 552; for an overview over experimental research results, cf. also Frey 1988; Hogarth/ Reder 1987; Kahneman/Slovic/Tversky 1982; Thaler 1992; numerous ingenious and sometimes funny counter-examples from everyday life are reported in Schelling 1984, 57 ff., 83 ff.

[80] Cf. Simon 1982. For further considerations cf., e. g., Frey 1992, 1993a; Kliemt 1984, 1991; Lindenberg 1990; Lindenberg/Frey 1993; Margolis 1981, 1982; Mueller 1986, 1992; Tversky/Kahneman 1986; Zintl 1989.

[81] Still instructive on this model: Dahrendorf 1968.

original premises include attempts to introduce the possibility of preference change into the model's premises[82] and even the assumption that compliance with norms may itself generate utility.[83] Another proposal amounts to the conception of 'nested' or multi-level decisions where the model of rational utility-maximization is believed to be applicable only to specific 'segments' of a person or certain 'levels' in the decision-making process.[84]

On the other hand, it is our specific purpose which makes *homo oeconomicus* appear as an unsuitable model of behaviour. We want to explain how morality and a sense of social commitment can grow and flourish among the citizens of a secular, interest-dominated society. And in regard to the concept of moral action as it has been introduced above, the model of *homo oeconomicus* is basically unable to account for such action. Moral action was characterized as an action where the actor adopts an internal point of view towards some norm. That means that he voluntarily uses that norm as a standard for his behaviour without calculating in each case the benefit or disutility connected with compliance or non-compliance. A person who in that way acts 'genuinely' morally not only has an 'extrinsic' motivation to act morally because of the expected advantages or disadvantages of doing so. He also has a specific 'intrinsic' motivation which operates independently of eventual external incentives.[85]

If we use an economic model of behaviour along the line of *homo oeconomicus*, then we must explain compliance with a norm in each case with the rational decision-making of a utility-maximizing actor. There is then only *one* good reason for the addressee of a norm to comply with that norm, and that is because it is the utility-maximizing choice in the specific situation. In principle, the behaviour of *homo oeconomicus* is diagonally opposed to compliance with norms. He decides anew in each and every situation and the criterion of choice is always which option can be expected to have the best possible consequences. Regular conformity to norms by a *homo oeconomicus* thus can be explained only as repeated "situational norm compliance"[86] which occurs as the result of a sequence of rational decisions on the basis of similar incentive structures. Structurally, such situational norm compliance is not different from other rational and utility-maximizing behaviour. Under the premises of an economic approach it is the *only* possible form of norm compliance, because a *homo oeconomicus always* decides on the basis of a situational assessment and weighing up of his options.

[82] Cf. Elster 1979, 77 ff., 1983, 109 ff.; Frank 1987, 1988; Hegselmann/Raub/Voss 1986; Schelling 1984, 83 ff., 93 ff.; Sen 1986; von Weizsäcker 1971, 1984.

[83] Cf. Coleman 1987; Opp 1983, 9, 214, 218; 1986; M. Taylor 1993.

[84] Cf. Coleman 1990, 503 ff.; Frank 1987; Kliemt 1993a; Schelling 1984; Vanberg 1988a, 1988b.

[85] Of course, one is not *forced* to define the concept of moral action in this way. It can also be defined in a way that makes it compatible with the model of *homo oeconomicus*. But in the present investigation we are exclusively interested in the question to what extent 'genuinely' moral behaviour in the defined sense can be expected in a liberal society. The reason for this is the assumption that it is precisely such 'genuinely' moral behaviour – as distinct from the compliance with moral norms merely for external reasons – which is essential for the viability of a liberal society. *That* assumption, in turn, is not further justified in what follows; it is rather taken as our basic premise. On the relevance of the concept of 'intrinsic' motivation in contemporary economic theory building, cf. Frey 1992, 1993a, 1993b.

[86] Vanberg 1988b, 152.

A *homo oeconomicus* will, therefore, *never* adopt an internal point of view towards a norm. He will never accept a norm as a binding standard of behaviour or as a 'personal' norm in the sense that he 'blindly' follows it without considering the consequences for his interests. Moreover, a *homo oeconomicus* is *incapable* of adopting an internal point of view towards a norm. In a certain sense he is 'condemned' to check anew on every occasion whether he is really choosing the best possible option. His behavioural repertoire simply does not contain 'genuinely' moral action for 'intrinsic' reasons. He necessarily regards all norms from an external point of view and complies with a norm because of an 'extrinsic' motivation only if the norm-compliant behaviour is his utility-maximizing option in a given situation. That means that the model of *homo oeconomicus* is basically unsuitable for our purpose – even if we leave aside its possible shortcomings as a tool for empirical explanation. It is for *conceptual* reasons that we cannot reach the goal of this investigation with that model, because 'genuinely' moral action is excluded *a priori* by its premises.

However, in our search for an alternative model we must keep in mind another important aspect of our explanatory aim: we want to investigate whether morality and a sense of social commitment can be explained as resulting from the actions of *self-interested* individuals. We must therefore carefully avoid setting out in the wrong direction by choosing a model of behaviour that cannot be regarded as 'modelling' self-interested action. The necessary modifications of the economic model must be designed in such a way as to make the modified behavioural model still applicable to persons who, in 'pragmatic acceptance of the world', rationally pursue their individual interests. Despite all its shortcomings, this forces us to stay relatively 'close' to the economic model of *homo oeconomicus*.

IX. Outline of the Investigation

We do not need to start from zero in our search for a model of behaviour that is adequate for our present purpose. As I have already pointed out, there is a growing tendency to revise the original model of *homo oeconomicus* within the tradition of economic theory itself. In addition we can go back to *the* classic author of sociology, that is, to Max Weber. From Weber we can learn that the model of rational utility-maximization can be broken down into several, independent components. It can thus be partially revised while at the same time still providing a theoretically plausible concept of rational, self-interested actors.

This will be the task of the first chapter, *Utility-Maximization and Commitment to Norms*. We will modify the economic model of behaviour in such a way that, though manifestly deviating from the 'standard' model of *homo oeconomicus*, it will still be applicable as an adequate model of interest-based action. We will see that the model of *homo oeconomicus* has distorted the image of the human actor in an important aspect. The core of an 'economic' conception of man must, in any case, be the assumption that people consistently act according to their self-interest.[87] But whereas the classics of eco-

[87] That is "The Soul of Modern Economic Man" (Myers 1983, 11).

nomics – just like ancient ethics – always included the *personality and character traits* people develop to that avail,[88] their modern successors discuss the pursuit of individual interests almost exclusively as a problem of situational rational choice, i. e. what *behaviour* a prudent actor chooses in particular situations. With an extended model of interest-based action, however, it can be shown that it may be in a person's long-term interest to acquire stable dispositions and a 'commitment to norms' which lead to a case-independent behaviour, rather than aspiring to make the best possible choice on each single occasion.

In the second chapter, *Norm-Commitment and the Emergence of Norms*, we will analyse in more detail under what conditions and in what situations such dispositional, norm-directed action may have beneficial consequences for an actor. We will see that personal norms can have significant advantages as instruments of self-control, as rules of thumb and as virtues. Especially personal norms as virtues are of central importance to a theory of the genesis of morality. The evolution of such virtues is facilitated and fostered, above all, by a person's participation in specific forms of collective action, i. e. in 'cooperative enterprises'. The reason for this is that in cooperative enterprises a mechanism of reputation becomes effective. Individuals who through their behaviour demonstrate that they possess certain virtues can thus enjoy substantial advantages over others who do not possess these virtues.

However, the conclusions in the second chapter are reached only with the help of a strong idealization: it is simply assumed that people's dispositions can be easily inferred from their observable actions. In the third chapter, *Deception and Trust*, this idealization is abandoned. We will discuss the consequences of the fact that observing someone's behaviour often allows only very doubtful and uncertain conclusions about that person's character and dispositions. The analysis in this chapter attempts to show, however, that despite the temptations of deception and hypocrisy there are sufficient possibilities to distinguish frauds and hypocrites from authentic, morally reliable persons. This is especially true in cooperative enterprises. Hence, in view of its costs and risks a strategy of deception generally does not seem to be a promising prospect. It can very well be in someone's self-interest not only to *appear* to be, but actually to *be* an honest person.

The considerations in the fourth chapter, *Moral Point of View and Moral Identity,* attempt to show how the virtues acquired by the members of a cooperative enterprise will, under certain conditions, have beneficial consequences for the existence of a social order as a whole. Their qualities as 'moral personalities' must not necessarily be restricted to traits that are only of use to the limited collectivity of the respective cooperative enterprise. They can entail a general disposition to moral behaviour which benefits the entire society. To the extent that the members of cooperative associations are guided by universalistic principles of interpersonal respect and social equity, they will contribute to the protection and conservation of individual and collective goods outside of their respective enterprises too. The evolution of such a universalistic morality, however, depends on the fulfillment of certain preconditions: it can only flourish in an open society

[88] Again, this can be seen most clearly in Hume: „'Tis evident, that when we praise any actions, we regard only the motives that produced them, and consider the actions as signs or indications of certain principles in the mind and temper" (Hume 1739, 529).

where people are protected from arbitrary power and the violation of norms is met with sufficient sanctions.

The fifth and last chapter, *The Market of Virtue*, begins with a consideration of the question whether these conditions can, in principle, be satisfied and offers some speculation about their historical evolution. The chapter concludes with a final assessment of the vision of liberalism. It is argued that this vision can be successfully defended only if the common picture of the basic features of a liberal society and its social mechanisms is corrected. A more realistic picture shows that market exchange and competition among individuals are by no means the only, or the only prominent, features of a liberal social and economic order – although the critics of such an order have often, and not without success, painted such a one-sided picture. In modern liberal society, not only trade and exchange have been 'liberated'; the self-determined association with people, their voluntary union in communities and groups has also experienced such 'liberation'. The citizens of a liberal society not only enjoy the freedom of individual economic activity by their own decision, the basic rights to a sphere of privacy and the protection of their property. They are also free to assemble and associate with other people as they see fit, whether in establishing an economic enterprise in order to further their material prosperity, an association for the representation of common political or economic interests, a club for the pursuit of some kind of ideal, or a community whose *raison d'être* are the 'internal goods' of a common practice themselves. Historically, the multi-faceted development of free associations and unions for the pursuit of self-determined ends, in self-designed ways and with self-chosen partners is just as much a genuine product of liberal society as the universal diffusion of market relations. A liberal society is characterized by a free market *and* free associations.

This is where a defence of the vision of liberalism must start and with it the explanation how the 'demand for morality' of a liberal social order can be met in an interest-dominated society. The result of the present investigation is that the protection and promotion of the freedom of association is decisive for the 'moral productivity' of a liberal society. Where that freedom flourishes without constraints, besides an economic market a 'market of virtue' can arise with a demand for 'virtuous' persons who are therefore suitable partners for cooperative enterprises. If such a market of virtue exists, it can with *its* invisible hand bring about the production of that measure of morality and social commitment which is needed for the existence of a liberal society as a whole. On that basis, we can then also dismiss the specific communitarian objections: neither does a liberal society necessarily lead to the 'individualist isolation' of its citizens, nor does it necessarily end up in relativism and blind decisionism in its treatment of moral problems.

However, it will also become evident that precisely those conditions which are typically found in modern industrial societies are among the necessary foundations of a well-functioning market of virtue: a great number of members, anonymous and functionally oriented relations between actors, and a high mobility, geographically as well as between social groups. This is quite the contrary of what is widely believed to be the case. According to a common conception, the orientation towards individual self-interest together with the way of life in modern 'mass society' is the source of cultural, political and moral evils. In the following investigation I attempt to show, on the contrary, that those very conditions are indispensable prerequisites for the empirical establishment of a morality in which the interests of all members of society will find consideration, and therefore also indispensable prerequisites for a social order in which ideological enlightenment, political freedom and economic prosperity are conceivable at the same time.

CHAPTER 1

UTILITY-MAXIMIZATION AND COMMITMENT TO NORMS

I. Learning from Max Weber

1. INSTRUMENTAL RATIONALITY AND VALUE RATIONALITY: A DUAL MODEL OF ACTION

Max Weber attempts to explain social facts and processes as the 'aggregated' results of individual actions, just as modern methodological individualism does. For Weber, too, the conception of rational action plays a central role. But there are also important differences between Weber and modern methodological individualism. The reason he gives for his approach is partly different, as is the way in which he elaborates its details. The most obvious difference from today's perspective is that with his typology of rational action Weber formulates from the very beginning a *dual* conception. With his famous dichotomy of 'instrumental rationality' *(Zweckrationalität)* and 'value rationality' *(Wertrationalität)* he introduces *two* fundamental modes of rational action. Weber regards both 'models of rationality' as equally necessary for sociological theory building.

It is interesting to note that Weber's 'ideal types' of instrumental and value rationality are basically equivalent to the two models of what sociologists today call *homo oeconomicus* and *homo sociologicus*. Thus, Weber thought it necessary to combine two conceptions which later in sociological theory-building gave rise to two independent and rival research programmes, based on different methodological principles as well as on different models of action, namely: a 'rationalistic' and 'individualistic' programme, on the one hand, and a 'normativistic' and 'holistic' programme, on the other.[1] The theoretical foundations and central theses of Weber's sociological work, however, can be adequately understood and assessed only if one takes into account that both models were equally important to him as 'basic concepts of sociology' and that, unlike some of his successors, he particularly did not attempt to reduce one of them to the other.

Nevertheless, Weber's typology of action has its weaknesses. First of all, it lacks internal consistency, a consequence of this being that the distinction between instrumental rationality and value rationality in its original form cannot account for all sociologically relevant kinds of action. Besides, it also neglects an important dimension of rational action. It will, therefore, be our first task in what follows to elaborate an *extension* of Weber's typology of action.

2. ENDS AND NORMS, IDEAL VALUES AND SUBJECTIVE UTILITY

The idea that Weber's typology needs to be complemented is suggested at first sight by the simple fact that his concepts of the 'instrumentally rational' and the 'value-rational'

[1] On these two basic currents in sociology, cf. e. g. Bohnen 1975; Vanberg 1975; Raub/Voss 1981.

each combine *two* logically independent features of actions. The question thus immediately arises whether these features are also *empirically* independent and whether, therefore, other combinations than those considered by Weber can possibly occur. The two characteristics can be classified as 'decision rules' and 'reasons for action'. Weber mentions two kinds of decision rules:

1. Teleological orientation. In this case, the actor decides with a view towards ends, means and secondary consequences: "this involves rational consideration of alternative means to the end, of the relations of the end to the secondary consequences, and finally of the relative importance of different possible ends", on the basis of his "expectations as to the behaviour of objects in the environment and of other human beings".[2]

A 'teleological orientation' implies that in a decision situation the actor assesses his options and their probable consequences and then chooses that option which according to his own standards is the best. The rational justification of the *choice* of a particular end or purpose is, according to Weber, explicitly a *constitutive element* of an instrumentally rational decision process. Weber's conception contains – if only as an intuitive sketch – all relevant aspects of the modern rational-choice model. According to this model, a rational decision-maker chooses from his given set of alternatives that option which, given his empirical knowledge about the probable consequences of different actions, has the highest expected value relative to his own criteria of assessment.[3] In order to make it perfectly clear that Weber's conception of a teleological orientation is not to be understood in the sense of a fixation on somehow predetermined ends, I will speak of a 'consequence-based orientation' in its broadest sense, instead of a 'teleological orientation'.

2. Commitment to norms. Unlike in the case of a consequence-based orientation, in case of a commitment to norms the actor acts according to "commands" or "demands" prescribing a certain way of action, "independently of its prospects of success", i. e. without considering "the behaviour of objects in the environment and of other human beings".

'Commitment to norms' means that the actor's decision is not based on the comparative assessment of alternative actions and their consequences; rather, from among the options he has on a particular occasion he chooses that which is prescribed by some norm. If in a purely formal approach we understand by acting 'rationally' simply acting in a predictable, 'non-arbitrary' way, then in the case of a consequence-based decision arbitrary action is avoided by systematically *weighing* all available options, whereas in the case of a commitment to norms arbitrariness is avoided by the normative *emphasis* on one option.

For a precise delimitation between the two different decision rules, it is important to note that an actor's regular compliance with a norm because of his being committed to norms is to be clearly distinguished from regular conformity with a norm which comes about as the result of a sequence of consequence-based decisions. In the latter case, regular conformity with a norm only takes place because *in every single situation*

[2] Unless otherwise indicated, the following citations are taken from Weber 1968, 24 ff.

[3] For concise presentations of this model, cf., e. g., Opp 1983, 31 ff.; Elster 1986, 1 ff.; Becker 1976, 1 ff.; Schoemaker 1982.

complying with the norm turns out to be the best possible choice from the given set of options. A paradigmatic example of such an "order which is adhered to from motives of pure expediency"[4] is the compliance with a norm because the actor expects sanctions or rewards in a particular context of action. Structurally, there is no difference between such a 'situational conformity' with a norm and other consequence-based actions. After all, in each single case it is the result of an individual assessment of all competing and conflicting ends and consequences. There is no reason for subsuming the situational compliance with norms under a decision rule of its own, since it can always be traced back to a consequence-based mode of decision.

This is fundamentally different in the case of a commitment to norms, i. e. the "genuine compliance with norms".[5] In this case, the choice of an action does not depend on the assessment of available options. Instead, the actor decides according to some norm which predetermines what action he is to perform. In normatively relevant situations he acts in compliance with that norm regardless of the consequences this will have in the particular case. Norm-compliant behaviour *by definition* excludes the individual assessment of the particular case in the sense of the decision-theoretic model. Hence, repeated or regular compliance with a norm because of a commitment to norms cannot be reduced to a sequence of consequence-based decisions.

Besides the two *decision rules* Weber also distinguishes two types of *reasons for action*:

1. Subjective utility. In this case, the reason for an action is the utility the actor himself can expect to gain from it. If the actor is rational, he arranges his "subjective wants [...] in a scale of consciously assessed relative urgency" and then "orients his action to this scale in such a way that they are satisfied as far as possible in order of urgency, as formulated in the principle of 'marginal utility'".

The criterion an actor uses for assessing his options in such cases, i. e. for determining his 'preference order' over a given set of alternatives, is the expected subjective utility. Relating a person's order of preferences to expected utility in such a way constitutes a deviation from today's theory of rational decision. According to the latter, the preferences a person utters or actually 'reveals' in making a decision for certain goods are usually *by definition* identified with an evaluation of those goods in terms of their subjective utility. In this conception, preferences are *represented* by a subjective 'utility function' rather than being *determined* or *generated* by subjective perceptions of utility.[6] On this assumption, every preference order someone actually has *implies* a subjective utility function; or, in terms of the theory of 'revealed' preferences, every rational decision can be explained as the maximization of some utility function: 'utility' is regarded simply as an abbreviation for 'preferences', and thus utility maximization for the choice of the most preferred alternative.[7]

It is important to note that the concept of utility Weber uses in his typology of action does *not* coincide with that concept of preferences. For Weber subjective utility is

[4] Weber 1968, 31.

[5] Vanberg 1988b, 138; on the distinction between the commitment to norms and 'case-dependent adaptation', cf. especially Kliemt 1984, 32 ff.; 1985, 203 ff; 1987.

[6] Schoemaker 1982, 532; Harsanyi 1986, 86.

[7] Elster 1982, 118; for a critique of this procedure, cf., e. g., Kliemt 1984, Sen 1986.

only *one* of several possible criteria according to which an actor may assign values to his options and thus generate preferences. In this conception the subjective utility of options is a separate causal determinant of preferences, existing independently of how alternatives are finally ranked in a rational choice of action. Only if subjective utility is thus distinguished from preferences does it make sense to assume that *besides* the attainment of subjective utility there can also be *other* reasons for rational action.

2. *Ideal value*. In this case the reason for an action is the realization of values which cannot be reduced to subjective utility. Examples would be the actions of persons "who, regardless of possible cost to themselves, act to put into practice their convictions of what seems to them to be required by duty, honor, the pursuit of beauty, a religious call, personal loyality, or the importance of some 'cause' no matter in what it consists".

'Ideal values' provide us with criteria for the evaluation of the most diverse objects. Depending on the respective ideal standards, social relations, events, actions, persons, goods, objects of art, or social norms may be more or less valuable. A person may be noble and good, a painting beautiful and moving, a way of action praiseworthy, or a normative order just. Just as with subjective utility, ideal values too may be used as standards for a person to rank options in a preference order and determine what is preferred most.

Subjective utility and ideal values share an important formal feature which explains their functional equivalence in decision processes and justifies the designation of both as 'reasons for action': 'good', 'bad', 'beautiful', 'just', and 'useful' all belong to the class of *evaluative concepts*.[8] Just as in the case of subjective utility, an ideal value constitutes a standard of evaluation which an object may satisfy to a higher or lower degree. Thus, we can say both for utility-motivated and for value-motivated action that it is based on a 'value judgment' reached by an assessment of 'values': either of the value of subjective utility in terms of the actor's empirically given needs and individual interests, or of ideal values whose realization the actor has chosen as the unselfish end of his action. Reasons for action are always 'values' in this broader sense; and in terms of reasons for action an action is rational only if it serves the realization of the actor's personal values, i. e. if it is either *subjectively useful* or *ideally valuable*.[9]

3. *HOMO OECONOMICUS* AND *HOMO SOCIOLOGICUS*

In each of his two modes of action, which he calls 'instrumental rationality' and 'value rationality', Weber combines one of the two reasons for action just presented with one of the decision rules, as shown in *Diagram 1* below. Instrumentally rational action combines the consequence-based decision rule with subjective utility as a reason for action. According to Weber, an action is oriented "wholly to the rational achievement of ends" only when "the end, the means, and secondary consequences are all rationally taken into account and weighed" according to the criterion of "subjective wants". The "ideal of purposeful action", he says, is the "principle of marginal utility", taken as the "standard of evaluation".[10] On the other hand, for value-rational action Weber combines ideal

[8] On the formal analysis of evaluative concepts, cf. Kutschera 1973, 85 ff.; 1982, 10 ff.
[9] For a more detailed analysis of different standards of evaluation, cf. von Wright 1963b.
[10] Weber 1922, 329.

values as a reason for action with a commitment to norms as a decision rule. Purely value-rational action is action without regard to foreseeable consequences, "it always involves 'commands' or 'demands' which, in the actor's opinion, are binding on him". Those who act value-rationally do not reflect on the cost of their action but "exclusively" on its "intrinsic value". "Value-oriented" action is by definition not "expectation-oriented".[11]

Diagram 1: *Max Weber's Ideal Types of Rational Action*

		Decision rules	
		consequence-based	*norm-committed*
Reasons for action	*subjective utility*	1 "instrumentally rational" (homo oeconomicus)	2 ?
	ideal values	3 ?	4 "value-rational" (homo sociologicus)

In the ideal type of instrumentally rational action we can easily recognize the model of *homo oeconomicus*, since for a *homo oeconomicus* all that counts is the consequences of his actions on each particular occasion, and his only motivation is the maximization of his subjective utility. Likewise, the historical model of value-rational action is easily identified and can explain why it seems to have been almost self-evident for Weber that there is a close connection between ideal values as reasons for action and a commitment to norms. We find this model in Immanuel Kant's moral philosophy. In Kant's view, a person's actions have moral value only if they "categorically" comply with the prescriptions of a set of moral rules. In time that austere Kantian character developed into a personality no less famous than *homo oeconomicus*: namely, into *homo sociologicus*.[12] *Homo sociologicus* differs from his Kantian ancestor above all in that he does not conceive of ideal values as the "moving force of the pure conception of virtue" or the "iron voice of duty" which makes him "tremble". He simply acquires his values and his com-

[11] Ibid., 442.

[12] On the model of *homo sociologicus*, cf. Dahrendorf 1968.

mitment to norms in a 'process of socialization'. *Homo sociologicus* is motivated by certain social values and is committed to certain norms because he has 'internalized' them, that is, he "adopts them and converts them into a determinant of his behaviour".[13]

4. From *Homo sociologicus* to *Homo politicus*

Weber himself explicitly formulates the criterion for the usefulness of his "classification": "it can only be judged in terms of its results." The diagram shows directly what the "usefulness" of Weber's classification depends on: They are useful only if, from a socio-scientific point of view, there are no relevant kinds of action with such a combination of features that they fall into the – so far, empty – cells 2 and 3. Now, one can think of three reasons why the 'empty cells' might be irrelevant for sociological purposes: *first*, actions with these features might not plausibly be conceivable as *rational* actions. *Second*, it might be *empirically* impossible for these combinations to actually occur; in which case the corresponding types of action would be only logical constructs. *Third*, actions of that kind might be *irrelevant to social theory*.

In fact, however, there are neither empirical reasons nor reasons connected to the postulates of rationality which necessarily link utility-motivation exclusively to consequence-based decisions and value-motivation to norm-commitment. Especially the combination of value-motivation and a commitment to norms in the value-rational type of action is by no means self-evident. It brings together two independent features of actions whose combination depends on specific non-trivial preconditions, such as a process of socialization leading to the 'internalization' of social values and norms, or an actor's belief that his personal values can best be realized by committing himself to norms.

But the intention to realize ideal values must not necessarily lead to a norm-committed behaviour. On the contrary: if it is true that ideal values and subjective utility are functionally equivalent criteria, then we have no reason to assume *prima facie* that the intention to realize ideal values necessarily obliges a rational actor to follow a decision rule other than the one he would use if his intention were to maximize his subjective utility. If from a formal point of view subjective utility and ideal values fulfil the same function as criteria of evaluation, they should also be able to play analogous roles in an actor's decisions. Seen in this light, it is no more plausible to link the commitment to norms to value-motivation than to combine the latter with consequence-based decisions. As a type of action this combination is just as plausible as value-rational action in the Weberian sense. Rational persons desiring to realize ideal values may perfectly well make their decisions depend on "expectations as to the behaviour of objects in the environment and of other human beings" and use these expectations "as 'conditions' or 'means' for the attainment of [their] own rationally pursued and calculated ends". The only difference to instrumentally rational action in Weber's sense is that the *criterion* for weighing and assessing ends and options are ideal values instead of the subjective utility of the acting person.[14]

[13] Ibid., 163.

[14] Weber's discussion of his famous distinction between an "ethics of conviction" *(Gesinnungsethik)* and an "ethics of responsibility" *(Verantwortungsethik)* can be read, in one sense, as a plea for the recognition of the relevance of a kind of action based on a combination of value-motivation and consequence-based decision.

Therefore, according to the criteria of rationality, it makes sense to complement Weber's typology of rational action by introducing a 'pure' type of action based on the combination of value-motivation and consequence-based decision. That type is then a genuine counterpart to both instrumentally rational and value-rational action. To what extent it is also empirically and theoretically relevant need not concern us here, since for our purposes that type of action will not matter.

Diagram 2: *Partly Complemented Ideal Types of Rational Action*

		Decision rules	
		consequence-based	*norm-committed*
Reasons for action	*subjective utility*	1 homo oeconomicus ("instrumentally rational")	2 ?
	ideal values	3 homo politicus ("responsibility-oriented")	4 homo sociologicus ("value-rational")

The name 'homo politicus' has been chosen for this new type primarily because Weber considered it, at least implicitly, mainly by means of the example of the politician with a 'vocation', i. e. who acts in a morally responsible way. But it can also be justified with substantial reasons. In everyday life, most of the decisions we are faced with are repetitive, displaying the same relevant features over and over again. In such situations, decisions that are 'correct' from an evaluative point of view can be ensured through compliance with norms. Politicians, by contrast, often face new problems and changing constellations. In such cases decisions cannot be taken mechanically; they require the careful assessment of alternatives and their expected consequences. Thus, *homo sociologicus* in that sense represents the 'every-day version' of a value-motivated person, whereas *homo*

Using the example of a responsible politician, Weber himself declares in all clarity that besides the type of "absolute ethics" which prescribes certain actions categorically, without "asking" about the consequences (Weber 1921, 551), there is another, equally plausible type of ethics according to which one must morally "account" for the consequences of one's actions (ibid., 552). But for Weber, being morally "accountable" for the consequences of one's actions means nothing other than weighing the given options for action and their various consequences on the basis of moral values.

politicus represents the same kind of person in conditions which demand exceptional responsibility because of the high complexity of the matters that come up for decision.

5. *HOMO OECONOMICUS & HOMO SOCIOLOGICUS = HOMO SAPIENS*?

As we have seen, actions which are motivated by ideal values are not necessarily linked to a commitment to norms. The question is therefore whether the converse holds too, i. e. whether a commitment to norms can also do without ideal values as reasons for action. At least formally, the above diagram also allows the combination of *subjective utility* as reason for action with a *commitment to norms* as decision rule. The question is, in other words: does cell 2 have a 'tenant' too? If so, it would mean that a commitment to norms can be rationally justified by the aim of subjective utility-maximization. A look at socio-scientific scholarship seems to teach us that the question is not particularly interesting. At least until a few years ago there was practically no research on whether and under what conditions according to the criterion of subjective utility it may be rational for actors to commit themselves to norms instead of assessing their options and the consequences in each single situation. Does such a way of acting have no relevance to social reality? Is it perhaps ruled out for empirical reasons? Or does it contradict the postulates of rationality?

In any case, the reconstruction of Weber's typology of action makes it clear what alternatives are left if one does not wish to interpret action motivated by interests or utility in the sense of the economic model of *homo oeconomicus*. The switch to the models of *homo politicus* or *homo sociologicus* is impossible if explanations are still to be based on the rational pursuit of individual interests. However, according to the typology proposed above there is another possibility: by introducing a type of action which combines utility-motivation with a commitment to norms, we can develop a model of behaviour which departs in important aspects from *homo oeconomicus*, without at the same time moving too far in the direction of *homo sociologicus* or *homo politicus*.

For the purpose of defending the vision of liberalism, two points are of central importance here. For one thing, such a model of behaviour, although clearly different from the economic model, can still be understood as a model of the kind of action which serves the rational pursuit of individual interests. In this view, *homo oeconomicus* is not the only model for representing the way how people decide and act who, in 'pragmatic acceptance of the world', wish to increase their subjective utility. According to the conception of a rational behaviour which is motivated by subjective utility and committed to norms, an actor will act in a norm-committed way only if doing so will better serve his subjective utility than if he were to assess the consequences of his actions in each single case. In that sense, he pursues his interests just as consistently as *homo oeconomicus*. A world inhabited by such actors can be seen to fit the liberal vision of a secular and interest-dominated society just as well as a world of *homines oeconomici*.

For another thing, norm-committed action can be understood as action where the actor adopts an *internal point of view* towards some norm. Individuals who choose an action that has been prescribed by a norm regardless of its consequences surely are not 'opportunistic' utility-maximizers who comply with a norm only when doing so promises to bring more personal benefits than costs on that particular occasion. Rather, they 'accept' the norm as a standard of action which determines their decisions independently of the situational incentives and constraints. Hence, a model of rational utility-maximization complemented by a category of norm-committed action would, at least in principle, open up the possibility of explaining even genuinely moral action as a consequence of a rational pursuit of interests – provided one can argue that it is beneficial for people to commit themselves to the norms of *morality*. With such an extended model of behaviour we would have found the instrument we have been looking for, i. e. a tool for examining in more detail the thesis that acting morally can be compatible with an individual orientation towards interests. It would then no longer be excluded *by definition* that an interest-based point of view might coincide with a moral point of view.

But the fact that the 'new' type of action could possibly fulfil such a useful explanatory function does not prove that its potential advantages can actually be realized. For that, at least three problems must be solved:

First, it must be shown that it can in fact be rational from the point of view of the pursuit of individual interests to act with a commitment to norms, i. e. that this can be a way of acting which under certain circumstances optimally serves the interests of the actor in question and therefore is consistent with the criteria of rationality.

Second, it must be shown that a model of behaviour which includes norm-commitment is empirically adequate, i. e. that it does not contain any assumption about human capacities and characteristics which manifestly contradicts empirical facts.

Third, we must answer the decisive question whether in a liberal society people can have good reasons to acquire a commitment to the norms of morality in order to realize their personal interests.

Keeping in mind that a tenable theoretical foundation thus is still pending we can now complete our typology:

Diagram 3: *Extended Ideal Types of Rational Action*

		Decision rules	
		consequence-based	*norm-committed*
Reasons for action	*subjective utility*	1 homo oeconomicus	2 homo sapiens
	ideal values	3 homo politicus	4 homo sociologicus

Whether and to what extent the new model of behaviour deserves to be given the honourable title of 'homo sapiens', that is, whether it really contributes to an empirically correct concept of human capacities and whether it also constitutes a prudent strategy are questions the following examination will have to answer. Meanwhile, the term must be understood as an expression of the hope that an enlightened 'pragmatic acceptance of the world' is not only compatible with an individually rational way of life, but can also satisfy the requirements of the common good and the dictates of morality.

II. The Model of a Dispositional Utility-Maximizer

1. Situational and Dispositional Utility-Maximization

Being a rational utility-maximizer, *homo oeconomicus* chooses the option with the greatest expected utility at every opportunity. We can therefore also call him a *situational* utility-maximizer. As such, *homo oeconomicus* is *unable* to act according to any other decision rule. His ability to maximize his subjective utility in every situation is also his fate. He has no choice as regards to the rules under which he makes his choices. In contrast, the purpose of introducing a utility-motivated *and* norm-committed type of action into the economic model of behaviour is to give human actors two *additional capacities*:

First, they need not always act according to the decision rule of a consequence-based assessment of the particular situation. Instead, they can commit themselves to norms. They can acquire the *disposition* of choosing a normatively prescribed option regardless of the consequences compliance with the norm will have in a particular situation.

Second, they can adapt their way of decision-making to their respective interests. Whether in a sequence of situations they act dispositionally in commitment to norms or strictly in consideration of the consequences of each single act will depend on which decision rule is more advantageous to them.

I will call actors possessing these additional capacities *dispositional* maximizers of utility.[15] Just like situational maximizers, dispositional utility-maximizers are *rational* utility-maximizers, i. e. they make the best of the given circumstances in terms of their subjective utility. However, unlike situational maximizers, dispositional maximizers can realize gains by acting in accordance with a disposition. In pursuing their interests they can act *either* in a consequence-based way *or* in commitment to norms, and they will act according to the more promising of these strategies.

2. The Freedom to be Unfree

As has already been remarked, dispositional utility-maximizers, unlike situational maximizers, can adopt an *internal point of view* towards norms. Since they can *commit* themselves to norms, they can comply with a norm without calculating opportunistically the expected costs and benefits. Dispositional utility-maximizers can thus 'recognize' or 'ac-

[15] Similar models of behaviour are used by Frank 1987, 1988; Gauthier 1986; Kliemt 1987, 1990b, 1993b; Rowe 1989; Vanberg 1988a, 1988b, 1993a, 1993b.

cept' a norm as a 'personal' norm in the sense of regarding themselves as belonging to the class of norm-addressees.

The model of a dispositional maximizer implies an *expansion* of the possibilities and capacities of a rational utility-maximizer. It includes *new* options – autonomy is *enhanced*.[16] Of course, situational utility-maximizers can choose the option with the best possible consequences in each single choice situation. But they *cannot* decide in advance which option they will choose in some *future* choice situation even when doing so would be highly advantageous to them. *That* option they do not have, because they lack the capacity for 'self-commitment'. The apparent 'omnipotence' of a situational utility-maximizer which consists in his unlimited ability to make a new choice in every new situation is thus actually an 'impotence'.[17]

In contrast, a dispositional commitment to norms offers a form of 'behavioural automatization' by 'programming' persons to act in a certain way and thus making them independent of the influence of specific situational incentives. The capacity to act in a dispositionally predetermined way can serve to block another capacity – namely, the capacity for situational utility-maximization. Because of this, dispositional utility-maximizers can exert control over their future decisions and therefore have more options than situational maximizers – even if the additional option consists in the possibility to *constrain* their own *future* choices: „When he adopts a rule and ensures its enforcement, the individual is exercising his freedom, at a more comprehensive planning stage of choice, only through restricting his own freedom in subsequent potential choice situations."[18]

3. THE ADVANTAGE OF A COMMITMENT TO NORMS: THE 'RATIONALITY TEST'

However, to what extent the possibility of a dispositional commitment to norms can actually be regarded as a substantial expansion of a rational *utility*-maximizer's abilities depends on the extent to which it is, in fact, an adequate instrument for increasing an actor's individual utility. Does the 'freedom to be unfree' as a means of pursuing one's interests have any relevance as long as there is also the possibility of a strategy of situational utility-maximization? Thus the question is whether a commitment to norms can be rationally consistent with the utility-motive, i. e. whether there are cases in which actors can pursue their personal benefits better by norm-commitment than by consequence-based decisions.

At first sight, it may indeed seem doubtful whether it can *possibly* be desirable for individuals to predetermine their own choices and thus make themselves unfree to choose the best possible actions when it is time to act: "How can it ever be better to follow a rule which requires any actions other than those that are best?"[19] But there is nothing paradoxical in thinking that it may be advantageous *not* to choose the respective utility-maximizing option in every single case. That the elimination of the freedom of decision may have beneficial consequences for the actors themselves does not even re-

[16] This point is especially emphasized by Kliemt 1990a, 78; 1993a, 1993b.

[17] "There is a paradox. Full freedom entails the freedom to bind oneself, to incur obligation, to reduce one's range of choice." (Schelling 1984, 98)

[18] Buchanan 1975, 150.

[19] Rowe 1989, vii.

quire extraordinary circumstances. If it were *only* a matter of whether from the standpoint of individual interests it may be rationally justified in certain situations to *wish* that one's actions were committed to norms, then the prerequisites for such a way of action would often be satisfied.

The classic example of this is Ulysses. In his case it was undoubtedly a rationally justified desire and a rationally justified decision to have himself tied to the mast of his ship in order to protect himself against the temptations of the Sirens, and thus deprive himself of the freedom to fall prey to their lures. Innumerable other examples could easily be found,[20] from the well-known problem of sticking to a diet, regularly saving money or taking out insurance policies, to the battle against all kinds of addictions. In all these cases actors may have reason to desire the restriction of their own freedom of action. Examples can also be found of collective actors and collective decisions. For instance, it may well be in the long-term interest of the members of a democratic decision-making body to restrict that body's competence.[21]

And there are also rational grounds for desiring effective constraints on one's own decision-making autonomy in numerous constellations of interpersonal, strategic contexts. They come about whenever it is beneficial to 'precommit' oneself to a certain way of action *towards other people*. If, for example, I were in the hands of a ruthless kidnapper, it would certainly increase my chances of survival if I could credibly commit myself to not giving him away to the police if he released me. If my potential enemies know that I will retaliate against any attack, even if the costs of doing so are high, then there is a good chance that I can deter them from committing hostile acts against me. If it is known that I will never succumb to blackmail, then no would-be blackmailer will choose me as a victim. And if, when bargaining, a certain limit to my willingness to compromise is simply not negotiable, I can effectively withstand attempts to weaken my position.

The avoidance of damage and costs, however, is not the only potential advantage of self-commitment. If I can commit myself to keeping promises and contracts, no matter how advantageous it might be to break them when a golden opportunity arises, if I can 'condemn' myself to fairness and honesty, no matter how great the incentives for free-riding and cheating, then I can expect an advantageous cooperation with others even under conditions that would exclude cooperation if my freedom of decision were unrestricted. Those who can solve the 'problem' of self-commitment can, in fact, expect considerable advantages.[22]

Thus, obviously, for the rational pursuit of individual interests it is not always desirable to keep the freedom to decide among one's options in every conceivable situation: "It would make the outcome worse if we were always disposed to do what would

[20] In the next chapter I will try to offer a useful classification of such examples.

[21] Cf. Brennan/Buchanan 1985, 67 ff.

[22] Many more examples, as well as their game-theoretical analysis, can be found in the literature. Cf., e. g., Buchanan 1975, 93; Elster 1979, 37ff. and 88ff; 1983, 53ff. and 66ff.; 1988; Frank 1987; 1988, 4 ff., 47 ff.; Gauthier 1986, 157 ff.; Hegselmann/Raub/Voss 1986; Hirshleifer 1987; Mackie 1982; Parfit 1984, 12 ff., 20 ff.; Raub 1990; Rowe 1989, 36 ff.; Schelling 1960, 123 ff., 131 ff.; 1984, 83 ff., 98 ff.; Thaler/Shefrin 1981; Williamson 1983; 1985, 164 ff.

make the outcome best."[23] Purely situational utility-maximization cannot escape the 'paradox of hedonism', i. e. the fact that it is precisely by refraining from the restless hunt for personal advantage that personal advantages can be generated. In many cases refraining from instrumental calculation is the very precondition for instrumental success. Constrained freedom can achieve a greater net gain than unconstrained freedom. If rational decison-makers have a choice, they will therefore, under certain conditions, choose "on utility-maximizing grounds, not to make further choices on those grounds".[24]

The model of a dispositional utility-maximizer has thus successfully passed its first test. Since without doubt there are circumstances in which it is advantageous for an actor *not* to have complete decision-making autonomy, it would also be *rationally justified* for a utility-maximizing actor under such conditions to be norm-committed instead of consequence-oriented. Hence, it is conceptually and logically *consistent* to accept a utility-motivated and norm-committed type of action in a typology of rational action. An individual interested in increasing his subjective utility has good reason to welcome the opportunity to act not only as a *homo oeconomicus* but also as a *homo sapiens*.

However, the examples mentioned above not only show that it can be in an actor's interest to be norm-committed. They also show that such a disposition plays a rather important role in human behaviour. It can hardly be denied that people do not always act like consequentialist decision-makers. In many situations they act more or less 'blindly' according to social habits and personal routines. Without thinking about it they follow the norms of convention, customs, morality or tradition. Surprisingly, this applies to the market too – the prototypical domain of *homo oeconomicus*. The average consumer, for instance, does not compare the entire range of offers when he wants to buy a certain good. In many purchase decisions he simply sticks to habits he has grown 'fond' of. In view of the empirical evidence, a model which besides consequence-oriented decisions also takes dispositionally determined action into account hardly needs fear the competition of *homo oeconomicus*.

According to Friedrich A. von Hayek, "man is as much a rule-following animal as a purpose-seeking one".[25] This characteristic is systematically included in the model of a dispositional utility-maximizer.

First, both decision-rules are instruments for the pursuit of interests, therefore both can be linked to the pursuit of subjective utility as a reason for action.

Second, these decision-rules are not isolated from one another: the choice between them can also be explained as an interest-driven process.

Third, there is still one uniform standard of rationality, given that rationality not only means applying one of the two decision-rules, but applying that decision-rule which actually maximizes utility. Thus, for a dispositional utility-maximizer too there is always only *one* rational way of acting. The basic idea of the economic model of behaviour still holds: that rational persons always choose the way of acting that furthers their interests better than any other feasible alternative.

[23] Parfit 1984, 49.

[24] Gauthier 1986, 158.

[25] Hayek 1973, 11.

4. THE LIMITS OF SELF-COMMITMENT

However, if we take another look at the examples presented above in which it may be advantageous to have only limited freedom of decision, it becomes clear that in practice the desire to have one's freedom thus restricted can neither always nor easily be converted into an effective and permanent behavioural disposition. Often internal fetters are but an unreliable protection against the seductive lures of all kinds of Sirens. That is why kidnappers usually do not rely on their victims' promises that they will not inform the police if they are released, why blackmailers will hardly be deterred by the statement that one will not give in to them, and why, at least in the 'rationalized' Western world, neither a threat of life-long revenge nor an oath of eternal gratefulness greatly impresses others. The mere wish is not enough to ensure norm-commitment on one's own part, just as it is not enough to bring about norm-compliance in others. What is needed is a *real* modification of the relevant determinants of action. But the efficacy of the 'mental instruments' we possess for bringing about such changes is limited.

These limits are especially obvious and especially painful for those affected in cases where someone desires to have his freedom of decision restricted because strong incentives in future situations will constitute a danger for prudent choices (as in the example of Ulysses). A commitment to norms is not an unlimited substitute for the lack of willpower. As we know from experience, even deep-rooted 'principles' that have been acquired and cultivated over a long time can be overridden by sufficiently strong temptations. Disposition is not an insurmountable 'barrier' to the seductive power of the prospects of immediate gratification.

Therefore, it is typical that people often use empirical devices in their surroundings as a means of effectively restricting their own decision-making powers: "we temporally deposit our will in some external structure; [...] we set up a causal process in the external world that after some time returns to its source and modifies our behaviour."[26] That is the function of Ulysses's mast as well as of other 'artificial masts', such as an alarm clock, compulsory insurance, or a wife instructed by her husband to stop him from smoking whenever he has a weak moment.

Our world would look completely different if people actually had an unlimited supply of techniques of self-commitment. Social relationships would take a fundamentally different course if the 'protective shield' of disposition would enable us to commit ourselves unconditionally to keeping our promises, carrying out our threats, or firmly withstanding attempts at blackmail. In such a world it would in principle be unnecessary to take recourse to an external enforcement of the compliance with norms. Not only could the problems of ensuring the stable efficacy of norms then all be solved by 'contractarian' means with all individuals concerned committing themselves to comply with the corresponding agreements. A lasting social order would then also be possible even in large societies under conditions of anarchy.[27] It could no longer be plausibly explained why the establishment and maintenance of social order in fact often fails or why formal sanctions imposed by public institutions actually play such an important role for the enforcement of social norms.

[26] Elster 1979, 43.

[27] Cf. Kliemt 1987.

The empirical fact that the human propensity for self-commitment has obvious limits must be systematically taken into account when applying the model of dispositional utility-maximization. Thus, in the following examination of different cases in which a commitment to norms is, in principle, advantageous to a dispositional utility-maximizer, we must distinguish between those cases where he can satisfy his desire to commit himself to norms, and those others where he can not. In this context, the fact that for a dispositional utility-maximizer the commitment to norms, if it is to be permanent and stable, must continously generate greater benefit than the consequence-directed strategy of decision will be an important criterion. Since he has the ability to act on the decision rule which promises the greater rewards, he can always give up a commitment to norms should he consider such a modification of his mode of decision-making a promising move. Instead of being irrevocably committed to a norm, a dispositional utility-maximizer is bound by it only as long as the relevant incentive structures do not change and it is in his interest to keep his disposition. But at the same time this capacity to change his disposition marks the limits of his capacity for self-commitment.

5. The psychological and the sociological model of behaviour

The basic assumptions of the model of a dispositional utility-maximizer do not seem unrealistic or empirically inadequate, especially if compared to the assumptions of the model of *homo oeconomicus*. One should, however, beware of exaggerated claims in that direction. After all, it is not intended as a *psychological* model that could serve to describe and analyse the mental processes going on within a person. But even with respect to the 'external' process of the formation of dispositions, two additional observations are in order:

1. Inertia: human dispositions cannot be changed at once, without delay. While it is true that they can be acquired, modified, and overcome, they are also relatively persistent: they "cannot be switched on and off at will".[28] It takes a while until experiences with the advantages and disadvantages of behavioural dispositions lead to newly adapted dispositions. Generally, it seems adequate to think of a long process in which behavioural dispositions can be built up or suppressed only gradually and in which specific investment and deinvestment costs arise.

2. Adaptive and strategic modification of dispositions: people rarely change their personal characteristics as a consequence of conscious, deliberate assessments and decisions. In most cases the mental process of changing a behavioural disposition is not a decision-based event subject to the control of one's will. We cannot choose a disposition as we choose an apple from a crate. But neither is there any need to make such an unrealistic assumption in the model of a dispositional utility-maximizer. This model 'only' assumes that the outcome of changes in someone's personality are in the interest of that person and that, therefore, they can be treated *as if* they were the well-calculated result of a deliberate decision.[29] As a sociological model of behaviour, the model of a disposi-

[28] Mackie 1977, 192.

[29] Cf. Kliemt 1985, 205, 207; Vanberg 1988a.

tional utility-maximizer comprises the hypothesis that the decisive causal factors for a switch between consequence-based and norm-committed ways of action are their respective costs and benefits. It does *not* comprise a hypothesis about the mental processes and mechanisms involved in such a switch.

A process of personality change that is not rationally controlled and yet conforms to the person's interests is theoretically conceivable, because beneficial and functional personal characteristics can be explained not only teleologically but also by an evolutionary process of adaptation and selection.[30] In such a process, dispositions that have proved successful are reinforced whereas those which are not useful become weaker. Although such feedback processes do not require rational calculation on the part of the actor, they can produce outcomes that are in the actor's interest. The principle of rational choice that the best option should to be *chosen* is to a great extent equivalent to the principle of evolutionary selection that the best option will *survive*. If the adaptive generation and modification of dispositions can be an interest-driven development, then it is no longer necessary to explain the usefulness of dispositions with the dubious assumption that it is the result of a rationally controlled and consciously planned process.[31]

[30] Cf. Axelrod 1986; Elster 1983, 117f., 125; Vanberg 1993a, 1993b.

[31] According to Jon Elster, behavioural models operating on the assumption that certain dispositions are (strategically) advantageous are based on two questionable premises: "(a) persons can *decide* to adopt a disposition [...] and (b) others are able to detect this disposition" (Elster 1989, 43, n. 47). The first objection I have just attempted to refute; the second will still occupy us in what follows.

CHAPTER 2

NORM-COMMITMENT AND THE EMERGENCE OF NORMS

I. Personal Norms as Instruments of Self-Control, Rules of Thumb and Virtue

1. THE PROBLEM

In pursuing his interests, a dispositional utility-maximizer can act either in a consequence-based or in a normatively committed way. We thus have a model of behaviour which, unlike the model of *homo oeconomicus*, at least in principle enables us to reconcile the idea of moral action, in the sense of voluntary norm-compliance, with an orientation towards individual interests. It is no longer *by definition* impossible for self-interested action to be compatible with an internal point of view towards some norms and thus with 'genuine' moral action. The attempt to explain the emergence of morality and moral action in a liberal, interest-dominated society is no longer doomed to fail from the start.

Of course, in order to show that a dispositional utility-maximizer has a 'moral character' it is not sufficient to point out that under certain conditions it is rational for him to commit himself to personal norms because this is expedient. It is not enough to find just *any* example of personal norms. We must also be able to show convincingly that such personal norms can be *moral* norms. Therefore the basic question in what follows will be: can the commitment to moral norms be rational from the standpoint of the individual pursuit of utility?

In order to reach an answer to that question, in a first step we will need to analyse which empirical conditions are *generally* decisive for norm-committed action being in the interest *and* within reach of a dispositional utility-maximizer. In the previous chapter, several examples have already been given of situations where one can plausibly say that it is indeed in an actor's interest to precommit himself. Now we must find an adequate classification of those examples. Only then will we be able to recognize the different empirical factors on which the expediency and efficacy of norm-committed action depends.

Generally, a dispositional utility-maximizer's normative commitment can be useful *and* stable under any one of three conditions:

1. if the content of a norm is a way of acting which is *always*, i. e. in every single instance, in the actor's interest; or

2. if the content of a norm is a way of acting which *as a rule*, i. e. in most cases, is in the actor's interest; or

3. if the commitment to a norm is itself – either always or as a rule – in the actor's interest.

2. PERSONAL NORMS AS INSTRUMENTS OF SELF-CONTROL

If a norm prescribes a way of action which corresponds to an actor's interests in every single instance, then it is a way of action even a *situational* utility-maximizer would choose. A personal norm which satisfies this condition leads to the same results as a consequence-directed calculation. And yet, even in such a case, the desire to commit oneself to a norm may be rationally founded. Certain influences make it difficult even for basically rational actors actually to perform the actions they would regard to be in their own interest if they reflected on them reasonably from a detached perspective. This is so because human beings are *imperfect* decision-makers.

Their *volitive* imperfection is paradigmatically illustrated by the example of Ulysses and the Sirens. In this kind of situation, an actor may be able to recognize his options and their empirical consequences cognitively and to assess them correctly from an evaluative point of view. But because of his *akrasia*, and given certain strong incentives, he may still be incapable of actually choosing the best possible option in the light of his interests. This can be demonstrated by behaviour resulting from addiction to alcohol, tobacco or other drugs, but also from passions which sometimes overwhelm us even when we 'know better'.[1]

The *evaluative* imperfection of human decision-makers was already identified by David Hume who drew far-reaching conclusions from this weakness.[2] Hume recognized that, due to their *defective judgement*, people tend to ascribe an unreasonably high value to their immediate interests as compared to their future interests. They thus risk succumbing not only to the lures of the Sirens but to the 'lures of the presence' in general. The existence of such a disposition to overestimate short-term utility and to underestimate more remote costs and benefits is confirmed not only by our daily experience, but by numerous experiments conducted in empirical psychology.[3] The specific irrationality of such behaviour is not the attitude as such of valuing the possession of a good in the future less than its possession now. Rather, it is the inconsistency of the change of preference orders over time.[4]

Hence, an actor may face obstacles concerning his will-power as well as his judgement when it comes to choosing and performing the actions his rational self-interest would recommend. And when this is the case, he will wish for a constraint on his freedom of choice and for some *instrument of self-control* in order to compensate for his shortcomings. Such an instrument could well consist in an effective commitment to norms that will immunize the actor against powerful situational incentives. Under such conditions, constraining one's choices through a commitment to norms is not *per se* more advantageous than consequence-based decision-making. Its purpose is 'only' to help implement utility-maximizing decisions in particular cases.

Undoubtedly, *akrasia* and our defective power of judgement, the possible partial solution of these problems with the help of a commitment to norms and the modelling of

[1] Examples can be found in Elster 1979, ch. II.2; Frank 1988, 81 ff.; Schelling 1984, 63 ff.

[2] Cf. Hume 1739, 586 ff.

[3] Cf. the detailed exposition in Frank 1988, 76 ff.

[4] Cf. Elster 1979, ch. II.5; Frank 1988, 77 ff.

all these processes raise difficult empirical and theoretical questions. As instruments of self-management and self-control, norms are certainly important phenomena, but from the perspective of our present purpose, they are *not*. From this perspective they would acquire importance only if a commitment to norms on those grounds played a relevant role when people adopt an internal point of view towards moral norms. In this context, they do indeed play a role, but – as will be seen later – that is a secondary rather than a central role, the reason here being that in view of our volitive and evaluative weaknesses what is at issue is 'only' the stabilization of actions which are rationally justified even from the standpoint of a situational utiliy-maximizer. And for the emergence and stability of moral norms these are not the decisive questions.

3. PERSONAL NORMS AS RULES OF THUMB

We now come to the second condition under which a dispositional decision-maker's desire to commit himself to norms may be rationally justified and stable: if the content of the norm is a way of acting which *as a rule* is in his interest. This means that according to the standards of *situational* utility-maximization the action in question is in most cases a 'good' or even the best possible choice, but in some cases it may be a sub-optimal or even a 'bad' choice. Depending on what kind of action the norm is about, the balance of bad and good consequences following from norm-compliance will vary. If in order to avoid traffic jams one refrains from going downtown by car except between noon and 3 p. m., this will probably yield a better overall result than if, in order to assure good quality, one always buys the most expensive product of its kind.

It is highly probable that in complying with such norms the overall balance will not be quite as good as it would be if one made the optimal choice in each single instance. Nevertheless it can be (very) advantageous for persons to commit themselves to norms which, as a rule, prescribe good or satisfactory choices. Two reasons may be decisive here: the *costs* of case-by-case deliberation, and the imperfection of human decision-makers in a *cognitive* respect.

Within the economic research programme, attention to the problem of 'decision-making costs' has inspired significant improvements in the model of *homo oeconomicus*. This development was triggered by numerous observations of behaviour that was incompatible with a consequence-directed way of decision-making.[5] How could undeniable facts of human conduct such as habits, conventions, customs or routines be integrated into the economic model? Instead of denying the rationality of such ways of action (with the consequence that hardly anybody would then act rationally in everyday economic life), it was argued that even habitual and rule-oriented behaviour may have a utility-maximizing underpinning. This is the case if, *first*, the rule or habit in question cannot be replaced by another rule or habit with better results, and if, *second*, the potential decision-making costs (above all the costs of acquiring and evaluating information) are higher than the sporadic or regular utility losses incurred by complying with a norm. Whenever these two requirements are satisfied, it is better to abstain from the conse-

[5] Cf., e. g., Frey 1988; Hogarth/Reder 1987; Kahnemann/Slovic/Tversky 1982; Schelling 1984; Schoemaker 1982; Thaler 1992.

quence-based assessment of one's options and instead to act on the standard solution of a *rule of thumb*.

Besides decision-making costs, there is another variable of decision-making processes which turns out to be an important factor for the possible advantages of rules of thumb. If we take a realistic look at human capabilities, we must come to the conclusion that human beings are imperfect decision-makers not only with respect to their will-power and judgement, but also in *cognitive* terms. We cannot expect them to be able to *identify* in every choice situation what their best possible option would be. Generally, people have too little individual knowledge and too short a memory to allow them to base their decisions on a complete understanding of the complex interactions of numerous factors. The problem is aggravated by the fact that the reliable perception and processing of stimuli and information becomes impossible as soon as these surpass certain quantitative and qualitative thresholds. The unavoidable outcome of ignorance, a limited capacity for processing information, and an equally limited ability to learn is that consequence-based decision-making processes will be selective and error-prone. Given their finite brain, finite capacity of memory, and limited velocity of both 'data retrieval' and 'data processing', human beings are forced to economize on scarce resources even concerning their intellectual assets.

It is, therefore, the specific costs as well as the cognitive demands of decision-making according to the principles of situational utility-maximization that can make personal norms as rules of thumb useful. Norm-guided action drastically reduces the costs of decision-making as well as the complexity of the task of deciding. The only assessment it requires for a correct decision is whether or not the norm in question is applicable. All other circumstances and possible consequences can be disregarded. Such a 'selective' decision-rule enormously reduces the required effort and the risk of error.

There can be no doubt that many rules of thumb bring considerably better results in certain contexts of action than costly and error-prone case-by-case strategies. Over a wide range of issues, such rules apparently enable imperfect human decision-makers to compensate their weaknesses. Where empirical circumstances are sufficiently constant it will *continuously* be more advantageous to give up case-by-case decision-making and not constantly to attempt to assess all information and consider all possibilities. Hence, even over time a dispositional utility-maximizer has no reason or incentive to abandon decision-making based on a rule of thumb.

The importance of action by rules of thumb for human practice can therefore hardly be exaggerated. The great majority of our ordinary every-day decisions are based on such rules. Among representatives of economic approaches, this seems to be undisputed.[6] However, following a rule of thumb is a special case of norm-committed action. It constitutes, so to speak, a commitment to norms in a *weak sense*. Rules of thumb are located, in a way, at the 'threshold' to 'real' norm-commitment. After all, by following a rule of thumb an actor refrains from situational utility-maximization only because in his particular situation he *does not know* what the utility-maximizing options are – and it is too costly or too risky for him to find out. But if he could acquire the necessary informa-

[6] Cf., e. g., Esser 1990, 1991a, 82 ff., 1991b; Frey 1988; Lindenberg 1989, 1993; Lindenberg/Frey 1993; Tversky/Kahneman 1986.

tion from a reliable source at low cost, then he would no longer have a reason to follow the rule of thumb and thus, possibly make a suboptimal choice.

In contrast, a norm-commitment in the *strong sense* exists only if the actor accepts a norm as a reason for action and complies with it even if he knows that the norm prescribes actions which are certainly not optimal from the perspective of situational utility-maximization and if he knows what a better or even the best choice would be. A commitment to a norm in the strong sense must be effective even when the costs and risks of a situational decision-strategy are perfectly acceptable for the actor. Later we will see that a commitment to norms in that strong sense is necessary especially if there is to be a commitment to *moral* norms.

4. PERSONAL NORMS AS VIRTUES

Even if a dispositional utility-maximizer were omniscient, made no mistakes, and had a strong will, and if decision-costs were negligible, he would under certain circumstances still have good reasons to practice a norm-committed way of action. But here it is not a question of norms prescribing actions which are always or as a rule in the actor's interest. Rather, it is a matter of norms prescribing actions which, seen singularly, always or as a rule *run counter* to the actor's interests. In such cases, the specific reason for a norm-commitment is precisely the fact that the prescribed action does *not* coincide with the actor's 'situational' interests, i. e. that the prescribed actions are actions the actor would *not* normally choose in the respective situations. Nevertheless, there are conditions in which it is a rationally justified desire of self-interested individuals to commit themselves to such a norm. That is the case when the *fact of being committed to the norm* is itself in the actor's interest, even if the prescribed action is not. The fact of being committed to a norm, however, can only be in an individual's interest if that fact *as such* has beneficial consequences. But how is that possible? How can it be that action x in situation y is not in an actor's interest, whereas the fact that he has a *disposition* to perform action x in situation y is?

For other people, the fact that someone acts on the basis of a dispositional commitment to a norm has, above all, one important consequence: they can *predict* that in certain situations he will act according to that disposition, *regardless* of whether or not the respective action benefits or harms his interests. A dispositional commitment to norms makes it possible to predict that under certain conditions the actor will *not* act as a situational utility-maximizer, but will do what the norm prescribes. However, the 'external effect' of dispositional commitments is not such that observers or partners can now generally make predictions; rather, it is such that they can now expect certain actions which *without* the disposition would *not* be performed. This is the specific 'new' empirical phenomenon which results from a commitment to a norm as such. And, therefore, it is also this phenomenon to which the potentially beneficial consequences for the actor must be linked if it is to be rational for him to follow a norm prescribing actions which neither always nor as a rule are in his interest.

Here, in contrast to those cases where personal norms serve as instruments of self-control or as rules of thumb, we *must* have a special constellation within an *interpersonal, strategic context.* According to what has just been explained, being committed to a norm can as such be beneficial to an actor only if this precommitment to perform certain actions affects *other* persons and their decisions in a way that is advantageous to him. There must be a situation in which it is beneficial to the actor if those he interacts with assume that his actions are guided by norms and not based on case-by-case calculation. These gains must at least compensate the disadvantages resulting from the fact that, judging each single instance, compliance with the norm leads to a loss of utility.

From the examples given in the previous chapter, we already know that there are indeed many situations where the positive consequences a commitment to norms has on other people's actions clearly exceed the negative 'side effects' in the form of a utility loss in particular cases. A commitment to norms can deter an enemy, signal firmness in negotiations, or assure a partner of one's cooperation and fairness. In all these cases an actor can count on the usefulness of the corresponding dispositions, precisely because in certain situations others can or must expect him to act against his immediate interests. It is this *expectation* in his opponents or partners which will guarantee him advantages he cannot realize in any other way – particularly not by keeping his unrestricted freedom of decision. What causes the benefit is not the characteristics and empirical consequences of particular acts, not the actions performed in compliance with a norm, but the very fact of the norm-commitment *itself.*

Seen from this angle, the only 'addressees' of an actor's commitment to norms are other people. They are the ones who are to be influenced in their actions by a norm-commitment. A personal norm is thus converted into a specific instrument to commit and bind oneself *in respect to other people* and thus steer their actions in a certain direction. From this perspective, too, it is plausible to see the option to commit oneself to norms as an *extension* of an actor's abilities. It opens up an additional way of affecting expectations and thus the actions of others.[7]

A dispositional norm-commitment which serves an actor's interests not by guaranteeing or backing the principles of situational utility-maximization, but by determining him to act *against* these principles, I will call a 'virtue'. A virtue in this sense leads to behaviour which definitely cannot be explained with the model of consequence-based decision-making. Unlike personal norms of self-control or rules of thumb, virtues do not bring an actor closer to utility-maximizing behaviour. On the contrary, a virtue may prescribe actions which in certain cases benefit the interests of others rather than the interests of the actor himself. Practising a virtue provides utility for the virtuous individual *exclusively* by way of the others' *reaction* to it. Thus, the potential utility of a virtue always arises *indirectly,*[8] either because others fear it (to the extent that it is a threat to them), or because they appreciate it (insofar as it serves their own interests). For other people, the specific danger or usefulness of virtues arises from the fact that virtuous actions are performed without the consideration of the actor's own immediate interests.

Unlike situational utility-maximizers, a dispositional utility-maximizer can develop a 'personality' consisting of individual dispositions and character traits which significantly distinguish him from others, even if those others are themselves dispositional

[7] This aspect is underlined also by Nicholas Rowe 1989, 6, 22 ff., 40 ff., 73.

[8] That is what distinguishes this concept of virtue from that of antiquity.

utility-maximizers. For other people this fact is of particular importance with respect to his virtues, since virtues are precisely those behavioural dispositions which acquire special relevance to one's counterpart in interpersonal relations. In dealing with actors who have the ability to develop virtues, one can no longer expect that in similar situations – under the same 'constraints' – they will all act in similar ways. Rather, under similar external conditions their behaviour may be very different because it depends largely on factors rooted in personality. If behaviour is to be predicted, it is *these* factors that must be known. Dispositional utility-maximizers not only have a present and a future, but also a past and an individual biography which make an 'imprint' on their personal characteristics and co-determine their present conduct. For a future-oriented, situational utility-maximizer, past events, and in particular his own past decisions, have no immediate relevance to his present actions. For him, the *only* things that count are the expected consequences of his actions in the future.

The fact that the actions of a dispositional utility-maximizer are substantially linked to the past and that his personal 'history' is relevant to his present personality makes it necessary for his partners to know 'what kind of person' he is if they want to guess how he will behave in certain situations. From this it follows that, initially, the existence of norm-committed action considerably increases the complexity of social interaction. The possibility that different people adhere to different norms (or to no norm at all) results in a greater variability of individual reactions to similar situational conditions. Moreover, the decisive 'internal' determinants of action which must be known in order to predict the behaviour of a dispositional utility-maximizer are much more difficult to observe than the external characteristics of a situation:

(1) In contrast to directly observable facts and data, hypothetical elements are always involved in ascertaining dispositions.

(2) In order to obtain the necessary information for ascertaining someone's disposition, one must study that person's behaviour. Above all, one must know how people behaved in the past if one wants to predict their present or future conduct.

(3) All this involves a type of information which the actor himself possesses in a different and usually more reliable way than an observer. Knowledge about behavioural dispositions is not *per se* 'common knowledge', as is knowledge about the external characteristics of a situation; it is knowledge which an observer must make an effort to gain and which an actor can try to hide in different ways. But even if an actor expressly wishes to communicate this knowledge, it may be difficult for him to do so.

These few remarks already show that the the ability of dispositional utility-maximizers to commit themselves to norms is not easily put into practice. Its successful practice is obstructed by numerous barriers and traps. With slight exaggeration, one could say that instead of the transparent strategies and predictable actions of situational utility-maximizers we have the opaque strategies and unpredictable actions of dispositional utility-maximizers. This is a problem even for the actors themselves. Because whether or not an actor has an interest in a virtuous disposition is a direct consequence of how others *perceive* him. In the long run, whether cultivating a virtue is advantageous to him depends solely on their reactions.

Therefore, it must be carefully analysed under what conditions personal norms as virtues can play an effective role in social life. Such conditions must support a *reputational mechanism* through which a person known to be virtuous can gain substantial advantages over situational utility-maximizers and opportunists. Where such a mechanism is operative, those interacting with a dispositional utility-maximizer will make their own behaviour towards him dependent on their assessment of his virtues.[9] Virtuousness would be useless to an actor if others could not detect and reward it.

In order to grasp the core of the problem and to show what advantages a dispositional utility-maximizer can, *on principle*, gain from his ability to commit himself to norms, the analysis will begin with a strong idealization. Let us assume for the time being that all actors involved are 'transparent', i. e. that they can mutually detect from others' actions whether their behaviour is based on case-by-case calculation or on a commitment to some norm. Thus we will ignore all problems connected with the reliable *identification* of the relevant characteristics of a partner and will leave out all problems connected with the incentive to *deceive* or the attempt to *credibly demonstrate* a commitment to norms. We will simply assume that all actors involved can infer behavioural dispositions from observed behaviour without any problem.

However, the fact that these problems will be ignored for the time being is *not* meant to signal that they are more or less irrelevant *marginal* problems. On the contrary, we will see later that they are extremely *important*. This is so because the advantage of successfully dissembling the commitment to some norm may be substantial, while the deception itself may seem relatively easy. As a consequence, there is the risk of an atmosphere of permanent mutual *suspicion* which could prove a great obstacle to realizing the potential advantages from norm-commitment.

II. Cooperative Enterprises as Norm-Generating Situations

1. Collective action and organization among situational utility-maximizers

The special abilities of dispositional utility-maximizers enable them to enter into advantageous relationships of a kind generally denied to situational utility-maximizers. This is particularly relevant for certain forms of *collective* action. And, as we will see, precisely these forms of collective action are of crucial importance to the empirical theory of morality. That is why I will concentrate on them in what follows.

Collective action can be of fundamental advantage to human beings. Under certain conditions, pooling their individual powers into one single potential may be extraordinarily beneficial to them – even if it implies a restriction of their autonomy in using their personal resources. It is one of the basic conditions of human existence that for many tasks and projects joint action allows considerable efficiency gains, compared with isolated individual efforts. Without a concentration of individual powers in different forms of cooperation, fundamental social and technical achievements, the progressive

[9] For an analysis of the effects of mechanisms of reputation, cf., e. g.; Granovetter 1985; Kreps/Wilson 1982; Kreps/Milgrom/Roberts/Wilson 1982; Milgrom/Roberts 1982; Raub/Weesie 1990; Rowe 1989, 36 ff.; Wilson 1985.

shaping of our natural and social world, and indeed the entire development of civilization from the very beginning of human history would be inconceivable. *Organization* in the sense of purposeful cooperation in a more or less stable framework of rules is one of the major and indispensable driving forces of human civilization in all its forms.[10] It is exactly the pursuit of individual interests which frequently gives rise to incentives to found organizations in order to use collective means to facilitate the attainment of individual ends.

Leaving aside the possibility of involuntary membership, there are basically two ways in which an organization can be founded: someone with an interest in the organization either joins together with others who aim at the same goals and likewise regard the organization as a means to a common end; or he recruits others who, as members of the organization, should pursue the organization's purpose without themselves having an immediate personal interest in it. In the latter case, the actor interested in the organization will have to offer some other kinds of incentives to the members of his organization in order to reward them for their activities.

For situational utility-maximizers, however, the possibilities for organized cooperation, as well as its attainable stability and efficiency, are considerably constrained by specific restrictions. This is due to the conduct to be expected from a *homo oeconomicus* as a member of an organization. The success of an organization does not come about automatically. The ends of collective action can be attained only if the cooperating individuals contribute to the desired result. All organized cooperation – whether in the little flowershop down the street or in a huge transnational enterprise – functions by imposing certain duties and tasks on the participants; and only if these are fulfilled the goal of cooperation can be attained. However, precisely because the result of a collective action is the result of a *joint* effort and cannot be brought about by single individuals, individuals may have an incentive to shirk their duties and enjoy the fruits of cooperation only as consumers, leaving the costs to the others. Even if it is only four people carrying a cabinet, each individual may be tempted to save on his own effort and literally put the burden on the other three. Practically all organizations sooner or later offer opportunities to neglect one's duties and responsibilities without being noticed or found out, or even directly to enrich oneself out of the organization's funds: cashiers might take money from the cash register, salesmen steal merchandise, secretaries store documents in the wrong archive, judges protract cases, policemen be negligent on their rounds, or teachers go to their classes unprepared. Incentives for such 'free-riding' arise within organizations even if the realization of the organization's goals is actually in the interest of all its members, i. e. if the organization is not of the kind where there is a basic difference between the interests of 'principals' and 'agents'.[11]

Members of an organization with a common end will frequently be tempted to behave non-cooperatively, since most organizations are plagued by an internal *collective-good problem*.[12] The contributions made by individual members to the organization

[10] "Among man's innovations, the use of organization to accomplish his ends is among both his greatest and his earliest." (Arrow 1971, 224)

[11] On the so-called 'principal-agent problem', cf. Alchian/Demsetz 1972; Alchian/Woodward 1987, 1988; Eisenhardt 1989; MacDonald 1984; Milgrom/Roberts 1992; Pratt/Zeckhauser 1991.

[12] On the basic problem of collective goods, cf. Olson 1968; Hardin 1971, 1982; de Jasay 1989.

will often be insignificant: whether one does or does not actively participate in the renovation of the club house will be irrelevant to the result if there are dozens of other helpers anyway. But even if the overall efficiency of an organization will notably suffer, it may often still be advantageous to an individual member to refrain from contributing. If business in a grocery store is slow because of the bad quality of its vegetables, it may still be more profitable for a co-owner to accept bribes from suppliers in exchange for buying low-quality goods than to buy good products for the store. It will probably be the rule rather than the exception that the costs of individual contributions to the goals of an organization will exceed the expected utility from that contributions. In this context, we must not forget that what is at issue is not only the positive contributions to the immediate attainment of the organization's goals, but also the omission of 'negative' contributions such as, for instance, the embezzlement of the organization's funds.

Besides this *problem of insignificance*, there is also a *problem of interdependence* in many organizations, i. e. a problem resulting from a lack of 'density' and 'transparency' in interpersonal relations. In this case, there can then be no effective informal monitoring and sanctioning mechanisms that could guarantee a reliable contributory behaviour, because it will be impossible consistently to uncover non-cooperative activities of individual members without special, complicated and cost-intensive instruments. Only in rare cases will the members of an organization form a group which is sufficiently close-knit to ensure that at all times all sides are completely informed about the others' behaviour.

The collective-good problem within organizations is, above all, a problem arising from ignorance, anonymity, and a lack of transparency. This makes it possible to violate norms without perceptible consequences for the perpetrator. Under such conditions, a situational utility-maximizer, as a member of an organization, will deliver the contribution expected of him to the organization's goals either not at all or in a less than satisfactory way. And since the same applies to all members, the success and survival of the organization as a whole will be endangered.

In view of this danger, there are only two possibilities when dealing with situational utility-maximizers as partners or employees. One can try to make the members' self-interest coincide as much as possible with the organization's interest, for instance through a system of payments and rewards linking income directly to the quality of individual performance. However, it will probably be impossible to invent such devices for each and every conceivable kind of organization. Besides, the devices themselves are susceptible to all sorts of 'opportunistic' subversion.[13] And even if the problem of the insignificance of positive contributions to an organization's goals could reliably be overcome, it would hardly be possible to solve the problem of the insignificance of 'negative' contributions in the same way, since even though it may be individually rational for a member to fulfil his organizational tasks and duties, it may at the same time also be tempting for that very same member to obtain illegal extra benefits from the organization's funds and proceeds.

If an organizer is unable to harmonize the interests of the organization with those of its members, the only alternative left is the establishment of a hierarchy of formal

[13] Cf. Granovetter 1985.

structures of regulation and supervision. The problem with this is that an organizational structure aiming at the total control of the activities of all members of an organization will only as an exception be desirable also from an efficiency point of view. Normally, it will imply high costs and a considerable reduction in the organization's performance.[14] Exhaustive prescriptions are as difficult to formulate as they are to implement, especially if the regulated behaviour cannot be observed directly. An organization may be paralysed if mistakes are unrelentingly investigated, activities are constantly monitored and individuals are under a permanent danger of being made personally accountable. Its members may then be driven to invest more energy in covering themselves against blame and in justifying their decisions than in working for the organization's goals.

And indeed, the successful cooperation of people and the effective coordination of their forces does not necessarily require the complete regulation of all individual activities. On the contrary, depending on the organization's purposes and the external conditions, it may be much more efficient if organizational rules do not explicitly regulate every little detail, if the mechanisms of coordination and supervision are not perfectly rigid, and if individual members are given the competence to adapt their decisions flexibly to situational requirements.[15] Think, for example, of a rapidly changing organizational environment and complex tasks involving a plurality of different constellations and new, unforeseeable problems that cannot be analysed in advance. Such conditions may well require organizational structures that leave ample room for individual discretion, initiative and improvisation, foster the extensive delegation and decentralization of responsibilities, and thus permit a high degree of self-determination and self-control on all levels of decision-making.[16] In such organizations, however, the very fact that many members are in a position to take decisions on their own will regularly offer opportunities for the anonymous violation of norms that will remain undetected. Organizational structures of such an 'unbureaucratic' kind thus necessarily require that the members contribute to the organization's goals even if their actions are not constantly monitored and controlled.

Besides, quite apart from the question of efficiency and costs, it will be practically impossible to implement encompassing monitoring and control mechanisms in many kinds of organizations.[17] In addition, there is the important aspect that the success of joint ventures depends to a great extent on the fact that the actors involved fulfil their duties and tasks not only 'to the letter' but also 'in spirit', i. e. that they are willing to invest their capacities, special skills and knowledge, even when explicit provisions are inexistent or incomplete. However, whether or not a member of an organization really makes the effort required for achieving the common end can hardly be controlled. As

[14] "The measurement costs of constraining behavior are so high that in the absence of ideological convictions to constrain individual maximizing, the viability of economic organization is threatened." (North 1981, 44).

[15] The idea of 'lean production' which is being adopted by more and more businesses around the world is an example of the perceived superiority of a form of organization based on delegation and responsibility over one of detailed rules and hierarchy.

[16] Cf., e. g., Kieser/Kubicek 1992, 33 ff., 191 ff., 365 ff.; Hill/Fehlbaum/Ulrich 1992, 141 ff., 369 ff.; Mayntz 1982, 120 ff.

[17] "In joint ventures, practical difficulties almost always stand in the way of being able to monitor other people's performance." (Frank 1988, 50) "The quality and quantity of individual labor can only imperfectly be controlled by rules, because of measurement problems." (North 1981, 47) Cf. also Coleman 1990, 421 ff.

important as the participants' work morale is for the success of cooperation: being a subjective attitude, it cannot be measured objectively.

From all this it follows that among situational utility-maximizers collective action is possible only in a very limited way and at the price of considerable utility losses because of inefficient organizational structures, the high costs of monitoring and sanctioning devices and – never entirely excludable – phenomena such as shirking, deception, sabotage, negligence, fraud, embezzlement or theft. A 'veil of ignorance' often unfolds within organizations behind which anonymous deviations become possible that are too tempting for an 'opportunistic' *homo oeconomicus* to withstand.

2. COOPERATIVE ENTERPRISES

In many, if not in most cases, successful organization is possible only if, by and large, members fulfil their duties voluntarily, pursue organizational ends on their own initiative, work to their full capacity because of an 'intrinsic' motivation[18], and voluntarily accept a fair share of the burdens. Although within an organization voluntary cooperation in this sense may not be strictly *necessary* for the realization of certain goals, it is in any case *desirable*. The willingness of an organization's members to cooperate voluntarily will always have cost-reducing, efficacy-increasing, and stability-enhancing effects. Therefore, any actor interested in establishing an organization in order better to further his interests through collective action will give high priority to partners and employees who satisfy these requirements.

Organizations *based* on the voluntary cooperation and work morale of at least part of their membership I will call 'cooperative enterprises' or simply 'enterprises'. By definition, cooperative enterprises have an internal collective-good or monitoring problem. Those interested in an enterprise, therefore, *depend* on the fact that at least some of their partners or employees adopt an internal point of view towards the enterprise's norms and goals and perform what is necessary for the pursuit of its interests even in those instances when it does not coincide with their personal interests. Among situational utility-maximizers, cooperative enterprises cannot exist, even if they would be advantageous to all participants. Situational utility-maximizers are simply unsuitable as members of such enterprises, since whenever they see an opportunity they necessarily succumb to the temptation of behaving uncooperatively. Cooperative enterprises could not even come into being as a form of organization if those interested in their existence could not rationally expect the members of their enterprise to have an attitude which deviates from the principles of situational utility-maximization.[19] For the existence of cooperative enterprises and the realization of the specific benefits connected with this form of collective action, the existence of a sufficient number of persons with the special ability to commit themselves to norms is a necessary condition.

However, the fact that dispositional utility-maximizers are *in principle* suited to becoming members of cooperative enterprises does not mean that they will actually commit themselves to norms with the necessary stability and reliability. The stable exist-

[18] On the importance of such intrinsic motivations, cf. Frey 1992, 1993a, 1993b, and Frey/Bohnet 1994.
[19] This is a central argument in Gauthier 1986, 157 ff.; cf. also Frank 1988, ix f., 18 f., 46 ff.

ence of cooperative enterprises will be possible only if the 'entrepeneurs' have reason to assume that in a cooperative enterprise it is *in the interest* of dispositional utility-maximizers to accept the organizational norms of the enterprise as their personal norms.

3. COOPERATIVE ENTERPRISES, SELF-CONTROL AND RULES OF THUMB

For an entrepreneur it would be best if he could count on an 'invisible hand' that would bring about norm-commitment on the part of the members of the enterprise without his active intervention. This could be the case if personal norms as instruments of self-control and/or as rules of thumb would ensure the desired norm-commitment of the members. The advantageousness of personal norms as instruments of self-control or as rules of thumb is independent of the fact that other people expressly recognize and reward a commitment to those norms.

Personal norms as instruments of self-control or as rules of thumb are in the interest of a dispositional utility-maximizer only if their content refers to actions which always or as a rule bring about satisfactory results and if he has reason to fear the risks implied in his volitive, evaluative or cognitive deficits, or if information and decision costs exceed the benefits of a case-by-case decision strategy. In cooperative enterprises, these may indeed be relevant reasons.

The basis of any cooperative enterprise is that being a member of such an enterprise offers a positive net balance of utility, i. e. that the costs of fulfilling one's duties are less than the benefits from membership. Thus, regular norm-conformity guarantees each member at least the 'satisfactory' result of the legal gains from membership, whereas the attempt to reap additional gains through the violations of duties is accompanied by the risk of the corresponding sanctions. Hence, one of the necessary conditions for personal norms as rules of thumb is satisfied: if an actor, as a member of an enterprise, commits himself to the enterprise's norms as personal norms, he can assume that acting on those norms will *as a rule* lead to good results – even if he has to accept utility losses in the form of forgone opportunities for shirking, negligence, fraud, theft or embezzlement.

Given the risks and costs of a situational decision-making strategy, how are these losses to be assessed? By design, cooperative enterprises time and again offer possibilities for anonymous deviations. But in cooperative enterprises the 'veil of anonymity' is not impenetrable. A free-rider must carefully distinguish between opportunities for norm-violations with an acceptable risk, and opportunities where the risk is too high because there is a danger of detection. He must beware of 'greedily' seizing whatever chance apparently comes his way. That is why in the context of complex, nested organizational structures it can be difficult and costly to distinguish a dangerous 'trap' from a 'golden opportunity'. As a consequence, the informational requirements for a well-grounded decision may be prohibitively demanding and the risk of a wrong decision unacceptably high.

Thus, it is not unfeasible that it may indeed be rational for a dispositional utility-maximizer to convert the organizational norms addressed to him into personal norms in the sense of rules of thumb and instruments of self-control. 'Blind' compliance with those norms will then at least assure him that surplus of utility every norm-complying member of the enterprise can expect from membership, while at the same time protecting him from the danger of succumbing to spurious temptations at the wrong time.[20]

However, in view of the plurality and variability of possible organizational structures this conclusion holds only for *some* areas of activity within an enterprise. In other areas it may be relatively easy to detect opportunities for the more or less risk-free violation of norms, or at least opportunities where the risk is worth taking. We need only recall the simple example of the grocery store: from an interest-oriented point of view, it may be rational to adopt the personal norm not to take money from the cash register, since even if one feels unobserved someone may come into the store at any moment. But from the same point of view it may also be perfectly rational to accept bribes from suppliers because there's no one else in charge of supplies and the probability of detection is low. It will rarely be the case that in the context of the different activities in an enterprise the balance of risks will *always* tip towards the side of the dutiful fulfilment of one's tasks.

Therefore, in order to protect himself from temptations, mistakes and decision costs, on the one hand, and given the existence of 'golden opportunities', on the other, the best thing a dispositional utility-maximizer can do is to develop a 'mixed strategy'. In areas of activity where the risk of detection or error is high, he will fulfil his duties without exception, in compliance with personal norms, whereas in areas where the risk is lower he will prefer the situational assessment and calculation of his chances. It will be advantageous to him to carefully analyse the different areas and distinguish between those where a situational decision-making strategy is profitable and those where the risks and costs of such a strategy are not worth his while.

Hence, an entrepreneur can hardly expect that his partners and employees have reason enough to accept the enterprise's entire set of norms as personal norms merely because of their need for self-control or because of high information and decision costs. They may not always be waiting for an opportunity to violate their duties and enrich themselves. They will often routinely behave in a cooperative way and comply with norms. But an entrepreneur must nevertheless expect the existence of vulnerable areas in his organization which offer 'loopholes' that make opportunistic calculation attractive.

4. Cooperative Enterprises, Virtue, and Reputation

An entrepreneur, therefore, only has a chance of running a successful cooperative enterprise if a commitment to norms as such is in the interest of the members of the enterprise. This means that a mechanism of reputation must be in force by which dispositional utility-maximizers with certain virtues gain considerable advantages over situational utility-maximizers and opportunists. But such a mechanism of reputation can become operative only if the fact that an actor is committed to a norm is detected and adequately rewarded by other people. Thus, the entrepreneur can no longer rely on an 'invisible hand'. He must actively intervene.

What is decisive for an entrepreneur in this context is that he has considerable power in his dealings with people who wish to become members of his enterprise. He

[20] Cf. Frank 1988, 71 ff.

can reward their virtue by accepting them and he can sanction their opportunism by rejecting them as partners or employees. He can thus make a commitment to norms and the adoption of an internal point of view towards enterprise-specific duties a *condition* for membership in his enterprise. Thereby, he has the necessary leverage for a considerable modification of the norm-addressees' situational constraints in favour of their commitment to the norms.[21] If they wish to gain access to cooperative enterprises, they must first qualify as suitable partners in cooperative relationships.

For a correct assessment of the position of power entrepreneurs occupy, consider once again the extraordinary importance of collective, joint action. For all human beings, membership in organizations and enterprises, i. e. the chance to take part in cooperative relationships with others, is one of the irreplaceable necessities of life.[22] Every human being must have a fundamental interest in having access to such relations in order to be able to participate in the elementary benefits of human cooperation. This is by no means restricted to material benefits: wherever people join together, in marriage, family, clubs, or travel companionship, we have a cooperative enterprise in the broad sense of the term. People found a company in order to increase their wealth, they join together in associations in order to pursue common political or social interests, or they form a community in order to promote their ideals. Cooperative enterprises may be of a political, religious, ideological, economic or social nature. Whenever people have common interests or projects which can be pursued better by way of planned cooperation than by isolated individual action, it may be advantageous and useful to resort to organized activities. But access to cooperative enterprises is important not only because it enables one to pursue common ends. It is also important because one may indirectly profit from the gains of collective ventures by being rewarded for one's cooperation. If someone were completely excluded from cooperative enterprises and in pursuing his ends and interests had to rely exclusively on his own personal resources, he would face an enormous restriction of his opportunities in life.[23]

Thus, given the fundamental interest of all human beings in having access to cooperative enterprises, on the one hand, and the fundamental interest entrepreneurs must have in the virtue of their partners and employees, on the other, the precondition for the effective operation of a mechanism of reputation is basically satisfied. For a dispositional utility-maximizer who is a 'candidate' for membership in a cooperative enterprise, it will be rational to commit himself to norms, since that is the condition for his being accepted by an entrepreneur. He will obtain an entry pass to cooperative enterprises and be able to enjoy the benefits of that kind of cooperation only if other participants can trust that he will not use every possible opportunity to maximize his personal utility and gain a private surplus profit. If the benefits from participation in diverse forms of human cooperation are of such fundamental relevance for an individual, it will be in his self-

[21] The studies of Schüßler 1990 and Vanberg/Congleton 1992 show that such selective cooperation may be an effective strategy to make life difficult for defectors.

[22] "The experience of belonging is a basic form of social experience, the certainty of belonging is a basic form of social self-assurance." (Popitz 1992, 141)

[23] A detailed analysis of the idea that a moral disposition may be advantageous because it opens up opportunities for cooperation which otherwise would remain closed can be found, e. g., in Gauthier 1986 and Frank 1988; cf. also Baurmann/Kliemt 1995; Hoerster 1982; Kliemt 1993b; Vanberg 1988a, 1988b, 1993a.

interest to take on the burdens of virtue instead of risking losing the chance to be part of such relationships once and for all: "the gains from cooperation cannot be fully exploited here unless one adopts at the outset what everyone would call a genuinely unselfish point of view."[24]

For an entrepreneur, the question that is of vital importance here is whether he can count on the stability of his partners' and employees' norm-commitment. Virtuousness must continuously be in their interest, not only at the time of their admission to the enterprise, but also when it is put to the test in the course of their activities. But that expectation is indeed justified, since an entrepreneur himself can see to it, by his own action and with his own resources, that there will be no incentives for the members of his enterprise to renege on their commitment to norms. To this end, he can employ two complementary strategies:

First, he can make virtue a condition not only for the *admission* to the enterprise. In addition, he can make it a condition which will determine whether a person may *remain* a member. Just as it is a prudent strategy for an entrepreneur to make his initial decision to cooperate depend on his potential partners' or employees' commitment to norms, it is also a prudent strategy to terminate a cooperative relationship when it turns out that the other's character no longer satisfies the prerequisites for membership.

Second, an entrepreneur can actively *reinforce* his partners' and employees' virtue during their membership in his enterprise by offering trustworthy and highly motivated members 'career opportunities' within the organization. These may reach from special forms of monetary and non-monetary rewards, over participation in important decision and planning processes, all the way to entrusting them with management positions, with their own gratifications from authoritative, directive action.[25]

These strategies can only be successful, of course, if a member's behaviour can be monitored by the entrepreneur to such an extent that he can find out about a person's characteristics and dispositions. However, success does *not* require that the behaviour of a member can be *permanently* observed. After all, that would make virtue superfluous, since it is valuable for the entrepreneur precisely if and when he cannot have complete information about all his members' actions. What is required, therefore, is only partial social control. This requirement is easily satisfied in cooperative enterprises. Usually, it is even satisfied automatically: organised collective action without personal contacts and a certain amount of mutual information about the characteristics and behaviour of participants is inconceivable.

From all this it seems to follow that, given the special abilities of dispositional utility-maximizers and the operation of a mechanism of reputation, the basic conditions for the foundation and stable existence of cooperative enterprises are satisfied. This means that dispositional utility-maximizers have opportunities for cooperation in social contexts in which for situational utility-maximizers cooperation is generally precluded. The fact that dispositional maximizers are suitable partners for cooperative enterprises is important evidence for the assertion that dispositional utility-maximizers "can thus ob-

[24] Frank 1987, 602.

[25] On the factors that contribute to enhancing or displacing intrinsic motivation, cf. Frey 1992, 1993a, 1993b; Frey/Bohnet 1994.

tain cooperative benefits that are unavailable to straightforward maximizers, however farsighted the latter may be".[26]

This result was obtained, however, under the umbrella of a 'heroic idealization'. We had assumed that people are 'transparent, i. e. that underlying behavioural *dispositions* can be inferred without any problem from observable *actions*. It is obvious that, in principle, the possibility of such inferences is extremely important. It can be advantageous to a dispositional utility-maximizer to *be* virtuous only if others can detect that someone *is* virtuous.

In real life, however, such inferences encounter two severe and complementary problems: *deception* and *mistrust*. The inference from people's actions to their dispositions may be wrong because their actions are not 'authentic', i. e. because they only dissemble virtues. Or people's genuine virtues may be useless because others suspect that their actions are not authentic and therefore do not make the inference from the actions to the corresponding dispositions. Thus, our 'heroic idealization' consists in simply presupposing *credibility* and *trust*. In order to test whether our results are of interest even under more realistic assumptions, we must now make room in our theoretical world for deception and mistrust.

[26] Gauthier 1986, 170.

CHAPTER 3

DECEPTION AND TRUST

I. Appearance and Reality

For a dispositional utility-maximizer, virtue can only be useful in a strategic context, as an instrument for influencing other people's expectations. This sows the seeds of suspicion and mutual distrust. Up to this point, the seeds had lain dormant, since as long as we assumed that a person's actions reliably indicate whether or not they are based on a commitment to norms, the purely 'strategic relevance' of virtue had no negative consequences. We were able to ignore all the problems one actually faces in identifying other people's behavioural dispositions. And that is also why we have not yet encountered the problems of doubtful credibility, deception and lack of trust.

It is, however, one of the fundamental conditions of human existence and social relationships that the observation of isolated actions or practices usually offers a rather doubtful and unreliable basis for inferences about a person's character and dispositions. Hence, we must now take a more realistic look at the possibilities of obtaining reliable information about other people's behavioural dispositions. This is a truly pivotal issue. Because if the parties interacting with a dispositional utility-maximizer cannot, by and large, trust their conjectures about his dispositions, then his inclination to virtuousness can hardly have the expected measure of beneficial effects. The potential advantages of the capacity for a dispositional commitment to norms can be gained only if that capacity is complemented by the ability to identify virtuous persons and distinguish them from mere opportunists without any 'intrinsic commitment'.[1]

If actors must assume that observing other people's conduct does not permit them to draw cogent conclusions about their character and dispositions, credibility and trust become a central problem in situations where cooperation depends on a partner's virtue.[2] All participants must be greatly interested in solving that problem, i. e. in finding a way to convey sufficient information about those characteristics which determine their actions. In other words, virtuousness is only beneficial to actors *and* their partners if they can credibly signal *that* they possess that virtue.

II. Dispositional Utility-Maximizers as 'Sensible Knaves'

Among dispositional utility-maximizers, however, there seem to be fundamental reasons for maintaining one's distrust in other people's virtue. After all, the advantageous conse-

[1] „When cooperators and defectors look alike, genuine cooperation cannot emerge." (Frank 1988, 59)

[2] 'Trust' is here understood in the narrow sense of trust in a person's *virtue*, not in the broader sense, often used in the literature, of confidence that she will *act in a particular way*. On the relevance of trust for cooperation in general, cf., e. g., Barber 1983; Coleman 1990, 91 ff., 175 ff.; Gambetta 1988; Hardin 1991, 1992.

quences virtues can have for an actor depend *exclusively* on *assumptions* of others that he possesses those virtues. For a dispositional utility-maximizer, virtue is simply a means to an end. It does not have its own rewards, and has no intrinsic value. For someone to derive a benefit from a virtue, it is not necessary that he really *have* that disposition. Rather, from a self-interested point of view the optimal solution is merely to simulate norm-commitment in order to reap the extra benefits that can be had under the cloak of virtue.

From the fact that the appearance of virtuousness is just as beneficial to the apparently virtuous as actual virtue is to the actually virtuous one could draw the conclusion that for a rational utility-maximizer a strategy of deception is *generally* more expedient. But if that were the case, the consequences would be far from desirable, because then there would *neither* be any mutually beneficial cooperation based on trust *nor* would anyone be able to gain an advantage from dissembling virtue. No one could then expect anyone else to be *really* virtuous, and therefore both the virtuous *and* the frauds would come away empty-handed.

Because of the problem of deception and mistrust, dispositional utility-maximizers thus face a fatal *self-fulfilling prophecy*: Awareness of the strong incentives for deception must lead to general distrust, and that makes it difficult to demonstrate one's virtue credibly. But the less possible it becomes to dispel the existing distrust, the less advantageous authentic virtue will be, which in turn will lead to a justified increase in distrust. In the end, there will neither be a motive to become virtuous nor a motive merely to dissemble it.

The fundamental problem that a self-interested and rationally calculating person will hardly be able to withstand the temptation to adopt the role of a hypocrite and 'sensible knave' was already identified by David Hume: "That *honesty is the best policy*, may be a good general rule, but is liable to many exceptions; and he, it may perhaps be thought, conducts himself with most wisdom, who observes the general rule, and takes advantage of all the exceptions." Hume was not overly optimistic that such an attitude can cogently be refuted: "I must confess that, if a man think that this reasoning much requires an answer, it will be a little difficult to find any which will to him appear satisfactory and convincing."[3]

If it were really impossible to undermine the position of the 'sensible knave', this would have highly undesirable consequences for our enterprise. The capacity of dispositional utility-maximizers to commit themselves to norms would then be totally useless. If this consequence is to be avoided, it must be shown that Hume's worries were not warranted and that even from the perspective of mere self-interest, after a sober calculation of advantages and disadvantages, life as a 'sensible knave' is not necessarily the best option.

This could be ensured by two factors, namely, the personal *costs* and the *risks* involved in living as a deceiver. If, compared with the potential rewards, the costs of a strategy of deception or the risk of being discovered are excessively high, a dispositional utility-maximizer, being a rational actor, will discard such a strategy. But then his partners would no longer need to be extremely suspicious at all times, even if they did

[3] Hume 1777, 282 f. Even Plato already stated the problem precisely, cf. Plato, Politeia, Book 2, 362d ff.

not have any sure knowledge about his 'personality'. It would be possible at least to go back to a neutral, 'unbiased' position. The vicious circle could thus be broken, because if distrust can be overcome, then it also becomes potentially advantageous again for a dispositional utility-maximizer not only to *appear*, but really to *be* virtuous.

III. The Costs and Risks of Deception

Now, even superficial analysis will readily show that in fact every deception implies personal costs and considerable risks for the deceiver. There can be no doubt that the permanent successful feigning of personal characteristics is not easy and "that faking integrity runs a strong risk of being detected by some of the people some of the time".[4] This is all the more plausible if one takes into account that the dissembled characteristics are normally accompanied by emotional and mental reactions which are difficult to fake:[5] "carefully prepared insouciance, studied indifference, finely calculated generosity or thoughtfully planned spontaneity"[6] are constantly in danger of being detected, and it may also be true that "for any actor [...] there is some potential spectator clever enough to see through him".[7]

But we should be careful not to fall into the other extreme and make things look overly simple. It would be empirically wrong and theoretically a typical *ad hoc* assumption to rely on the premise that the personal costs and risks of a strategy of deception are *as such* prohibitively high. Rather, they vary greatly, depending on the specific conditions of each particular social context. That it is possible successfully and systematically to deceive others over years and even decades has been proven by more than one spy or 'decent' banking clerk who diligently climbed up the career ladder during most of his life only to pull off a big coup in the end. We cannot assume that, given its personal costs and risks, a strategy of deception will *always* be imprudent for a rationally calculating actor. On the other hand, systematic deception in fact seems to be less frequent than the number of existing occasions and opportunities would suggest. Apparently, there are weighty reasons why, despite the 'technical' possibilities and obvious incentives, people refrain from choosing a strategy of deception.

Hence, it seems that only under *specific* empirical conditions its costs and risks can turn a strategy of deception into a wrong choice. We must therefore identify the factors which determine how high those costs and risks will be. Once they are known, it becomes possible to estimate the advantages and disadvantages of a strategy of deception in a specific situation and to differentiate between the contexts where deception is likely and the circumstances which are conducive to honesty. But first of all it must become clear what the specific costs and risks of deception are. For this, it will be necessary to further complete the fragmentary picture of human nature typical of economic approaches.

[4] Elster 1983, 74.

[5] In this sense, cf. especially the arguments in Robert Frank 1987 and 1988, 109 ff.; related problems are also discussed in Elster 1983, 66 ff.

[6] Elster 1983, 71.

[7] Ibid., 74.

IV. The Personal Costs of Deception

1. OBJECTIVE COSTS

The costs produced by a way of life based on deception are both objective and subjective. *Objective* costs consist in information and decision-making costs which arise for a deceiver in two kinds of choice situations: on the one hand, they arise in situations where the issue is a general decision about whether or not in some particular context he should try to exploit his guise. A prudent decision on this question requires a thorough investigation of the nature of the respective social relationships. A deceiver must carefully consider whether the expected gains are really worth the risks and personal costs involved in deviant behaviour. Such considerations presuppose ample knowledge of the empirical conditions in which the respective social relationships evolve as well as of the consequences to be expected should the fraud be discovered.

On the other hand, information and decision-making costs also arise in each particular choice situation, where the question then is whether or not, under the 'cover' of successful deception, the deceiver should 'go for it'. Such choice situations are typical of a deceiver's double life, since if his deception strategy is to pay off, he must first of all identify those golden opportunities that will allow him to collect the 'payment' for his deception with the least possible risk. However, it will often be rather difficult for him to distinguish the situations in which he should better keep up his disguise from those where he can act opportunistically without the risk of being 'unmasked'. Many situations which at first sight look like 'golden opportunities' turn out, on closer inspection, to be dangerous 'traps' leading to the discovery of imprudent deceivers. In fact, a deceiver always faces a kind of dilemma: if he wants to benefit from deception, he should, of course, grasp all convenient opportunities; but at the same time, in order to minimize the risk of being found out, he must be careful not to succumb to temptation too quickly. Maximum protection of one's disguise is guaranteed if one *always* acts in accordance with the dissembled disposition, whereas maximum gain from deception means not letting *any* good opportunity pass by.

What makes things even worse for a deceiver is that substantial gains from a strategy of deception often accumulate only after some time in which he *regularly* succeeds in profiting from the deception. A once-in-a-lifetime 'jackpot' rarely materializes. This is another reason why it is of the utmost importance for a deceiver to maintain his cover. In deciding whether or not to deviate from a norm in a particular situation, he cannot risk a high degree of uncertainty. Such caution, however, requires the costly inspection of the given conditions and the careful weighing of the respective chances and risks.

2. SUBJECTIVE COSTS

Subjective costs arise specifically with successful deception and are linked to the fact of secrecy as such. They consist in direct or indirect mental and psychic problems for the deceiver. Acts of hypocrisy and the faking of false personal characteristics are always accompanied by multiple emotional strains, intellectual efforts and nerve-racking consequences.

1. Loss of naturalness and spontaneity. A deceiver is forced to maintain more or less permanently a high level of concentration and a high degree of self-control. He must make a conscious 'effort' to produce those personal characteristics and manners which in the case of authentic virtue arise spontaneously. While an actor genuinely committed to norms benefits from the fact that a behaviour routinized by rules can make life much easier, a deceiver must not only be careful to avoid mistakes and to keep his true intentions to himself; he must also succeed in appearing just as 'relaxed' as someone who does not have to worry about such things. He must constantly concentrate on staying in character and not providing an uncontrolled view of his 'inner life'. Thus, he must not only bear the disadvantages of a *loss* of naturalness and spontaneity; he also has the additional problem of having to cover up this loss with *feigned* naturalness and spontaneity.[8]

A deceiver must be careful not to violate norms in unfavourable circumstances. And he risks giving away his cover through some careless remark or revealing reaction. Deceivers and hypocrites possess information no honest person would have and which they therefore must not reveal. They certainly know about their own deviations, but usually also about other kinds of facts, such as data that may be useful in identifying favourable opportunities for the violation of norms. For instance, a simple clerk at a bank would arouse suspicion if he revealed that he possessed detailed information about the bank's alarm system. Often, deceivers not only have the problem that they cannot tell the truth. They also have the problem that they must 'construct' a coherent picture of some pseudo-reality. The unfaithful spouse cannot simply be silent about his whereabouts; he must invent a plausible story, without obvious inconsistencies, that can withstand possible scrutiny by the deceived partner.[9]

Hence, deceivers are not only obliged to simulate certain personal features and characteristics; they are also forced to hide some facts and invent others. They live a disharmonious life, accompanied by lies and the fear of mistakes, miscalculations, and uncontrolled utterances. Inevitably, the resulting mental strain is aggravated by constant distrust, by the fear that other people might suspect something, that they already monitor and control the deceiver's behaviour and perhaps even deliberately set up traps. In comparison, someone who sticks to the truth and does not need to hide behind a cover saves mental energy and can enter into relaxed relationships with other people.

2. Loss of personal integrity. However, the subjective costs of a strategy of deception weigh on the mind of the deceiver not only in the form of mere 'inconveniences' resulting from the practical difficulties and complexities of his double life. In addition, successful deception has further negative consequences for the deceiver which have nothing to do with the basically 'technical' problems of maintaining his camouflage. Once again, David Hume provides the cue when he describes the advantages of a sincere and honest life: "But in all ingenuous natures, the antipathy to treachery and roguery is too strong to be counterbalanced by any views of profit or pecuniary advantage. Inward peace of mind, consciousness of integrity, a satisfactory review of our own conduct; these are cir-

[8] On the difficulties this involves, cf. the above-mentioned considerations of Elster 1983, 66 ff., and Frank 1987; 1988, 43 ff., 96 ff.

[9] Cf. Ekman 1985, 43 ff.

cumstances very requisite to happiness, and will be cherished and cultivated by every honest man, who feels the importance of them."[10]

In order to understand and find plausible the subjective value of an "inward peace of mind" based on the "consciousness of integrity", one does not need to associate it with vain self-satisfaction or link it to conceptions of things like 'bad conscience' or 'superego'. The value of such an "inward peace of mind" can also be seen as the result of the fact that personal integrity is a basic need directly rooted in human nature and the nature of human relationships: "a life of deception and dishonesty" would thus not only be "a furtive life, in which the possibility of discovery always clouds the horizon",[11] but also a life which, even if the efforts of deception were successful, would fundamentally harm the unique human *interest in authenticity*.

V. Personal Integrity as an Individual Good

1. EXTERNAL IMAGE AND SELF-IMAGE

What distinguishes individuals with integrity from deceivers or hypocrites? People have integrity if the image others have of them, of their personalities, goals, motives and attitudes – above all, regarding those aspects which are relevant to other people's interests – coincides with their self-image, with what they themselves know about their idiosyncracies and characteristics. To have an intact personality in that sense means that one leads an 'authentic' life free from strategic deception and hypocrisy, that one does not systematically try to hide one's attitudes and feelings in order to convey a false impression of one's personality and dispositions and to draw personal gains from that impression.

If the harmony between one's self-image and one's external image really is an important psychic need of human beings, and if the desire for personal integrity refers to an 'ultimate' interest *sui generis*, then the violation of that interest must be clearly distinguishable from the inconveniences a deceiver faces in terms of the subjective costs of a strategy of deception mentioned above. This must go beyond the destruction of naturalness and spontaneity and the mental strain produced by a permanently high level of concentration. And, in fact, it is possible to identify such fundamental damage: if a strategy of deception is successful, then it is precisely because of this success that the deceiver loses a specific ability, namely the ability to establish *authentic interpersonal relationships* with other people.[12]

2. AUTHENTIC INTERPERSONAL RELATIONSHIPS

By an 'authentic interpersonal relationship' or, for short, an 'authentic relationship', I understand an interpersonal relationship characterized by mutual trust and sincerity, in

[10] Hume 1777, 183. This is reminiscent of the ancient idea that only the just can be happy because only their souls are in harmony and equilibrium.

[11] Peter Singer 1979, 213.

[12] This concept is indebted to considerations by P. F. Strawson (1974, 6 ff). I have discussed Strawson's conception in more detail – albeit from a different perspective – in Baurmann 1987, 145 ff.

which, above all, none of the parties attempts to hide, to their own advantage, any relevant information about personal characteristics, motives or objectives pursued in the relationship. In an authentic interpersonal relationship there is room for 'imprudent' emotional or intuitive behaviour, i. e. behaviour which escapes the person's conscious, rational self-control. The parties in an authentic relationship must neither worry about revealing information the other side could take advantage of, nor do they have any secret knowledge they could use to harm each other. In such a relationship, the parties' behaviour will thus not only result from sober calculation and detached reflection, but also from spontaneous reactions and uncalculated emotions. Well-functioning authentic relationships spare one the effort of distrustfully calculating the possible consequences of one's actions.

Following Strawson,[13] we can distinguish a 'participant attitude', which is the attitude of the parties in an authentic interpersonal relationship, from an 'objective attitude'. To adopt an 'objective attitude' towards another person in an interaction means to regard him as a means towards own ends, as an 'object' to be influenced as effectively as possible. Such an 'instrumentalization' of another person obviously excludes spontaneous, emotional actions towards that person and requires a high degree of detachment and of control over one's own emotions.

Likewise, persons who attempt to get others to behave in a way that will benefit themselves by deliberately concealing their own intentions and dispositions also adopt an objective attitude in this sense. Their partners are reduced to objects of secret tactics. By intentionally hiding relevant information from them, the deceivers convert them into instruments to serve their own interests, making them objects of *manipulation*.[14] Hence, a deceiver is unable to enter into authentic interpersonal relationships with those he deceives. In that respect, a strategy of deception implies a specific *inability*: one simply *cannot* at the same time be a deceiver and reveal one's personality or true feelings.

Now, it is obvious that the party who is the *object* of deception is usually harmed by a manipulative, non-authentic relationship. Deception often provides a basis for exploitation and fraud. But what is decisive here is that a deceiver's inability to establish authentic relationships also generates substantial personal costs and losses *for himself* – even when *he* is dealing with a partner whose integrity is intact and when there is no fear of becoming the victim of deception and manipulation himself.

But what are the specific advantages of authentic interpersonal relationships that are inaccessible to a deceiver? Metaphorically speaking, they consist in the value other people may have as *mirrors* of one's own personality and conduct. This refers mainly to two phenomena: On the one hand, there is the fact that as human beings, for our self-image, our self-assessment and self-realization, we depend in many ways on other people's reactions to our personal features and peculiarities, and on their judgments of our abilities, talents and weaknesses. Without such a 'reflection' of our personality in the perception of others, an adequate self-perception, constructive self-critique and the development of our personality will hardly be possible. This aspect can be called the *epistemic* value of authentic interpersonal relationships.

[13] Cf. Strawson 1974, 9.

[14] For a concept of manipulation which refers especially to situations of 'asymmetric knowledge', cf. Baurmann 1987, 89 ff.

On the other hand, such relationships also have an important *emotional* value. This is so because in authentic relationships it is possible to satisfy one's desire for expressing emotions and feelings without running any risk. Expressing an emotion can be immediately satisfying, regardless of whether the emotion is positive or negative. Our relationships with other people are usually marked much more by emotional ties than by a similarity of interests. In his analysis, Strawson has emphasized precisely this emotional and expressive aspect of authentic relationships. In his view, what makes authentic relationships so valuable is above all the fact that they allow us to practice emotional, "non-detached attitudes and reactions" such as "gratitude, resentment, forgiveness, love".[15]

Basically, what is involved here is the rather trivial truth that people normally have a genuine need for *self-expression*, which has nothing to do with vanity. They can only obtain their 'inward peace of mind' through the authentic expression of their personality: their preferences, strengths, weaknesses, desires, needs, emotions and feelings. As Strawson puts it: "The central commonplace that I want to insist on is the very great importance that we attach to the attitudes and intentions towards us of other human beings, and the great extent to which our personal feelings and reactions depend upon, or involve, our beliefs about these attitudes and intentions."[16]

But, of course, a mirror can only reflect a truthful image of ourselves if we stand in front of it unmasked. Only honest persons, acting authentically in accord with their actual dispositions and revealing their true characteristics and feelings, can benefit from other people's reactions. Hypocrites and deceivers are barred from that possibility. In that respect, their lives are impoverished. They must cope with a specific kind of loneliness as an inevitable consequence of the fact that they cannot be frank with their partners and reveal their feelings, attitudes, fears, sorrows and hopes, except in a calculated and selective way. Deceivers are forced to forego the 'internal goods'[17] inherent in trusting communication: self-expression, self-knowledge, emotionality, but also amiable criticism, good advice, or consolation. Therefore, even and especially from a self-interested point of view, a life in "consciousness of integrity" may be preferable to a life lived 'in hiding'.

3. INSTRUMENTAL AND EXPRESSIVE INTERESTS

The disregard of the independent value of trust-based interpersonal relationships is another aspect of the limited vision of human nature as reflected in the 'classical' behavioural model of *homo oeconomicus*. This aspect is the exclusive emphasis on people's *instrumental, outcome-oriented* interests, at the expense of their *expressive, non-instrumental* interests. In the economic tradition, man is envisioned as a being whose desires are related almost exclusively to active and purposeful interventions in the external world, i. e. to the modification of that world. In fact, however, human beings do not only fix their attention on the empirical consequences and effects of their actions. The ability

[15] Cf. Strawson 1974, 4.

[16] Ibid., 5.

[17] Alasdair MacIntyre (1985, 188 ff.) has emphasized the fact that common 'practices' as such can produce 'internal' or 'inherent' goods for the participants.

to express their feelings and sentiments, their fears and hopes, has the same vital importance for them and constitutes a value *sui generis*. The expressive presentation of one's personality is an end in itself; it is important regardless of the positive or negative consequences such expressive behaviour may also have. The thesis that interpersonal relationships based on a 'participant attitude' of the parties is indispensable for the cognitive and emotional process of self-assessment and character forming is supported by psychological theories of personality development.[18] According to these, an individual can acquire and maintain a personal 'identity' *only* through open exchange with others. Just as one cannot speak a 'private language', one cannot have a purely private 'self-image' either.

In summary, then, there is convincing theoretical and empirical evidence supporting the assumption that one can develop and maintain a mentally mature and healthy personality only in spontaneous and frank relationships with others, and that such relationships are of great importance for our subjective perception of happiness. For our present purpose, this is the decisive result, because it means that all individuals must have a fundamental interest in establishing authentic relationships with others and will not behave like 'sensible knaves' towards *all* other people *all* the time. The 'inward peace of mind' of an intact personality can be understood as the mental state one enjoys in situations where in dealing with other people one does not need to be permanently on one's guard and is not under the constant pressure to keep certain things hidden, but instead can communicate openly and without restrictions – in situations, that is, in which the advantages of authentic interpersonal relationships can be obtained to the full.

4. THE IMPORTANCE OF EXPRESSIVE INTERESTS

But just how *important* is the desire for personal integrity, and in what kinds of social relationships will it prevail? In Strawson's view, the interest in having authentic relationships with others definitely cannot be replaced: "A sustained objectivity of interpersonal attitude, and the human isolation which that would entail, does not seem to be something of which human beings would be capable".[19] But, here as always, we should be careful not to overburden the theory with excessively strong premises. I will therefore use only a relatively *weak* version of the assumption that people have an intrinsic interest in leading an authentic life. In this weak version, it would indeed entail excessively high subjective costs for a person to deceive *all* of the people all of the time; but it may very well be acceptable – provided the expected benefits are sufficiently large – to fool *some* of the people all of the time. So the need for authenticity and integrity would not manifest itself equally in every social environment and towards every group of people. Although I think Strawson is right insofar as no mentally sane person can do *completely* without authentic interpersonal relationships, this plausible assumption does not imply that the personal costs of strategies of deception always and under all circumstances exclude the option of the 'sensible knave'.

[18] For instance, by the 'interactionist' theories of George Herbert Mead and Erving Goffman, or Leon Festinger's theory of 'cognitive dissonance' and its successors.
[19] Strawson 1974, 11.

From this weak version of the thesis that personal integrity is genuinely valuable, it can be inferred that in choosing between a strategy of deception and behaving authentically, an actor must consider two different aspects: on the one hand, in order to satisfy his interest in authentic relationships he needs a certain number of people with whom he can act in an open and sincere fashion; on the other hand, he must consider whether perhaps he also has relationships in which it may be worth his while to lead a double life because the specific costs of deception would be sufficiently low.

The first group can only consist of persons with whom the actor is in permanent and regular personal contact. Only such persons can know him well enough to be able to display significant responses to his personality. And only with them can he develop the trust and confidence necessary for an interpersonal relationship based not on calculation, but, among other things, on emotions. Those who satisfy these conditions are not only welcome 'positive candidates' for the group of persons which may constitute an actor's relevant 'environment' for authentic relationships. They are, at the same time, 'negative candidates' for the group of potential objects of a strategy of deception. What matters in this context is not only the opportunity costs implied by the loss of possible partners for authentic interpersonal relationships. Another important aspect must also be taken into account: in order to deceive others, one must in a certain sense isolate and shield oneself from them, keeping them 'at arm's length' and hiding one's own thoughts and feelings. But the closer one interacts with a particular group of people, the more regular and intensive one's contact and the longer one's personal relationship with them, the more difficult and costly it becomes to build and reliably maintain such protective walls. The reason for this is not only that in the course of regular contacts the risk of detection is great and the measures necessary for successful camouflage become ever more complicated when the intensity of a relationship increases. It is also that, as a personal relationship becomes more stable and permanent, emotional bonds and mutual sympathy may develop which make it difficult to regard the other side only as a means to one's own ends. Therefore, the personal costs of a double life will, *ceteris paribus*, increase with the duration and intensity of one's contact to the deceived persons.

From this it follows that actors have important reasons to establish the authentic relationships they cannot do without among those persons with whom they have regular and permanent contact, *and* they also have reason *not* to choose the addressees of a possible strategy of deception from among that same group of people. That is why the potential victims of a strategy of deception will be found above all among those people with whom an actor has only a fleeting personal relationship and little contact.

VI. The Personal Risks of Deception

1. Loss of Reputation and Status

In analysing the personal risks of a deceiver, two aspects must be distinguished: the extent of the *damage* detection would cause him, on the one hand; and the *probability* that he will be detected and the damage will actually occur, on the other. Let us first take a closer look at the specific nature of the damage a deceiver must expect upon detection.

What behaviour one expects from a dispositional utility-maximizer in an interaction depends on what personal characteristics and dispositions one believes him to have. This assumption determines whether or not one will trust him in cooperative relationships. Therefore, a dispositional utility-maximizer's actions are important to his partners not only because of their particular positive or negative consequences in the respective case, but also as indicators of his virtues or vices. The informational content of a dispositional utility-maximizer's violation of a norm will be almost of more interest to his present and potential partners than the particular damage he may have caused by this behaviour. From an unequivocally identifiable deviation they can and must infer that his apparent virtue had only been a pretence. In this case, they will not only react by imposing a sanction on him for that single non-compliant act. They will also exclude him from participating as a partner in future relationships that require sincere and virtuous personalities. By violating a norm, he will thus have destroyed his reputation.

But with one's reputation, one also loses, so to speak, one's 'passport' to society. A loss of reputation is a loss of *social status*, i. e. of opportunities to participate in advantageous cooperative relationships. With respect to the past, such a loss means to a dispositional utility-maximizer that his investments have been wiped out. The costs involved in acquiring a good reputation in the first place are worth his while only if they can be converted into an instrument for influencing others to his advantage. His reputation is a capital which is expected to yield interest – and for a deceiver, interest at twice the normal rate – in the form of the corresponding status and the participation in profitable enterprises.[20] If his reputation is destroyed, his past investments will mostly have been made in vain since the really profitable fruits of a good reputation can usually be reaped only after a prolonged period of time. In addition to the immediate short-term damage, the deceiver therefore risks suffering the long-term damage of his permanent exclusion from cooperative relationships. The loss of utility following from such a loss of trust may well be a much more severe 'punishment' than the deliberate imposition of a harm as a direct reaction to non-compliant behaviour.

2. ONCE A LIAR ...

Besides, a loss of reputation is potentially a severe damage because once a reputation is lost the chances to restore it are not very good. The damage is likely to be *irreversible*, because the loss of a 'good' reputation does *not* mean that in the future one simply has 'no' reputation. Rather, what one will have is a 'bad' reputation. But whereas it is quite easy to lose a good reputation, it is very difficult to reconvert a bad reputation into a good one. The assumption of others that one is a trustworthy, sincere personality can be 'falsified' by one single wrong move; in contrast, the belief that one is a deceiver cannot be cogently refuted by any number of norm-complying, virtuous actions.

Once an actor has been exposed as a deceiver and thus acquired a bad reputation, the situation changes considerably to his disadvantage. Henceforth, an observer will (and must!) always interpret his behaviour on the basis of the hypothesis that he is dealing with a dishonest person. After all, the suspicion that the actor in question will con-

20 „[...] deliberately forgoing potential gains from rule violation may be considered an investment in the human capital of a good reputation." (Vanberg 1988a, 23)

tinue to deceive others is not unfounded: once people have been caught at deceiving, they lose their chance of participating in cooperative relationships. But an investment in virtue would be worthwhile only because of that chance. When those chances decrease, so do the incentives for making such an investment. Because of that 'prejudice', it will be difficult for a repentant sinner to convince an observer of his newly found integrity.

A detected deceiver will thus be subject to 'labelings' which defy direct refutation. This leaves him trapped in a vicious circle. The people around him know how bad his prospects are and will therefore be all the more suspicious if he makes a demonstration of behaving well. As already explained, distrust in someone's credibility has the quality of a self-fulfilling prophecy because it reduces the utility of honesty for that person and thus provides additional motives for sparing himself the expense of it.[21] This can have the further fatal consequence that even genuinely positive character traits will no longer be useful for him since they too fall under the 'deception hypothesis' and are no longer rewarded. In the end, the entire 'moral' personality can be destroyed. The process is similar to the well-known phenomenon of the 'criminal career' – a central topic of the theory of deviant behaviour.

3. THE PROBABILITY OF DETECTION

In estimating the risk of a strategy of deception, one must take into account not only the extent of the potential damage, but also the *probability* that the damage will actually occur. What factors determine whether a deceiver will be found out and as a consequence will suffer a loss of reputation and status?

Three factors, above all, make it difficult for a deceiver to lead a double life: *first*, with only one wrong move, he will give himself away – at least if it is an obvious case of attempted defection. In that sense, a deceiver plays an all-or-nothing game. In order to be successful he cannot risk making a single mistake. *Second*, it is not easy for a deceiver to make no mistake at all. Decision situations are often complex, difficult to analyse, and deceivers are likely to be confronted with problems of self-control and weakness of will. *Third*, even if a deceiver actually does not make any mistake, in the sense of the violation of a norm that can be imputed to him, he is not fully protected from discovery. It would be wrong to assume that a deceiver is capable of simulating *all* indicators of personal integrity. While he may be able to do so for the *primary* characteristics, i. e. manifestly norm-compliant ways of action, this is not the case with respect to the *secondary* characteristics intact personalities also display. These secondary indicators – or 'symptoms', as I will also call them in what follows – which are necessary elements of the overall impression people intuitively gain of someone with personal integrity basically escape our voluntary control and are therefore difficult to feign.

4. THE ALL-OR-NOTHING PRINCIPLE

A deceiver who goes into the trap of just once acting manifestly against a feigned disposition in a situation where his behaviour is monitored has usually already lost the

[21] „One of the most interesting but disturbing consequences of labels is that they can lead to self-confirming stereotypes." (Axelrod 1984, 147)

game. He must expect to lose his entire reputation as a consequence of only one miscalculation and wrong decision. One single bad judgment can have irreparable consequences for his image and may bar him forever from cooperation with others. An "endowment of ingenuity and politeness" (Hume) accumulated over long years can be completely lost through a single wrong step. One is discredited and one's guise is destroyed, no matter how many times one had acted in a honourable way before.

Hence, the loss of reputation is not a process one can direct and keep under control. Either one manages to keep the state of deception totally intact, or it is lost entirely. There is no step-by-step unraveling, no downward slope on which one could, at least in principle, stop and even return. The probability of being unmasked as a deceiver, and of the ensuing loss of reputation, equals more or less the probability of being caught on a single occasion, i. e. of *once* performing a norm-violating action when unprotected by anonymity. In other words: for a deceiver, the probability of success is more or less equal to the probability that he will *never* make a mistake and will *never* wrongly try to take advantage of a spuriously favourable opportunity. The extent to which under these conditions one may realistically assume that there is a certain chance of success for a strategy of deception depends on the role the other two factors play in different contexts of interaction.

5. WEAKNESS OF WILL, PRESSURE AND COMPLEXITY

Compared to someone with personal integrity, a deceiver has to bear *extra* costs as long as he finds no opportunity to reap the benefits of his strategy of deception. As long as he does not see such an opportunity, besides the costs related to the deception itself a deceiver must pay the same price for virtue as an authentically virtuous person. He will therefore be under considerable pressure not to 'miss' any good opportunity. Because of this pressure, it will be difficult for him to carefully weigh up the pros and cons in every particular decision situation. Besides, since the gains from defective behaviour are immediate whereas the possible negative consequences will be felt only in an uncertain future, apparently good opportunities for cheating constitute a temptation that is hard to resist.[22] The longer a deceiver is forced to act in accordance with his camouflage, the more dangerous becomes the temptation 'at last' to enjoy the benefits. In any case, a wrong decision in either direction has unpleasant consequences: on the one hand, there is the risk that the efforts spent on the strategy of deception will not be compensated, and on the other, the danger that imprudence will trigger immediate detection. Therefore, the dangers resulting from the volitive and evaluative imperfection of human decision-makers threaten deceivers in a special way.

But the emotional volatility of a deceiver and the temptations 'of the moment' also increase the dangers connected with the cognitive deficiencies of human decision-makers. The insufficiencies of an individual's knowledge, memory and capacity for the perception and evaluation of information lead to dangerous errors in decision processes which get worse when the complexity of the situation increases. And a deceiver will frequently be confronted with rather complex choice situations. He must often collect and

[22] This danger for the deceiver is emphasized especially by Frank 1988, 66 ff.

process a multitude of empirical data. Besides, he must expect that others, who perhaps already mistrust him, may have taken special, not easily perceptible measures precisely in order to make things difficult for potential deceivers. He must reckon with 'invisible' controls, hidden traps and similar devices. What matters for a deceiver, above all, is that he must be careful to avoid all *indirect* indicators of his true nature. Because besides manifest defections, there are many other ways of giving himself away. In a context where not only individual actions but also dispositions are sanctioned, the risk for an opportunist to commit a revealing mistake or error increases enormously.

From all this it follows that not infrequently deceivers must make their decisions under conditions which are not very favourable for the making of correct judgments, thus increasing the probability of mistakes: temptation by the prospect of immediate gains, mental pressure because of the rising costs of an unprofitable strategy of deception, the additional pressure because of the great, often irreparable damage resulting from errors, complex and confusing choice situations with their danger of miscalculation.[23] The problems for a 'sensible knave' are made even more complicated by the fact that there is hardly a strategy for avoiding wrong decisions that does not itself have properties which, in turn, increase the danger of detection. He can minimize the risk of error only by collecting as much information as possible and carefully analysing and assessing it. But these will be analyses an honest person would not be interested in. A deceiver must therefore not only protect himself from making wrong decisions. He must also keep secret the entire information, calculation and decision process which is to protect him from such errors and mistakes. After all, a dispositional commitment to norms manifests itself, among other things, precisely in the fact that the actor does not calculate his 'chances' in each particular case.

6. SYMPTOMS

The probability that a deceiver will be successful depends not only on how well he manages to do the right things at the right time. He must also come to terms with the phenomenon that sincere persons possess a number of 'secondary' characteristics. By such secondary indicators or 'symptoms' I mean characteristics and reactions which, besides the 'hard' facts of manifestly norm-compliant or norm-violating behaviour, serve as additional indicators of a person's authenticity.[24] They are valuable to an observer not because they enable him to draw cogent conclusions about a person's character. Symptoms alone are not sufficient proof to unmask a deceiver. But such indicators may well emit 'signals', reinforce one's trust or distrust towards a particular person, arouse suspicion, and significantly increase the risk of going into a trap.

In view of the objective and subjective problems of leading a double life it is plausible that there are symptoms by which honest people can be distinguished from deceivers. Because of the pressure caused by these problems, the mental and emotional situation of a deceiver will be considerably different from that of an honest person. He

23 Cf. Ekman (1985, 280) who emphasises „how hard it is to lie without making any mistakes". The difficulties increase exponentially when one is dealing not with a single lie, but with the permanent faking of personal characteristics.

24 Cf. Frank 1988, 96 ff.

must constantly watch out and mistrust those around him, he must keep his emotions under control and cope with the frustration and isolation which inevitably accompany a strategy of deception. Even if a deceiver succeeds in avoiding manifestly defective behaviour, his state of mind will be exposed by specific indicators which he cannot completely control at will. Certain emotions and reactions that are difficult to hide are typical of a deceiver. One will hardly be able to appear natural and spontaneous if one must constantly hide one's true intentions. And there are also clear physical signs to be detected in many people when they try to lie or cheat, such as blushing or turning pale, sweating, changes in facial expression, velocity of speech, voice pitch and body language, nervousness and restlessness in dealing with the people one is about to deceive.[25]

The problem for an observer in assessing and interpreting such symptoms is that indicators of emotions and states of mind cannot reliably and with certainty be identified and classified, and that they vary from one person to another and with people's cultural and social environment. On the part of the observer, experience, a good knowledge of human nature and a considerable degree of sensibility and empathy are required. The problem for the deceiver is that it is much more difficult intentionally to produce symptoms than to perform specific actions, and that symptoms often appear without the control or awareness of their bearer. They are, by nature, not the result of purposive action, and that makes them hard to imitate intentionally. Not least because of this, good actors must have a highly specific qualification which cannot entirely be acquired by intensive training but must partly derive from a special talent.

An additional difficulty for the deceiver is that it will frequently be necessary for him to display exactly the *opposite* of his actual state of mind. He must appear unconcerned and spontaneous while he is actually frantically calculating, he must seem indifferent when he actually perceives a great opportunity, calm and cool when he is nervous and agitated, acting routinely while actually carefully weighing his chances. He must simulate sympathy and attachment towards people whom he actually exploits without blinking, 'love' of truth while actually being a liar, satisfaction when he is really disappointed, anger and fury while actually feeling satisfaction and triumph.[26]

However, experience teaches us that despite all these problems with successful deception, observers do sometimes make bad mistakes. Knowledge of human nature and capacity for perception vary. People 'demonstrate' their personalities in many different ways, and they can show a considerable talent for mimicry. After all, secondary characteristics can never be more than 'symptoms' of what really matters. There is simply no necessary relationship between them and a person's actual character. But that does not mean that taking symptoms into account may not be a useful way of protection against deceivers and hypocrites. Symptoms can arouse and focus suspicion, they can increase mistrust or confirm trust. They thus contribute to improving one's prospects of detecting the decisive primary evidence. However, what relevance secondary characteristics and symptoms will have in the end for judging other people depends fundamentally on the respective context of action and on the kind of interaction involved.

[25] Cf. Ekman 1985, 80 ff., 123 ff.; Sommer 1993, 119 ff.

[26] „Most often lies fail because some sign of an emotion being concealed leaks. [...] Looking unemotional, cool, or neutral is the hardest appearance to maintain when emotions are felt.“ (Ekman 1985, 21 and 33).

VII. Again: the Costs and Risks of Deception

A deceiver thus faces numerous inconveniences, difficulties and dangers. And they are mutually reinforcing. For instance, subjective and objective costs increase considerably with the awareness that even a single mistake can have 'catastrophic' consequences. The personal costs and risks for a deceiver appear to be generally high. This aspect was emphasized already by Hume when he remarked that an honest person has "the frequent satisfaction of seeing knaves, with all their pretended cunning and abilities, betrayed by their own maxims; and while they purpose to cheat with moderation and secrecy, a tempting incident occurs, nature is frail, and they give into the snare; whence they can never extricate themselves, without a total loss of reputation, and the forfeiture of all future trust and confidence with mankind."[27]

Hence, even in a world of basically self-interested persons, a certain degree of *prima facie* trust may be perfectly adequate. Paradoxically, precisely the fact that trust in others can so easily be shaken is an additional reason for trusting someone. Since one must be so very careful not to forfeit the 'good impression' one has made, it is often more expedient really to *be* trustworthy than to make all the necessary efforts to dissemble trustworthiness. On the other hand, however, one must not forget the substantial gains a successful deceiver can expect. We can therefore not assume that a strategy of deception is imprudent for a dispositional utility-maximizer *in all circumstances*. Now that we have gained a *general* overview over the cost and risk factors of a strategy of deception, we must look at the *specific* costs and risks of such a strategy in certain situations, i. e. we must analyse how the costs and risks for a deceiver vary with the social framework. In doing this, we are, of course, primarily interested in the conditions of cooperative enterprises, since our purpose is to find out to what extent the preconditions for the development of morality and virtue are satisfied in such a setting.

VIII. Deception in Cooperative Enterprises

1. THE 'STANDARD ENTERPRISE'

Cooperative enterprises are characterized by a structure in which participants regularly find opportunities to violate their obligations to their own personal benefit. Social control is never complete. An entrepreneur depends on his partners' and employees' voluntary cooperation. At least a considerable number of them must adopt an internal point of view towards the objectives of the enterprise and their own tasks. The integrity of the actors is therefore of central importance. If one had to assume that incentives for a strategy of deception are strong or that protection against deceivers is hardly possible, cooperative enterprises would not be established in the first place.

Cooperative enterprises, however, come in the most diverse forms and variants, in very different sizes and with as many different purposes. Three men carrying a table constitute a cooperative enterprise just as the association of practically all states in the

[27] Hume 1777, 283.

UN. In order to facilitate a more or less systematic discussion, the following considerations will be based on the idea of a 'standard form' of a cooperative enterprise. Such a 'standard enterprise' will consist of a relatively large group of people cooperating, in direct personal contact with each other, over a prolonged period of time, within the framework of a fixed organizational structure. The consequences of deviations from that standard form for the issues treated here will easily be seen once the decisive causal factors have been identified.

2. THE HIGH RISK OF A LOSS OF STATUS

In case of detection, a deceiver participating in a cooperative enterprise must expect *maximal* damage: on the one hand, the loss of membership in the respective cooperative enterprise itself and therefore also the loss of all future benefits from *that* membership; on the other, the total loss of his reputation and social status and therefore also the loss of all future benefits from membership in *other* cooperative enterprises.

The involuntary loss of membership in one cooperative enterprise alone can already be very damaging since many enterprises offer the prospect of long-term cooperation. Not infrequently, membership in an enterprise is for life and includes periodical improvements of one's position within the enterprise. Hence, even exclusion from only *one* enterprise can result in considerable losses. But the special danger for a deceiver in a cooperative enterprise who is exposed is the potential total loss of his reputation and status. He must reckon with losing access to cooperative enterprises *in general*. This is mainly due to two factors:

(1) Membership in a cooperative enterprise often involves a mutual long-term commitment. Entrepreneurs therefore have good reason to be very careful and to invest considerable resources in checking the reputation of a potential new partner. Whenever possible, they will make reliable information about his conduct in *other* cooperative enterprises a prerequisite for accepting him. He will have to present a 'curriculum vitae', recommendations and certificates. The entrepreneurs themselves will check his reputation, investigate his past and ask other entrepreneurs. A deceiver who has been exposed in one enterprise will therefore hardly be able to keep this fact from others for a long time. If he presents a curriculum with 'gaps' in it, that will, on the contrary, arouse suspicion right away.

An additional difficulty for a deceiver is the fact that every truly honest candidate has a fundamental interest in proving *his own* trustworthiness and integrity. Such a candidate will therefore voluntarily present all imaginable facts that might serve as evidence of his authentic virtue. For that purpose, 'high-cost situations', i. e. situations in which certain ways of action imply such high personal costs that a deceiver would be unlikely to take them on, will be especially useful.[28] When the issue is professional qualification, that function can be fulfilled, e. g., by a diploma from a prestigious educational institute; when moral qualities are in question, by proof of membership in institutions and associations known for their high standards concerning their members' character. Max Weber

[28] Former US president George Bush, Sr. used to see to it that in parades held in his honour there would be an airplane of the type in which he had been shot down during World War II. Part of Bill Clinton's often diagnosed 'character problem' has been the fact that there is no such plane for him.

mentions the example of the Quakers in North America who were welcome partners everywhere because it was known that no-one would seek to become a member of such a morally rigid and ascetic sect without actually having the corresponding characteristics.

(2) It is much easier to obtain relevant information about the reputation someone has earned in an enterprise than information about behaviour relating to other social contacts. If only because of its duration and the number of participating actors, membership in a cooperative enterprise is a much more visible phenomenon than relationships between individuals. Besides, from a purely quantitative perspective, memberships in enterprises are much less numerous in the life of an individual than isolated social contacts, and it is therefore easier to investigate them exhaustively. Take the case of a car dealer: it is much easier to find out how he behaved in school, in his pigeon breeders' club, during military service, as a member of the church board and of the car dealers' association than to investigate whether in countless car sales he has regularly been a fair and reliable partner.

Thus, while in a person's life there are many opportunities to establish contacts and relationships with other people which only those directly involved will know about, it is much more difficult to hide one's membership in a cooperative enterprise in similar anonymity. And that implies that it will be easier for others to obtain information about an actor's behaviour as a member of certain enterprises. The social network resulting from membership in various cooperative enterprises is more likely to be perfectly intact than the social network made up of individual actions.[29]

Because of the intensive checks performed before someone is accepted into a cooperative enterprise and the good chance that through such checks the relevant data about an individual will actually be obtained, a deceiver must expect that his chances of future participation in profitable and prestigious enterprises may be entirely and irrevocably lost if he gets a 'dishonourable discharge' from even a single cooperative enterprise. From one moment to the next, his social status can change for the worse. And such a deterioration of one's social status constitutes an existential threat. For most persons, access to cooperative enterprises is the main source of their material well-being. But, as already indicated, when talking about cooperative enterprises we must not only think of economic enterprises with material objectives. Certainly, the pursuit of economic ends plays an important role in a person's life. But cooperative enterprises are just as indispensable for a person's political, social, religious and private interests – not least because they provide the 'internal good' of the participation in authentic interpersonal relationships.

A high social status in the sense in which the concept is used here is therefore not identical with its usual sense, meaning a high income, a socially prestigious job or membership in a certain social class. In the sense used here, persons have a high social status if they are believed to be honest and therefore have access to cooperative enterprises which offer them relevant material *as well as* immaterial benefits. According to this criterion, the social status of a factory worker who is a member of the corresponding union, of the local rifle club and the men's choir is no different from the social status of

[29] In modern society, the "sea of anonymity" (Axelrod) is thus partly drained by the networks between cooperative enterprises.

an executive who has a top income, chairs the board of a huge company and is a member of the local Rotary Club.

A person's loss of reputation and status, and along with this the trust in his or her 'sociability', thus means much more than the loss of the possibility to find a well-paying and prestigious job. A *complete* loss of reputation and status is equivalent to the exclusion from all forms of social community, because practically in all communities it is expected that members and beneficiaries have certain community-enhancing virtues. Someone without reputation and status has an 'a-social' position, because such a person is *generally* denied access to the different forms of social cooperation.

3. THE GREAT RELEVANCE OF PERSONAL INTEGRITY

Long-term cooperation in an enterprise entails regular and permanent personal relationships between the members. Rather than entering only into brief, fleeting contacts, they often cooperate over years in a shared context of life and work. In analysing the subjective costs of a strategy of deception, it was assumed that every individual has a fundamental need for authentic interpersonal relationships and that in order to satisfy this need he must have a group of partners with whom he stands in close personal contact over a longer period of time. Only in such a group will he find people who know him well enough to be able to react to his conduct and character in a personally relevant way. And only in such a group will he, for his part, be able to develop the trust that is necessary for non-calculated relationships characterized, among other things, by emotions.

These prerequisites are satisfied by the members of a cooperative enterprise in an exemplary way. They constitute a social community which, because of the intensity of personal contacts, promises participants the 'internal goods' of authentic interpersonal relationships. An actor who chooses a strategy of deception in a cooperative enterprise has to bear at least the cost of forfeiting these internal goods. But the members of cooperative enterprises are not only 'positive candidates' for authentic interpersonal relationships. They are also 'negative candidates' for a strategy of deception. In order to deceive others, one must hide one's thinking and feeling from them. One cannot openly communicate with them. Such alienation from others will affect one's 'inward peace of mind' all the more, the more durable and intensive one's interaction with them. This will cause rising costs on the emotional side as well, since personal closeness can lead to emotional ties and mutual sympathy which make it difficult to abuse the other person as a mere object of manipulation. Maintaining an 'objective attitude' in Strawson's sense towards another person requires an effort which increases exponentially with the frequency of contact. The longer a deceiver must do without authentic relationships with the people in his immediate social surroundings and the longer he must remain in a kind of 'internal emigration', the greater the mental strain on him.

Considering his interest in personal integrity and in the participation in authentic interpersonal relationships, a dispositional utility-maximizer therefore has good reason not to choose the victims of an eventual strategy of deception from within the cooperative enterprises of which he is himself a member. Within such enterprises, a double life and a strategy of systematic deception are inevitably linked to high subjective costs.

4. THE INEVITABILITY OF SYMPTOMS

By hypothesis, cooperative enterprises do not permit the complete monitoring of the *primary* indicators of a person's virtue, i. e. they do not permit the permanent control of each and every action of their members. They do, however, allow a high degree of social control of the *secondary* indicators of personal integrity. Regular contact with persons inevitably leads to an intensive confrontation with their personal forms of expressive behaviour. In a cooperative enterprise, the indirect indicators of personal integrity, the marginal symptoms of a person's emotional and mental states, which are often perceptible only in an intuitive, non-conscious way, are exposed to permanent observation. This permits above all the detection of changes in a person's behaviour.

Of course, symptoms do not enable an observer to draw absolutely certain conclusions about another's character. But especially in the positive case – that is, if personal integrity is actually present – they generate additional trust and a higher degree of intuitive security. People who over a longer period of time engage in regular mutual contact will often feel very sure about their judgment of their partners' reliability and integrity even if they cannot produce any conclusive proof of it. In the negative case, however, symptoms will cause a person to become the subject of closer scrutiny and the topic of gossip and rumours. They will arouse distrust and give rise to speculations. In order for this to happen, it is not even necessary that the person in question exhibit manifest symptoms, e. g. in the form of conspicuous personal inaccessibility and self-isolation. The mere lack of certain *positive* symptoms may already be considered 'suspicious'. Someone who does not regularly participate in enterprise-sponsored social events or who refuses to have a drink with his colleagues once in a while will be regarded as a strange fellow from whom not much good can be expected in other respects either.

It is hardly reassuring or consoling for a deceiver that this kind of social control can lead to grotesque misjudgments. Rather, he will see an additional threat and cause for concern in the unpredictability of human reactions and opinion-formation with respect to the judgment of other people, so often marked by emotions and prejudices. He must spend a great deal of effort on avoiding to the best of his ability *any* peculiarity or anomaly. But it will hardly be possible for a deceiver to avoid such undesired signals completely. There is a considerable risk that he will exhibit symptoms that make him suspect and also that, in a cooperative enterprise, in such dangerous moments he will be under the scrutiny of others.

But the danger of giving oneself away as a deceiver through secondary indicators is a serious threat in cooperative enterprises not only because of the relatively tight control. Besides, once his suspicion has been aroused, an entrepreneur has good chances to confirm his doubt. After all, the opportunities one may have in an enterprise to act secretly against the enterprise's interests do not arise naturally. They exist because, for reasons of cost if nothing else, it is impossible to monitor the members' conduct in an even approximately complete way. But once particular members have become suspect, it is perfectly possible to increase the controls at least for some time, in order to monitor especially these persons and their activities or even deliberately to *set up* traps for them. Even if there are only vague doubts, the prolonged duration of cooperation in an enterprise leaves ample time for confirming a suspicion. Particularly in the framework of an enterprise, even the less reliable secondary characteristics and symptoms can therefore be helpful and ultimately effective instruments for unmasking potential deceivers.

In any case, in a cooperative enterprise a deceiver must expect high subjective costs. He must cope with a severe loss of natural serenity. Given that social relationships in enterprises often take place in relatively personal 'intimacy', during his entire membership he will have to cope with self-control, self-discipline, concentration, tension and stress. Not least of all, a deceiver will need to mobilise a considerable acting ability.

5. THE GREAT COMPLEXITY OF CHOICE SITUATIONS

A deceiver in a cooperative enterprise runs a great risk. The damage to be expected from losing his reputation and status can easily take on fatal dimensions. The prospect that under certain circumstances maximum damage can result from just one wrong move increases the pressure not to make any mistakes and to take the right decision in each and every situation. Consequently, a deceiver must meet very high standards concerning the quality of his decisions and will therefore have to bear equally high information and decision costs. In addition, his choice situations will often be characterized by a high degree of complexity and uncertainty. Some degree of complexity is inevitable in a cooperative enterprise of a certain size in any case. Organizations structured along the lines of some degree of division of labour, with several centres of coordination, different levels of control and decision-making, a multitude of participants and an intricate web of interrelated functional processes do not present a clear and simple picture that could be comprehended at one glance. Of course, that kind of complexity also offers chances for a deceiver. But in any case it forces him to plan his decisions and strategies carefully and assess his possibilities thoroughly.

Besides the – as it were – 'natural' causes of the complexity of the workings of an enterprise, which are connected with the organization of collective action as such, there are also 'artificial' causes of that complexity. This phenomenon is especially dangerous for a deceiver and therefore requires his special attention. After all, he must expect that in addition to the 'official' structures, enterprises may have another, hidden structure of secret controls and monitoring mechanisms. For a deceiver, this danger increases his uncertainty still more. He must either fear that special measures for monitoring his own person have been taken or that, even without any particular suspicion, secret controls and checks on randomly selected members of the enterprise are periodically performed.

Because of such 'natural' as well as 'artificial' uncertainties, the information and decision costs of a deceiver in a cooperative enterprise will generally be high. And since under such conditions he is also forced to avoid all errors and mistakes, he must make substantial investments in the quality of his decision-making. In addition, he must cope with the general insecurity about whether he will always be able to maintain the high level of self-control and sober self-restriction which will enable him to withstand spurious temptations and make well-reflected choices even in difficult situations.

The complexity of the circumstances of action, the ensuing error-proneness of decisions which is still further increased by great psychic pressures, and high information and decision costs thus tip the balance still more against using a strategy of deception in a cooperative enterprise. But to which side the scales will tip in the end can only be estimated by weighing up all the relevant aspects. This requires especially the consideration of a factor we have so far neglected, namely the possible *gains* an actor may hope to reap from a successful strategy of deception within a cooperative enterprise.

6. WHY ARE THERE DECEIVERS IN COOPERATIVE ENTERPRISES?

The long list of costs and risks a deceiver faces in a cooperative enterprise suggests that, for a dispositional utility-maximizer who has acquired a satisfactory social status and who is integrated in profitable enterprises the reasons in favour of personal integrity and authentic virtue clearly outweigh those on the other side. There is simply too much at stake for him. It may therefore seem that it will actually be difficult to answer the question "why are there so many dishonest people in the world?".[30]

But we must not generalize too hastily. The dangers and disadvantages of a strategy of deception are countered by the potentially high gains a clever deceiver may hope to make especially from his successful intrusion into a cooperative enterprise. As a member of an enterprise he will have to make a greater effort than in other social contexts to maintain a double life and, as we have seen, will have to take considerable risks. But even in cooperative enterprises the 'technical' problems of a systematic strategy of deception can be overcome. And if successful, this may offer fantastic prospects. In an enterprise, a deceiver has the chance to enrich himself by exploiting not merely the property of single individuals but the surplus jointly produced by a large group of people. And this may be possible over a long period of time. Hence, just as, seen in isolation, the costs and risks of a deceiver in an enterprise *ceteris paribus* look particularly deterring, the prospects of gain, also seen in isolation, *ceteris paribus* look especially tempting.

Besides, between the members of a cooperative enterprise there may be great differences concerning their positions within the enterprise, their functions and 'ranks'. Such differences will have considerable consequences for the advantages and disadvantages of a strategy of deception. It will depend decisively on a person's position in an enterprise and the tasks implied by that position what benefits he can expect to gain from norm-compliant or norm-violating behaviour, respectively, and what problems he will encounter if he chooses a strategy of deception. There will also be great differences in the status the members of an enterprise enjoy, and therefore in the amount of the damage they risk by a strategy of deception. The greater the 'capital' of reputation and social status one has accumulated, the more one has to lose. Virtue can be more or less rewarding, just as opportunism can be more or less rewarding. However, persons with a good reputation and a high status can also expect to encounter especially tempting opportunities should they choose deception. Where trust is great, abuse of trust can also be great. Last, but not least, it must be taken into account that cooperative enterprises, besides the 'standard version', come in countless other variants. With different organizational structures, the gains, costs and risks for deceivers and for honest members will vary enormously.

[30] Frank 1988, 56.

In view of the great differences in the social status of actors, in their positions, their duties and tasks, and in the types of enterprise they belong to, a *general* assertion about whether virtue and integrity in a cooperative enterprise are more advantageous than opportunism and hypocrisy may therefore seem totally out of place.

But such a pessimistic conclusion would still be premature. We must look at the problem of integrity within enterprises from the point of view of the entrepreneur, i. e. the person interested in the optimal functioning of an enterprise with a minimum of losses due to deceivers and freeriders. It then becomes obvious that just as there is a great variability in the conditions on which the incentives for a strategy of deception depend, there is also a great variability in the measures an entrepreneur can take to counter such incentives. Among the factors that affect the gains, costs and risks of a strategy of deception in an enterprise, there are many which depend mainly, or at least to a great extent, on the entrepreneur's own decisions. Three strategies are of particular relevance to an entrepreneur in this context: *First*, he can reduce the position-specific advantages of a strategy of deception and/or the position-specific burdens of norm-compliant behaviour. *Second*, he can adapt the probability of exposure, and thus the risk for a deceiver, to the different positions. *Third*, he can directly reinforce and reward the personal integrity and virtue of the members of his enterprise. The entrepreneur can thus intervene in a number of ways in order to compensate, at least potentially, the temptation to which the members of an enterprise, because of their different status, their different positions and their different duties, are exposed in different degrees.

The first group of measures listed above take into account that the possible gains from a strategy of deception can be won in two different ways: on the one hand, a deceiver may reduce his performance and 'passively', by omission, shirk his duties and tasks; on the other, he can make an effort and actively attempt to generate benefits for himself. An entrepreneur can therefore lower the corresponding incentives by reducing particularly burdensome duties and tasks and/or by eliminating opportunities to abuse positions and resources to one's personal advantage.[31] In both cases entrepreneurs do, of course, have only limited possibilities of intervention. Many features are dictated by the nature and purpose of the respective enterprise. 'Technical' barriers against fraud, embezzlement or theft cannot always be insurmountable. Not every cash register can be emptied often enough. The command of people over resources belonging to the enterprise often cannot be effectively restricted without, at the same time, endangering their efficient use in the interest of the enterprise. In a cooperative enterprise the request 'Lead me not into temptation!' can never be completely satisfied. But an entrepreneur may be successful even with limited means. Even if all he can bring about is a slight shift in the weight of the aspects which are relevant for an actor's decisions, that change may be decisive.

This applies also to attempts to counter the incentives for 'passive opportunism' by reducing the burdens, for example by distributing 'unpleasant' duties on the shoulders of several persons, or by introducing technical modifications and innovations in order to reduce the overall load. An entrepreneur can also take advantage of the fact that regularly monitoring the performance of difficult tasks may require much less personal

[31] Cf. the references to the 'principal-agent problem' in ch. 2, n. 11.

effort on the part of the controllers than the controlled activity itself. The same applies to the imposition of sanctions on behaviour that violates duties. An entrepreneur will therefore allow control-free zones primarily in the areas of organizational coordination and controlling, where extensive resources are managed and monitored at relatively low personal cost.

More important than the reduction of temptations and burdens, however, is the second instrument entrepreneurs can rely on, that is, increasing the probability of detection for deceivers by intensifying controls at carefully selected, specific points of operation. This is an instrument an entrepreneur will put to use primarily where measures of the first kind are of little avail. He will then increase, at least sporadically, the control and monitoring of those members of his enterprise who, because of their positions, could obtain considerable personal benefits at his expense. This does not at all imply that the respective group of people will need to be subjected to permanent monitoring and inspection of their activities. It is perfectly compatible with decisions and actions on one's own authority that under certain circumstances these decisions and actions will be examined and the respective position-holders will be obliged to account for them in detail.

With the selective intensification of controls, the entrepreneur possesses a flexible instrument that can be employed and adapted as needed. In principle, he thus seems to be in the situation to increase the costs and risks of a strategy of deception in each case to that level where they will adequately counter-balance the incentives for such a strategy. But will an entrepreneur be able to employ this instrument in such a way as to approximate the situation where a strategy of deception will *generally* be unprofitable in his enterprise? *Prima facie*, this does not seem implausible if one takes into account that such a favourable outcome would by no means require perfect control. In order to shift the calculation of a potential deceiver sufficiently into the 'right' direction, it would only be necessary to increase the *probability* of exposure to a level of risk that will seem unacceptable to him. And in view of the other costs and risks a deceiver always faces anyway, it may well be that with relatively moderate measures an entrepreneur could generate an effective level of deterrence.

However, deceivers could be completely driven out of an enterprise by honest persons only if the costs which always accompany even imperfect measures of control and scrutiny were negligible. As soon as these costs must be taken into account, there will be 'ecological niches' for deceivers in a cooperative enterprise, and therefore opportunists and honest members will co-exist, side by side, in some stable proportion.[32]

The costs prevent an entrepreneur both from establishing a perfect system of control and from increasing the probability of exposure to such a level that even the last potential deceiver will be deterred. The relevant criterion for an entrepreneur rather is to step up his investment in monitoring and control only to the point where an additional investment to deter still more deceivers would be more costly than the damage to be expected from them. In this context, he can assume, on the one hand, that at the beginning of the introduction of devices of control relatively small investments will already have considerable effects. Given the costs and risks connected with a strategy of deception in

[32] Cf. Frank 1988, 56 ff.

any case, many potential deceivers will already 'give up' when the risk of exposure increases only slightly. On the other hand, the entrepreneur must expect that the effect of additional investments will continuously decrease. There will always be some persons to whom deception offers extraordinarily attractive opportunities, who have no high status to lose, who are already covering up a past exposure, or who are able to maintain their camouflage without much effort. In other words: there will always be people who have much to gain from deception and/or little to lose by exposure. In order effectively to deter even such persons from a strategy of deception, the corresponding costs of scrutiny would likely be much higher than the damage to be expected from this minority of 'obstinate opportunists'. Therefore, as a rule it cannot be a realistic objective of an entrepreneur to create an entirely 'deception-free' enterprise; rather, his aim must be to create an enterprise with a 'tolerable' level of deception and free-riding.

For the effectiveness as well as for the limits of measures of control in enterprises, the decisive factor is that there is not one single 'critical' probability of detection applicable to all potential deceivers that will cause them all jointly to refrain from a strategy of deception. Because of the multitude of very different idiosyncratic factors on which the gains, costs and risks of such a strategy depend, the critical threshold will basically be a different one for each single actor. This is why in every enterprise there will be an enterprise-specific mix of honest and dishonest members. However, it is unlikely that such a mix will be stable. The external factors of influence which co-determine the risk behaviour of potential deceivers do not remain constant. An entrepreneur must therefore expect that the proportion of deceivers infiltrating his enterprise will change. There will most likely be a permanent process of adaptation between mechanisms of control and opportunities for free-riding and deception.

Finally, besides the possibility of reducing the prospects for deceivers by means of measures based on *distrust*, an entrepreneur can also improve the prospects of honest persons through measures based on *trust*. For this purpose, he not only has the option of making admission to his enterprise generally depend on whether a candidate possesses personal virtue and integrity. He can also deliberately reinforce and reward virtue and integrity *during* someone's membership. Just as authentic interpersonal relationships offer specific 'internal goods' to the parties within the framework of individual action, this is also true of cooperation in a collective context. An organization based on mutual trust between its members can produce 'intrinsic' motives for cooperation which an organization counting only on external incentives will not be able to generate.[33] This presupposes, among other things, that desirable positions are assigned and designed with a view to the criterion of trustworthiness. Virtue and integrity must give access to additional chances essentially related to these qualities, for instance to decisions and activities with a high degree of self-determination and responsibility. An essential mechanism for the reinforcement of integrity and virtue is based on the fact that the reliability and trustworthiness of persons enable one to 'entrust' them with tasks which offer a great amount of intrinsic satisfaction and self-esteem. *Trusting* can contribute to the creation of *trustworthiness*. The congenial reward for integrity is the assignment to a task whose fulfilment presupposes integrity.

[33] For an analysis of the different factors which contribute to the reinforcement or displacement of intrinsic motives, cf. Frey 1992, 1993a, 1993b; Frey/Bohnet 1994.

But the strategy of *awarding* trust in order to foster integrity and virtue seems to clash head-on with measures of *controlling* trust in order to deter opportunists and deceivers. In fact, 'blind' trust most benefits those who want to abuse trust. If awarding trust really is to reinforce integrity and virtue and not only to create a free zone for opportunists and deceivers, it must be 'clearsighted', i. e. *selective* trust and may not benefit everyone equally, without distinction. The award of trust and the control of trust are not colliding strategies at all; rather, the award of trust necessarily depends on the control of trust. What matters, however, is that the entrepreneur distinguish between measures of control and scrutiny which presume that a person will actually exploit every chance of opportunistic behaviour, and measures designed to confirm the assumption that a person has characteristics which, on the contrary, exclude such opportunistic behaviour. If persons are permanently treated as if they were opportunists, they lose every reason for actually being anything else.

Keeping all this in mind, a rational entrepreneur will not act on the principle 'Trust is good, control is better', but on the principle 'As much trust as possible, as much control as necessary'. However, his trust will never be unconditional; it will be trust which is partly based on the result of control efforts and, in that sense, derived from his mistrust. Even if he lived in a world in which at some point in time there were no deceivers at all, it would be advisable for him not to reduce these efforts. But the fact that human decision-makers are imperfect will have negative effects on entrepreneurs too. A temporarily satisfactory state of affairs will make their attention slip, since control and scrutiny require investments that will only pay off in the future: „In a world in which no one cheated, no one would be on the look-out".[34] As a consequence of this negligence, the risk for many potential deceivers will then drop below the critical value. Only as a reaction to that development will he take heed again. To some extent, such 'reactive' proceeding even makes sense. Since it is impossible to predict the calculations of potential deceivers exactly, the adequate 'equilibrium point' between control and *laissez faire* can only be found by trial and error.

Hence, the conclusion from the analysis of the costs and risks of deceivers in cooperative enterprises can neither be that it will never be rational for a dispositional utility-maximizer to prefer a strategy of deception to authentic virtue nor that we must entirely give up the idea of formulating a general statement about the proportions of deceivers and honest persons. Instead, the conclusion is that the flexibility with which entrepreneurs can react to the dangers emanating from deceivers and opportunists will lead to enterprises in which the ratio of deceivers to honest persons is in equilibrium at a point where the realization of the enterprise's goals is normally not endangered. 'Normally', there will be members for whom it will be worthwhile to act as deceivers, as well as members who find it advantageous to be authentically virtuous.[35] And there will also be persons for whom it will be advantageous to be entrepreneurs because they have a good chance of cooperating selectively with those who are *really* virtuous and to exclude and keep off those who, being deceivers and opportunists, only pretend to possess

[34] Frank 1988, 9.

[35] This means that persons with authentic virtue will be able to persevere in an 'evolutionary stable' way, provided the identification of another's personal integrity is not excessively costly or unreliable; cf. Güth/ Kliemt 1993, 1994.

personal integrity. Normally, entrepreneurs can modify the determinants of their partners' and employees' actions sufficiently to make it rational for a great number of them not only to *appear*, but to *be* honest.[36]

[36] The preceding considerations have shown that the problems of deception and distrust can be overcome not *only* in ideal-typical 'standard enterprises'. To the extent that other forms of cooperative enterprises and other kinds of social relationships promote the demand for personal integrity and are unfavourable for the 'survival' of opportunists, they will also become norm- and virtue-generating settings. Thus, for example, Granovetter (1985) correctly points out that economic transactions are often 'embedded' in a structure of durable social relationships. Hence, they take place in a context in which opportunistic behaviour may be just as effectively exposed and sanctioned as in the social community of an enterprise. But – for reasons that will become apparent later – as a morality- and virtue-generating institution, the cooperative enterprise plays a role of special importance.

CHAPTER 4

MORAL POINT OF VIEW AND MORAL IDENTITY

I. Regional and Global Social Orders

The preceding analyses have shown that in a world populated with dispositional utility-maximizers norm-generating situations seem to be feasible under conditions in which they would be impossible in a world inhabited exclusively by situational utility-maximizers. And this picture does not basically change even on taking into consideration phenomena such as deception and distrust. Cooperative enterprises generally provide sufficient opportunities for people to tell the difference between deceivers and honest persons and credibly to demonstrate their own virtue at the same time. They offer honest persons the chance to cooperate selectively with others of the same kind, thus protecting them from the dangers of exploitation as well as from the devaluation of their virtue.

But how will a dispositional utility-maximizer, for whom a commitment to certain norms *within* cooperative enterprises is expedient, behave *outside* of such enterprises? If a dispositional utility-maximizer's genuine commitment to norms is sufficiently rewarded only within cooperative enterprises, it seems that one cannot expect the 'diffusion' of norm-compliance beyond their boundaries. A look at the interests of entrepreneurs seems to confirm this scepticism. It is mainly in their hands whether a cooperative enterprise pursues above all the interests of its members and disregards the interests of outsiders, or whether it forges personalities who, besides the well-being of their own group, also keep in mind the 'common good' in general. In the former case, from the point of view of an outsider a cooperative enterprise would be a menace. Outsiders would not only have to expect that the members of the enterprise will pursue their ends without any consideration towards the interests of others and that they will in no way act more 'morally' towards them than anyone acting in isolation; they would also face the threat of an aggregation of forces to which, as individuals, they have nothing they could oppose it with. In this case, from the point of view of an outsider the fact that the members of a cooperative enterprise are honest people who genuinely commit themselves to the norms valid within the enterprise is not an advantage, but a disadvantage which further endangers their interests.[1] In the latter case, in contrast, outsiders would have good reason to hold the members of cooperative enterprises in especially high esteem, because as honest persons they would not only be trustworthy; one could also expect them to take the interests of 'strangers' into consideration even in anonymous and impersonal social relationships.

It is, however, not immediately clear what motive an entrepreneur who is a rational utility-maximizer could have that would induce him to adopt a 'business ethics' which, besides his own interests and those of his enterprise, also takes the interests of

[1] One can probably put more 'trust' in the members of the mafia than in a single criminal, for instance with respect to the question whether they can be 'relied on' to carry out a threat to kill someone.

others into account.[2] For a cooperative enterprise to be successful, it is necessary that its members adopt an internal point of view towards the enterprise's ends, and that they accept the norms which determine their obligations and tasks within the enterprise as personal norms. Of course, the contents of such norms will not be exclusively *specific* to the enterprise (as would be the obligation to perform certain actions in order to produce a certain good). They will also demand general moral virtues, that is, conduct which is needed in *every* social order. After all, for the stability and the success of an enterprise it is not only important that its members are oriented towards the respective purposes of the enterprise. It is also important that, as participants in a cooperative context of action, they do not kill, hurt, cheat or steal from each other, that they practice fairness and solidarity, and that they do not try to shift common burdens onto the shoulders of others.

But why should an entrepreneur require his partners and employees to have more than 'local' virtues with respect to these norms? Why should he attempt to expand the sphere of such norms beyond the confines of the enterprise? For his enterprise's efficiency, all that is needed is that the members of his enterprise do not *mutually* kill, hurt, rob, cheat or deceive *each other*. It may even be extremely advantageous for an entrepreneur if they are only 'selectively' virtuous. If they feel committed exclusively to the enterprise they belong to, a 'ruthless' entrepreneur may be able to define goals, and to choose methods for achieving them, which are incompatible with a respect to the interests of outsiders – in the extreme, he might even found an enterprise which relies *exclusively* on a 'hostile' strategy. If, instead, the members of the enterprise possess a 'global' virtue which shows consideration for everyone, entrepreneurial strategies based on a general disregard for the interests of outsiders are impossible to implement.

If what has just been said were conclusive, the special capacities of a dispositional utility-maximizer would result merely in the better realization of the interests of particular groups and not in the better achievement of the common goals and interests of all members of a society. Based on the solidarity practiced within them, different cooperative enterprises would then have an incentive to fight each other for power and predominance rather than to contribute to a global social order which is in the interest of the members of other cooperative enterprises too. In other words, the assumption of the critics of liberalism that in an interest-dominated society there is no room for a morality that benefits the community as a whole would not have been refuted by our reflections and results.

II. The Scope of Morality and Virtue: Universalism or Particularism?

1. Norms of Limited and of Unlimited Scope

However, these conclusions are premature, because we are dealing with two different questions which must be carefully distinguished. *First*, one can ask *under what condi-*

[2] In the present context, the concept of a 'business ethics' is taken in a different sense than in common theories of business ethics. Here, I do not mean the *normative* or *moral* foundation of norms for enterprises, but the *empirical, explanatory* question as to which entrepreneurial norms are in an entrepreneur's interest. In this sense, even the 'morality' of the mafia is a 'business ethics'.

tions it is rational for a dispositional utility-maximizer to commit himself to certain norms. The answer is that such conditions hold within cooperative enterprises. But that does not yet answer the *second* question, which concerns the *scope* of those norms. By the 'scope' of a norm I understand the set of people who, as beneficiaries of the norm, have an immediate gain if the norm is obeyed.[3] The beneficiaries of the norm 'One should not kill other people' are all people, i. e. the scope of that norm includes everyone. The beneficiaries of the norm 'One should honour one's parents' are all people with children, hence the scope of that norm is limited to persons who have children. And the beneficiaries of the norm 'One should not torture sentient beings' are all persons and many animals, and therefore the conjunction of these groups also constitutes the scope of that norm.

The scope of a norm depends essentially on what interests are taken into account in its formulation. I will say that a norm has *unlimited* scope if and only if its beneficiaries are *all* those who in the relevant sense – that is, with respect to the behaviour prescribed by the norm – share the same interest. In contrast, I will say that a norm has a *limited* scope if its beneficiaries are *not* all those who have the same interest in regard to the prescribed behaviour, i. e. if the interests of *some* of them are not taken into account in the formulation of the norm.

It is not always obvious whether a norm is of limited or unlimited scope. Thus, norms prescribing that certain benefits should accrue only to a particular class of people as norm-beneficiaries may well have unlimited scope – for example, that one should first and foremost be concerned with the welfare of one's relatives, or that one should support the poor and the weak. Although compliance with such norms serves only the interests of a limited group of people, these beneficiaries may include all those who in the relevant respect have the same interest. This also implies that whether a norm has unlimited or limited scope does not depend on whether all, most, or only a few individuals gain from compliance with it and thus belong to its beneficiaries. A norm can be of unlimited scope even if its implementation benefits only a single individual, as long as that individual is the only one with the relevant interests.

2. UNIVERSALIZATION AND THE MORAL POINT OF VIEW

According to the currently predominant conception of morality, from an ethical or normative point of view norms of limited scope are to be rejected. In this view, it constitutes an extraordinary achievement in human history that in the creation of social and moral norms, in the course of time the welfare of ever larger groups has been taken into account and that individual and social rights have been continuously extended beyond the limits of certain groups such as families, clans, tribes, nations, religious communities or races. There is a great demand for social and moral norms of unlimited scope which give due consideration to the well-being and the interests of all concerned, of people from other social communities, strata or classes, of the members of other races, religions or nations, of the weak, the elderly and the mentally retarded, of infants, of the members of future generations, and even of non-human beings.

[3] Cf. for the following Mackie 1977, pp. 83 ff., 193 ff.

According to this conception, since they give priority to the interests of a particular group of individuals, norms of limited scope are unacceptable *particular* norms which arbitrarily discriminate against certain individuals and their interests. They violate the basic requirement that norms should be *universalizable*. This requirement claims that a norm, in order to be justified, must be based on the impartial consideration of everybody's interests and give equal treatment to all individuals who are similar in some relevant respect. Whatever benefits or burdens a norm confers on *some* individuals it must also confer on *every other* individual who is equal in the relevant respects. Thus, the principle means that "what is right for one person must be right for every *relevantly* similar person in *relevantly* similar circumstances".[4]

The requirement that norms should be universalizable can also be interpreted in the sense that individual decisions for or against the acceptance of a norm should be 'universalized', i. e. that a norm is justified only if it can be accepted not only from the particular point of view of a single individual, but from that of *all* those actually or potentially affected. According to this interpretation, the principle of universalization entails a 'reversal of viewpoints': "to decide whether some maxim that you are inclined to assert is really universalizable, imagine yourself in the other man's place and ask whether you can then accept it as a directive guiding the behaviour of others towards you".[5] To take into account the perspective of others with the same right as one's own can be called a *moral point of view*. Persons with such a moral point of view will pursue their own interests only to the extent that this is compatible with the pursuit of the interests of others and will endorse only norms of unlimited scope.[6]

Whether and how the principle of universalizability and the moral point of view can be argued for and ethically justified is a fundamentally important question of moral philosophy. My purpose at this point, however, is not a discussion of *normative ethics*. Here, I am merely interested in an *empirical, explanatory* question, namely the question how the behaviour of a dispositional utility-maximizer compares to the ethical principle of universalization and whether under certain conditions it will be compatible with that principle. Could it be possible that the acceptance of norms of *unlimited scope* may be rational from the point of view of individual utility-maximization? Or, in the language of ethics: can one expect a dispositional utility-maximizer to accept the principle of universalization and to adopt a moral point of view, i. e. – since a dispositional utility-maximizer only does what is in his interest – can one expect it to be in the *interest* of a dispositional utility-maximizer to accept the principle of universalization and to adopt a moral point of view? Should we succeed in giving affirmative answers to these questions, we will not only have made some progress in defending the vision of liberalism against communitarianism, we will also have provided evidence that the request for universalization and the adoption of a moral point of view, far from belonging to some unrealistic utopia, may have a chance of realization even under the 'hyper-realistic' conditions of a world populated by strictly self-interested individuals.

4 M. Singer 1961, pp. 19 f.

5 Mackie 1977, p. 90.

6 The moral point of view is often thought to be expressed in the 'Golden Rule' ('Do as you would be done by') or the 'categorical imperative' ('Always act in such a way that you can wish the maxim of your behaviour to become a universally valid law').

3. THE MORAL POINT OF VIEW, AS SEEN BY NORM-ADDRESSEES AND NORM-GIVERS

But that is as yet speculation about uncertain variables. After all, for a dispositional utility-maximizer it is by no means obvious that he should adopt a moral point of view. The claim of universalist ethics that he should pursue only the realization of 'universalizable' interests must appear utterly strange to him. *Ex hypothesi*, he cares only about his own interests and his own advantage. The maxim that he should take the interests of all other people impartially into account seems to be diagonally opposed to his starting point. Rather, a dispositional utility-maximizer seems to be the prototypical partisan of a particularistic morality who couldn't care less about the needs and desires of others. Of course, even a dispositional utility-maximizer is forced to take other people's interests and points of view into account, to the extent that their behaviour is relevant to his own interests. But any extension of this group must be justified to him by the advantages to be expected from such a move.

This seems to imply an insurmountable barrier to extending the scope of the norms a dispositional utility-maximizer will comply with. The line will be drawn between those norm-beneficiaries who have a bearing on his own interests – i. e. those beneficiaries who are *relevant* to him – and those others to whom this does not apply. Why should a dispositional utility-maximizer comply with norms which cater to the interests of people who are of no relevance to his own interests since they can neither benefit nor harm him? Why should a self-interested actor, by adopting a moral point of view, grant advantages to people who are unable to reciprocate his behaviour? For a dispositional utility-maximizer that ability seems to be the only feasible criterion for an 'equal treatment' of others. And this seems to imply that out of all potential norm-beneficiaries the group of those relevant to a norm-addressee is *automatically* identical with the scope of the norms he complies with.

But this conclusion would be premature. It is always only a limited group of people who are relevant to the interests of a dispositional utility-maximizer. However, it does not *necessarily* follow from that fact that the norms he will comply with will likewise only take into account the interests of those same persons. After all, the scope of the norms which are addressed to him does not depend on *his own* decision. Rather, it depends exclusively on what scope those norms should have *from the point of view of the norm-giver*. Certainly, a dispositional utility-maximizer as a norm-addressee will not voluntarily include into the scope of a norm those beneficiaries who are irrelevant to him. But compliance with such a norm may still be rational for him if those norm-beneficiaries who *are* relevant to him demand this extension.

It is thus at least *possible* that a dispositional utility-maximizer as a norm-addressee complies with a norm which takes into account the interests of *all* those affected by it. But whether that possibility will indeed become effective depends on the norm-givers who are relevant to him, *and on their interests*. Instead of focussing on the decision of a norm-*addressee*, we must focus on the decision of the norm-*giver*. In order to answer the question whether for a dispositional utility-maximizer it may be rational to *obey* a norm of unlimited scope, one must first answer the question whether it may be in the interest of a dispositional utility-maximizer to *enact* a norm of unlimited scope – in other words, whether it may be rational for him as a *norm-giver* to adopt a moral point of view.

But what reason could a self-interested actor have to enact norms which besides himself also benefit all other people? Why should he guarantee on their behalf that they are not excluded from the scope of a norm? Doesn't that seem just as implausible as the idea that a norm-addressee might voluntarily take into account the desires of persons who cannot affect his interests? The cursory remarks made above about the interests of entrepreneurs seem to confirm this impression.

But again, we must not draw premature conclusions. The universalization of a norm by a self-interested norm-giver presupposes that it is not only in the self-interest of individuals that certain norms are obeyed in regard to *themselves*; it must also be in their interest that these norms are respected in regard to *other people*. In principle it is not difficult to prove this. It is by no means true that from the point of view of his own interests it can never be rational for a norm-giver to demand compliance with norms for any other purpose than his own immediate personal benefit. There are, above all, two reasons why even a strictly self-interested norm-giver may be willing to take the needs and desires of others into account in determining the scope of the norms he endorses.

The first is that they may belong to the set of actually or potentially relevant partners of interaction for the norm-giver. In this case, protecting their interests will indirectly benefit the realization of his own interests. In a broad conception of 'cooperation' including personal and emotional relationships with others, one can say that the interest of a norm-giver to enforce norms for the benefit of others extends as far as his *cooperative interests*. He will want norm-addressees to comply with social and moral norms in their dealings with all those who either are already part of, or who some day could become relevant to, a cooperative relationship with him. Altruistic motives need play no role in this. A norm-giver will want to enact norms whose scope includes his actual and potential partners of cooperation, if only in order to ensure that their interactions will be undisturbed by third parties. The stability and predictability of cooperative relationships with others depends decisively on the fact that in the social environment in which the relationship is embedded basic moral norms are respected vis-à-vis these persons too. An economic relationship with a partner whose life and property is not respected is as unlikely to prosper as a loving relationship with a person who is socially discriminated or persecuted.

Thus, in many situations it may very well be in the genuine interest of a norm-giver that norms are complied with even with regard to certain other persons. As far as that goes, he also has an incentive to guarantee the enforcement of these norms. However, not every norm-giver will therefore become an advocate of *universalized* norms which include *everyone* in their scope. Cooperative interests can themselves have very different scopes. In fact, they are always limited and will never include *everyone*. And the decisive criterion for the selection of the norm-beneficiaries remains the *relevance* of their interests to the norm-giver, and not their interests *as such*.

And yet, under special circumstances and in conjunction with other factors, the cooperative interests of a norm-giver can contribute to the effective universalization of norms. The additional factors are related to the second reason why a self-interested norm-giver may be willing to guarantee norms for other people.

This second reason is that by an 'invisible hand' certain norm-givers will unintentionally, in pursuing their own interests, also promote the interests of some or even all other potential norm-beneficiaries. Such norm-givers would thus *involuntarily* adopt a moral point of view. That may appear almost paradoxical, because a norm of unlimited scope is, by definition, a norm whose beneficiaries include all those with an identical interest. So how could it be that a norm formulated by someone in order to serve his own interests to an optimum and without the conscious consideration of the interests of others turns out to take everyone's interests equally into account?

In any case, *one* thing is clear from the start: from the point of view of a dispositional utility-maximizer the question whether norms should be of limited or unlimited scope will never arise for him *in that form*. His motivational repertoire simply does not include 'universalizable' interests. For him there can be no doubt that his willingness to take other people's interests into account will end where these people no longer affect his own interests. It can certainly not be the explicit *end* of a dispositional utility-maximizer to include all people with identical interests in the scope of a norm. And that is why it must be possible to describe the difference between a norm of limited scope and a norm of unlimited scope in other terms than those concerning the norm-beneficiaries and their interests. And indeed, such terms can be found.

III. Substantial and Contingent Norms

It is an important difference whether the conditions under which a norm prescribes some conduct – its conditions of application – are *substantially* or only *contingently* related to the interests of the norm-beneficiaries. For brevity's sake, in what follows I will speak of 'substantial' or 'contingent' norms, and of the 'substantial' or 'contingent' conditions of application of a norm.

In the case of a *substantial* norm, the norm's conditions of application correspond to the norm-related interests of the norm-beneficiaries. Such correspondence can be ensured either by making the existence of norm-related interests explicitly the condition of application ('If someone is in need, help him', 'If someone needs advice, share your knowledge with him', 'If someone is in despair, console him') or by determining circumstances which are related empirically to these interests as the condition of application ('The poor should receive financial aid', 'Promises should be kept', 'Children should be educated').

Substantial norms require their addressees to behave in a certain way *if and only if* the norm-related interests of the norm-beneficiaries actually exist. Given such an intrinsic correspondence between a norm's conditions of application and the interests of its beneficiaries one can count on the prescribed behaviour whenever a person has the respective interests – but, of course, where the intrinsic correspondence is based on empirical relations this certainty cannot be the same as in the case where the intrinsic correspondence is based on the conceptual identity of the conditions of application and the interests.

In contrast, a *contingent* relation between the norm's conditions of application and the interests of a norm-beneficiary holds if the conditions of application contain a set of circumstances in *addition* to the existence of norm-related interests as necessary preconditions. A contingent norm therefore does *not* require a norm-addressee to perform a certain action whenever persons have the relevant norm-related interests. In other words, the potential beneficiary of a contingent norm will not be able to enjoy the benefits of norm-compliance merely because of having the relevant interests. Additionally, he will have to satisfy a 'contingent' condition – a condition which neither corresponds, nor has an empirical relationship to his norm-related interests. Thus, in contrast to what happens in the case of substantial norms, in the case of a contigent norm one can *not* expect others to comply with the norm merely because someone has the corresponding interests. If the conditions of application of a norm are related to the norm-relevant interests only contingently rather than substantially, then it is logically and empirically possible that a person has the respective interests and yet an application of the norm will *not* take place.

As examples of contingent norms, one can think especially of norms which determine their actual beneficiaries by reference to their membership in certain natural or social groups, where this membership has no consequences for their norm-related interests – such as norms stipulating discrimination or privileges on the basis of belonging to a certain species, race, nationality, class, social stratum, clan or family. Therefore, norms stipulating that one should tell the truth, help others, keep one's promises or take on a fair share of communal burdens only if the norm-beneficiaries are members of the same cooperative enterprise belong to the class of contingent norms too. Membership in a cooperative enterprise is just as irrelevant to a person's general interest in not being deceived, cheated or treated unfairly as is race or nationality.[7]

Now, the distinction of norms according to whether their prescriptions are substantially or contingently linked to the norm-beneficiaries' interests happens to correspond precisely to the distinction between norms of limited and unlimited scope. That is so because, on the one hand, if there is an intrinsic correspondence between the conditions under which a norm prescribes a certain conduct and the interests of its beneficiaries, then the beneficiaries of this norm will include all those who in the relevant sense share the same interests. *Vice versa*, a norm of unlimited scope must be a substantial norm which stipulates conditions of application that coincides with the interests of the norm-beneficiaries. On the other hand, if the conditions of application require that the norm-beneficiaries must not only have the relevant interests, but must also satisfy additional conditions, then this norm does not include as beneficiaries all persons with the same interests. Therefore, a norm which is to exclude from its scope some people with identical interests must stipulate some kind of contingent conditions of application.

But although the classes of substantial and contingent norms coincide with the classes of norms of unlimited and of limited scope, respectively, from the point of view of a norm-giver the difference between substantial and contingent norms presents a fundamentally different picture than the difference between norms of limited and of unlimited scope.

[7] However, independently of that general interest people may *additionally* have a specific interest in not being deceived or cheated by their *partners*; hence, there may be norms geared to the *particular* constellation of interests of someone as a member, for instance, of an enterprise or a family, which nevertheless are substantial norms because their conditions of application are intrinsically related to the existence of that specific constellation of interests.

IV. Substantial and Contingent Norms From a Norm-Giver's Point of View

1. THE STRATEGY OF DISCRIMINATION

As a norm-giver, a dispositional utility-maximizer can have only one reason for wanting a norm to be imposed, and that is because in certain circumstances he benefits from the prescribed conduct, either as a direct beneficiary of that conduct, or because he can expect indirect advantages from the fact that certain other persons who are relevant to him as actual or potential partners of cooperation benefit from the norm. Thus, in his view, the norm's conditions of application must ensure to the highest possible degree that the norm applies whenever he himself or his actual or potential partners have the respective interest. This is guaranteed in each case if the norm is a substantial norm and its conditions of application *generally* coincide with the norm-related interests.

Only on one condition will a rational actor be ready to give up this intrinsic correspondence between the norm's conditions of application and the norm-related interests, in favour of a contingent norm: on the condition that the additional restrictions contained in the contingent norm do not exclude him and those relevant to him from the class of the norm's beneficiaries. It will be of utmost importance to him that in the case of a contingent norm there is a reliable and permanent relationship between those conditions under which he directly or indirectly benefits from the prescribed conduct and those conditions which make the norm applicable to a particular situation. However, from his point of view the norm's conditions of application need not guarantee that the prescribed conduct is imposed *whenever* there is a norm-related interest. All they must guarantee is that the norm is applied whenever he himself or his partners have such an interest. And that is why, in principle, a norm-giver might consider enacting a contingent instead of a substantial norm in order to further his interests. For this purpose, he can choose between two different ways how to formulate a contingent norm:

1. He may *individualize* the desired set of norm-beneficiaries by stipulating individually designated persons as the norm's beneficiaries.
2. He may *classify* the desired set of norm-beneficiaries by stipulating persons fitting a general criterion as the norm's beneficiaries.

In both cases, the task is to formulate 'discriminating' conditions of application for a contingent norm in such a way that the norm applies whenever the particular group of people privileged by the norm-giver have the relevant interests. Such a 'strategy of discrimination', however, entails certain basic inconveniences and risks for the norm-giver.

2. THE RISKS OF A STRATEGY OF DISCRIMINATION

(1) The correspondence between a norm-giver's interests and a norm's conditions of application

In regard to the strategy of discrimination where in the content of a norm the norm-beneficiaries are classified, two kinds of discriminating characteristics can be distinguished:

those that are and those that are not *invariably* connected with a person. As an example of a *variable* characteristic, think of a prohibition of lying as a contingent norm, such as: 'One ought not to lie to Catholics'. In order to be a beneficiary of this norm, one must fulfil the condition of being Catholic. The relationship between the discriminating feature of being Catholic and having an interest in not being lied to, however, is only contingent: being Catholic does not cause one to have an interest in being told the truth; that interest is shared by Protestants and atheists alike. Hence, a rational norm-giver will enact such a norm only if those who he wants to include as norm-beneficiaries are, and are likely to remain, Catholic. Only if this is the case will there be a reliable and permanent relationship between his interests and the conditions which make the norm applicable.

However, the use of variable characteristics as contingent conditions of application for norms raises a fundamental problem. Since the characteristic may change – after all, even a Catholic might some day become an atheist –, the empirical relationship between the norm-giver's interests and the norm's conditions of application may eventually be lost: he or some of his partners of cooperation may some day find themselves excluded from a norm's protective shield. That risk increases proportionally with the probability that the norm-giver or the persons relevant to him will some day cease to fulfil the condition which now includes them in the beneficiaries of a contingent norm. In that respect, the Catholic faith may be relatively immune against erosion. But membership in other social groups often undergoes quick and frequent changes. And, in any case, where a characteristic is variable, it is by definition impossible to exclude the event that one may lose it.

Of course, in the case of *invariable* characteristics this risk does not exist. Examples of such characteristics are blood-relationship, hereditary traits such as membership in the aristocracy, race, geographic or national origin, or membership in the human species. In such cases, one can rest assured that anyone who has such a characteristic at one time will also keep it at any later time. Once someone has gained the status of a norm-beneficiary because of such a characteristic in the norm's conditions of application, he need not be afraid of losing this status again.

Nevertheless, even with such invariable characteristics the norm-giver runs certain risks – at least concerning other persons' status as norm-beneficiaries, if not his own. The reason for this is that from his point of view it matters not only whether certain partners of cooperation continue to possess the discriminating feature. It also and above all matters to him whether he can expect that the group of people who are relevant to him as actual or potential partners will remain identical with the group of persons who have the respective characteristic. But how sure can the aristocrat, the patriarch, the tribal chief, the anglophone or the white man be that those people who will be relevant to his future cooperative interests will always come from the aristocracy, or from his family, tribe, language community, or race?

Hence, in formulating contingent norms, what is decisive for a norm-giver is the stability of his relationships with the classes of people included or excluded by these norms. Even if discriminating characteristics are invariable, this is not necessarily true of cooperative relationships: relevant partners with a certain characteristic may become irrelevant, and irrelevant persons without the respective characteristic may become relevant. Thus, what matters most for a norm-giver of a contingent norm is not that the criterion of discrimination he chooses should be as invariable as possible, but rather that his criteria of discrimination and his cooperative interests should *coincide* as reliably and permanently as possible. But not always will there be such a stable social or natural relationship between an actor and the group of his actually or potentially relevant partners that this bond will yield an adequate criterion of discrimination.

Hence, the main question seems to be whether and to what extent a norm-giver can expect a discriminating criterion to continue to select those persons who will acquire relevance for him as partners of cooperation. His cooperative interests will have to remain within the limits drawn by this criterion. Whatever the probability for this may be, the norm-giver can never be entirely sure that there may not in the future be persons who become relevant to his interests and who are not accounted for by a contingent norm. Quite to the contrary, depending on external circumstances it may even be very likely that the evolution of an actor's cooperative interests will not 'conform' to contingent personal characteristics, as we will see later.

Obviously, this problem will become even worse if a norm-giver chooses the strategy of individualization in order to link a contingent norm as closely as possible to his own interests. At first sight, such a strategy may appear to be well suited. How could one protect the interests of particular norm-beneficiaries more effectively than by explicitly listing them individually, one by one? But in this case, the rigidity of the contingent norm will be even more at odds with the possible dynamism of cooperative interests, because here the group of people from which the norm-giver will be able to recruit his partners will, as a rule, be considerably smaller than in the case of discrimination by general characteristics. And hence, from the outset, the probability that the correlation between the contingent norm and the cooperative interests of the norm-giver will be lost, because persons who do not fall under the norm's criterion of application become relevant to him will be considerably higher.

All this means that for a norm-giver the empirical contingence of the relationship between his cooperative interests and a contingent norm is a disadvantage which, *ceteris paribus*, speaks in favour of the promulgation of substantial norms.

(2) The moral point of view as a byproduct

If one looks at the situation of a norm-giver *exclusively* from the point of view of the disadvantages and risks of contingent norms, it seems to be better for him to enact only substantial norms. They give him the highest possible degree of certainty that the conduct prescribed by a norm will be forthcoming whenever it is in his interest that the norm be complied with. Although this result would be less obvious if we were also to take into account the *advantages* contingent norms may have for a norm-giver, it is still, as such, remarkable. As we have already seen, the difference between substantial and contingent norms perfectly corresponds to that between norms of limited and norms of unlimited scope: contingent norms are necessarily particularistic, substantial norms are necessarily universalistic. And that means that it is not entirely out of the question that it might be to the benefit of a norm-giver to endorse a norm of unlimited scope, i. e. a universal norm. It may indeed be in a person's *interest* to adopt the moral point of view.

Therefore, a mode of behaviour for which at first sight there seemed to be no reason at all has now become at least conceivable. And it has become conceivable, because a distinction which, from the perspective of a self-interested actor, is totally irrelevant acquires direct importance to him if it is 'described' in a different way, that is, if the alternative between universal and particular norms is translated into the alternative between substantial and contingent norms. Thus, an 'invisible hand' brings about the unintended side-effect that a norm-giver, through his purely self-interested decisions, will take care of *everybody's* interests. Even in a world inhabited exclusively by self-intested actors, it is therefore not at all impossible that the decisions of a norm-giver express 'universalizable' interests. And the same applies to norm-addressees to the extent that they have reasons to comply with substantial norms. Hence, under the right conditions, both norm-givers and norm-addressees will behave *as if* they had consciously adopted a moral point of view and acted on an impartial consideration of everybody's interest.

V. Substantial and Contingent Norms From an Entrepreneur's Point of View

1. Criteria of Discrimination and Cooperative Interests

For our present approach, it is of decisive importance how *entrepreneurs*, as norm-givers, will deal with the alternative between substantial and contingent norms. Because only if cooperative enterprises produce norms of a scope that goes far beyond the confines of the respective enterprise can we expect from them a substantial contribution to the establishment of non-particularistic social and moral norms in a society.

For an entrepreneur, just as for any other norm-giver facing the decision whether to enact a substantial or a contingent norm, there are two groups of relevant persons: on the one hand, the group which through a potential criterion of discrimination would be constituted as the 'in group' of privileged norm-beneficiaries; and on the other hand, the group which is determined by the entrepreneur's cooperative interests – that is, those people with whom he already maintains cooperative relationships or who in the future may become possible partners for such relationships.

The second group will, above all, encompass those persons who in the immediate or distant future are potential candidates for membership in the enterprise of the entrepeneur. Thus, it is of vital importance for him that his chances to cooperate with these persons will be enhanced and protected through their inclusion in the norms of social cooperation and morality. But the cooperative interests of an entrepreneur also include other persons who, as individuals or entrepeneurs, are relevant to the enterprise's ends – for instance, as partners in exchange or trade. Therefore, with respect to them too he will not want his cooperative relationships with them to become endangered because others exclude them from the protection of social and moral norms. Finally, an entrepreneur will usually be a member of more than just *one* enterprise, and he will also be integrated not *only* in cooperative enterprises, but also in other kinds of private and social communities. And again, it must be in his interest that the members of these other enterprises and groups will also be included in the scope of social and moral norms, since they are relevant partners for him. Thus, the cooperative interests of an entrepreneur will almost always go beyond the confines of the respective enterprise. And this implies that the scope of the norms he will enact as a norm-giver will encompass significantly more persons than the actual members of his enterprise.

Now, when an entrepreneur considers enacting a contingent norm, it will be of decisive importance for him that the group of norm-beneficiaries who will be privileged by this norm has, and continues to have, the greatest possible overlap with the group of actual and potential partners of cooperation. The contingent norm's conditions of application should, if possible, include all those who, now or in the future, belong to this group. Denoting the desired norm-beneficiaries by individualization has not proved to be a very promising strategy. Instead, an entrepreneur will have to find a characteristic which he shares with the group of his actual and potential partners and which links him to that group as permanently and invariably as possible. That is the only way for him to ensure that his criteria of discrimination always correspond to his cooperative interests.

Of course, an entrepreneur runs the same two risks as any other norm-giver of a contingent norm: *firstly*, the correspondence between his criteria of discrimination and his cooperative interests may get lost because the former are variable, and persons who are relevant to him may lose the respective characteristic. *Secondly*, the correspondence may disappear because of a change in the composition of the group of relevant people. Persons who fulfil a criterion of discrimination can become irrelevant and persons who do not fulfil this criterion can become relevant. In both cases, the empirical bond between the entrepreneur and the group of relevant partners would turn out to be too weak. And the two dangers may even reinforce each other: for instance, a Catholic entrepreneur who wishes to work only with Catholics may witness that many Catholics become atheists, while at the same time a growing number of Protestants acquire the specific skills he needs in his enterprise.

But the risks to a stable bond with his partners of cooperation may also emanate from the entrepreneur himself. He may lose the features he once shared with them – he may abandon his religion, leave his village or country, change his political affiliation or move up the social ladder. Alternatively, there may also be a change in his interests, ends or projects, with the consequence that for the realization of his purposes people who are not encompassed by a given criterion of discrimination become relevant. And even if his ends remain the same, there may be a change in the skills and abilities required of his partners. Besides, the group of an entrepreneur's partners of interaction outside of his enterprise, in his personal relationships, may change. This may happen entirely without his own doing, merely because new people 'come into' his life. But it may also be the case that he intentionally reconstructs his social contacts.

The invariability and stability a norm-giver requires of a useful criterion of discrimination may thus clash with the potential variability and instability of the group of people who are relevant to an entrepreneur. While the beneficiaries of a contingent norm constitute a rather static group, with fixed boundaries separating them from other groups, the group of an entrepreneur's relevant partners of cooperation may be open and flexible, its composition constantly changing. But the extent to which this potential conflict between criteria of discrimination and cooperative interests really materializes depends mainly on *external* factors which an entrepreneur can hardly influence. It is the 'statics' and the 'dynamics' of a society as a whole which determine the degree to which the necessary statics of discrimination will conflict with the potential dynamics of co-operative interests.

2. CLOSED AND OPEN SOCIETIES

(1) Closed societies

The relevant contrast can be brought to light by comparing the ideal types of 'closed' and 'open' societies. I will use 'closed society' to refer to a 'traditional' society with static social structures whose members live in stable communities with clearly drawn boundaries and in relationships based on personal ties. Closed societies display little mobility – whether social, political, economic or geographic. Typically, in such societies the infrastructure, the means of communication, science and technology are poorly developed, and incentives to raise the existing level are weak. Life is constrained by narrow social and natural confines. Such societies are characterized by individual and collective continuity and stagnation rather than change and dynamism.

In closed societies, individual life prospects are basically predetermined by one's membership in some group and one's social role. This concerns the acquisition of skills and knowledge as well as the accumulation of material goods and the social contacts and relationships open to an individual during his lifetime. Individual freedom is subjected to collective constraints. In a closed society, especially the ways and means of pursuing economic interests are determined by descent and social origin: whether one becomes an 'entrepreneur' or a day-labourer does not depend on personal desires and talents, but on whether one comes from a family of merchants or is the son of a labourer; and whether as a merchant one deals in fabrics or in spices does not depend on one's individual preferences but on which town one was born in. The education and training one receives depends on one's social status, birth, religion or region – either because the free transmission and dispersion of knowledge is impeded by a practice of professional secrecy or because 'guilds' defend their monopolies, excluding members of other groups from acquiring certain skills and practicing certain professions. In a closed society, an entrepreneur[8] cannot freely choose his ends and means. The ends and ways of collective action are socially prescribed. This implies, among other things, that an entrepreneur is unable to redirect his interests and plans in the course of his life and to pursue new projects in a new social or geographic environment. In closed societies it is often prohibited or factually impossible for people to change a profession once acquired, or their social position, or the place of residence determined by birth.

Consequently, an entrepreneur in such a society will not be able to choose his partners and collaborators according to his own criteria. He will have to make do with the persons available in his immediate social surroundings or who are assigned to him. If nothing else, the geographic immobility typical of traditional societies may already make it impossible for an entrepreneur to establish contacts with people beyond his immediate social context. Similar constraints will exist with respect to cooperative relationships with other entrepreneurs or individuals outside of his enterprise. This circle too will not

[8] In this context, the term ‚entrepeneur' is, of course, used in the broadest sense of the word.

develop 'spontaneously' or through his own initiative. Besides, in closed societies compulsion and involuntariness also reign in areas which do not concern the acquisition of economic goods. Generally, as members of a closed society people are 'born into' the communities which serve non-material, social or personal ends and do not have the chance to leave them if they so desire, or to found new communities according to their own ideas.

But what is decisive for the situation and the interests of an entrepreneur is that the primordial communities and social groups to which he usually belongs simply by birth will be largely identical with the communities and groups in which he will spend his entire life. There is no clear separation between economic, social, private or religious spheres. In the ideal type of a closed society, private and 'public' life constitute one and the same context. Particularly, economic relationships are not autonomous with respect to those community relations in which every actor has been firmly integrated anyway. For individuals, the consequence is that concerning all matters and in all their social relationships, they will mainly be dealing only with the members of the same few social groups: with *them*, they will found cooperative enterprises if they are entrepreneurs; in *their* enterprises they will become members; *they* will be their partners in trade and exchange; and with *them* they will satisfy their religious, emotional and political interests. One's partner in the shop will at the same time be one's brother-in-law, drinking companion and neighbour in the pew as well as in the trenches.

Such social circumstances leave hardly any space for individually designed curricula. They basically define the social existence of all members of society, drastically restricting the choice of persons with whom they can establish contact and relationships. In closed societies, the confines of the clan, tribe, village or town, region, nation, class, social stratum, guild or race may, for natural or social reasons, be insurmountable for the individual. On the other hand, this also means that they do not have to fear that their social ties, that their constant and calculable cooperative relationships, may be destroyed or fundamentally modified. If anonymity and mobility are *dangers* of modern society, they are dangers which the members of traditional societies are not exposed to.

Due to their immobility, closed societies will have many social characteristics which are more or less invariably linked to an individual: membership to a social class or stratum, profession, wealth, place of residence, religion, way of life, or skills. And not only will those characteristics themselves be more or less invariable. Together with characteristics such as social or geographic origin, birth or race, they will constitute a more or less invariable empirical link between people.

From the point of view of an entrepreneur or norm-giver, this means that the more the actual social circumstances approach the ideal type of closed society and, therefore, the more the empirical links between the members of social groups are robust and permanent, the more he can expect that there will be no dangerous gap between the criteria of discrimination of a contingent or particular norm and his cooperative interests. Rather, it will be relatively easy for him to find a discriminating feature which is reliably linked precisely to those persons who in the course of his life will be relevant to him as partners in economic, social or personal relationships. In a closed society, there are numerous social and natural 'bonds' which tie people together in a practically indestructible way. In such circumstances, the cooperative interests of an entrepreneur will, from the outset, be *locally restricted*: his actual or potential partners of cooperation will come from a set of persons who can be distinguished from others by some clearly perceptible criterion, such as membership in a clan, tribe, class, race, religious congregation, or nation.

Hence, an entrepreneur in a closed society can expect the group of norm-beneficiaries privileged by an appropriate criterion of discrimination very likely to remain identical with the group of his relevant partners of cooperation. He will therefore be able to choose the content of a particularistic norm in such a way that its protective scope will, with great certainty, encompass all his potential partners, now and in the future. Neither will the persons relevant to the entrepreneur lose the feature by which they are privileged as norm-beneficiaries, nor will people become relevant to him who do not possess this feature. Nor will the entrepreneur himself give rise to such dangers. It will be impossible for him to abandon his religion, leave his village or tribe, move up into another social stratum, or modify his interests and goals. His biography will not be a matter of his own choice. In a closed society, the required invariability and stability of the criteria of discrimination of contingent norms are in harmony with the factual invariability and immobility of the group of people who are relevant to an entrepreneur. An entrepreneur will not need to renounce his chances to enter into possibly advantageous cooperative relationships with persons who happen to be excluded from the scope of a particularistic norm.

Therefore, in a closed society, no 'invisible hand' will induce a rational utility-maximizer to act as if he pursued 'universalizable' interests and to adopt a moral point of view. If he lives in social circumstances in which he only comes into contact with a certain 'category' of people, then the potential disadvantages and risks of contingent norms will hardly concern him. Since he can be confident that only persons satisfying a certain criterion will be possible partners of cooperation for him, he only needs to demand compliance with particularistic norms of an appropriately limited scope from norm-addressees, without having to fear that this may harm his own cooperative interests.

(2) Open societies

If we switch from the circumstances of an ideal-typical 'closed' society to those of an ideal-typical 'open' society, the calculus of an entrepreneur as a norm-giver must change fundamentally. In an open society, change and dynamism take the place of static social structures. People do not live in stable, strictly delimited communities and in relationships based on personal ties. Social groups are flexible and 'osmotic', their membership fluctuates, the boundaries and composition of groups are constantly shifting. In open societies, infrastructures, means of communication, science and technology are constantly developing. Instead of continuity and stagnation, there is private, social, political, economic and geographic mobility.

Open societies are characterized by a high degree of *individualization*. There is no stable link between the fact that individuals belong to a certain group and their life prospects. One's course and way of life are not predetermined by group membership and social roles. They depend on subjective interests, personal qualities and talents, and the 'contingencies' of individual biographies. In an open society, the fate of individuals is no longer the fate of their family or class, but their *personal* fate. The living conditions of individuals are determined by their own decisions and not only by the social framework. One is not 'born into' certain communities and social relationships once and for all. Rather, individuals can choose the communities and social relationships they wish to participate in and shape them according to their own criteria. Above all, they can change their interests, projects and goals in the course of their lives.

In an open society, increased personal liberty and autonomy affect all spheres of life. Education and professional training depend mainly on personal qualities and dispositions and are not linked to birth, religion, region or social status. Also, in an open society it is not predetermined by family and social origin how one may pursue one's economic interests. The day-labourer's son may learn to be a merchant, and the merchant from a town which traditionally produces fabrics may move to a sea-port and trade in exotic spices – and he will be able to decide for himself who his partners and collaborators will be in running the enterprise and who to establish trade relationships with. He no longer depends on the persons in his immediate surroundings. Similarly, freedom and voluntariness also characterize the spheres of life which have nothing to do with the acquisition of material goods. One's own decisions and desires basically determine who to believe in, who to pray with, who to marry, who to play cards and drink with, or who to cooperate with in social or political matters.

Besides, only in an open society will there be a clear separation between the different social spheres in which people pursue their economic, social, private or religious interests. Only in such a society, can the 'private' and the 'public' part of a person's life go on in separate social contexts, and the different kinds of social relationships and community links acquire a certain degree of autonomy. This has the important consequence that in their social relationships individuals in an open society are not dealing with members of one and the same group all the time. The people one cooperates with in the economic sphere are not the same as one's private partners, and in private relationships one does not necessarily also pursue religious or political interests. A man's partner in the shop will *not* at the same time also be his brother-in-law, his drinking companion and his neighbour in the pew as well as in the trenches.

Hence, in an open society individuals certainly have greater liberty and more options, in all respects. The group of people with whom they can come into contact in the course of their life is not restricted by 'artificial' barriers. But this also means that reliable community links with constant and calculable personal relationships will be less frequent. The mobility within an open society unavoidably leads to more anonymity and a greater 'substitutibility' of social partners.

But in any case, from the point of view of entrepreneurial interests the circumstances in an open society have the beneficial consequence that an entrepreneur can establish cooperative relationships basically without being constrained by natural or social bounds. As a member of an open society, he is free to associate with others, design common projects, abandon them and set up new ones as he pleases. He is free to employ his personal resources exactly where it seems most effective for his purposes. And that applies to entrepreneurs both with material and immaterial ends. Whatever the ends an entrepreneur pursues – in an open society, in his search for partners he does not need to consider any criterion other than the question of which persons will best be suited for his ends and projects. He does not depend on those persons who happen to be members of his family, clan, tribe, village, social stratum or class. The owner of a trade shop can employ those best skilled in the trade, the merchant can do business with those who make him the best offer, a private person can found a club with those who have the same cultural preferences – and one can marry the person one loves.

Such freedom can only develop if the 'statics' and the typical social structures of a closed society are overcome, if the 'personal' bonds existing between people on the grounds of their social origin, family, sex or class become irrelevant to their cooperative ventures, and if people can choose their place of residence and their context of life exclusively on functional grounds, i. e. according to where and in what context they will best be able to realize their ends. Individual mobility and dynamism of social relationships are necessary preconditions for the full exploitation of the potential of human cooperation. They permit people who are strangers and reside in different places to associate and cooperate if they have common projects and mutually useful skills and talents.

However, these circumstances which, from the point of view of an efficient realization of an entrepreneur's cooperative interests, *prima facie* look advantageous are at the same time circumstances in which the disadvantages and risks of contingent or particular norms are especially great. A stable correspondence between potential criteria of discrimination and the set of persons who may become relevant to an actor in the course of his life as possible partners is particularly difficult to ensure, since the members of an open society are constantly confronted with members of new social groups and communities in the different spheres of their lives. With the growing fluctuation and interdependence between social groups and the increasing mobility and flexibility of individuals who change their social and geographic positions depending on their interests and plans, it becomes less likely that the group of norm-beneficiaries who are privileged by some criterion of discrimination will remain identical with the group of an actor's actual and potential partners of cooperation. Since in an open society there is a general lack of empirical 'bonds' which tie people together permanently in their social relationships, an actor cannot expect that the people who are now, or some day will become, relevant to him can always be recruited from the same social group or community. A coincidence of ends, interests and abilities will not necessarily coincide with joint membership in some social or natural group. Rather, all kinds of coincidences and common features will be likely to undergo substantial changes in the course of time: people will reorient themselves from time to time, look for new ends and commitments, move to other places, and participate in different enterprises.

With a contingent or particular norm, the two general dangers threatening the harmony between the norm's criteria of discrimination and the norm-giver's cooperative interests will be the greater the closer the social framework resembles the ideal type of an open society. On the one hand, as a consequence of social and individual mobility, many features which in a closed society are more or less invariably tied to a person become variable – membership in a particular social stratum or class, profession, wealth, place of residence, religion, way of life, skills, but also political or ideological beliefs: all these are personal features which in the course of a person's life in an open society may change more than once. This means that the number of characteristics which one reliably shares with certain other people are generally more and more reduced.

On the other hand, in an open society neither variable nor invariable personal features such as birth, social or geographic origin, or race constitute a permanent empirical bond between individuals which would also create persistent relationships between them. There will hardly ever be a precisely definible group of people who in their economic, social or private relationships are permanently available for or dependent on each other. In an open society, the confines of one's family, village, town, tribe, region, nation, class, gender or race can be overcome. Hence, they cannot guarantee either that the set of people within these confines will continue to coincide with the set of people who are or will be relevant to an entrepreneur as possible partners of cooperation.

Thus, the evolution and dynamism characteristic of open societies, the permeability of social groups and social relations, the mobility of the entrepreneur himself as well as of those who are or may become relevant to him as partners of cooperation all contribute to the fact that the 'gap' between possible criteria of discrimination and the cooperative interests of entrepeneurs threatens to widen considerably. It will be practically impossible for an entrepeneur to find a discriminating feature that links him permanently to a group of persons who have qualities that are useful for his interests and purposes and, at the same time, does not exclude too many persons who also possess those qualities. In an open society, the 'statics' required for successful discrimination necessarily conflict with the dynamism of the social relationships. An entrepreneur who in such circumstances continues to rely on contingent norms will, in any case, have to subtract from the potential gains of such a strategy the opportunity costs implied by the fact that he can no longer recruit his partners from the totality of persons who would be suitable candidates.

All in all, an open society therefore seems to engender *non-local, supra-regional* cooperative interests. For many members of such societies, there simply will not be any reliable criterion of discrimination by which those encompassed by their cooperative interests can be delimited from all others. With the expansion of market relations and a well-developed division of labour, group confines become permeable and group membership varies. Social groups and communities are no longer isolated from their environment, their members fluctuate and are not bound to each other by unbreakable ties. The lack of static social bonds leads to a relatively frequent change of partners in cooperative ventures. In such an 'unbounded' society, one cannot confide in temporarily existing barriers and boundaries.

Therefore, when looking for suitable partners for a cooperative enterprise, in an open society one has good reasons not to look for people who practice their virtue only with respect to a *particular* group of persons, but for people who are *generally* disposed to consider the interests of all those affected by their actions and not only the interests of particular categories of people. Often, large societies, functional and impersonal relationships between people, great fluctuation between social groups, anonymity and mobility are seen as destructive forces undermining and dissolving once intact communities and personal relationships. But they also mean that people who at first have little in common can come into contact and establish relations; that people come to live and work together despite racial, national, social or cultural differences. And only when that is the case, will people who adopt social norms of unlimited scope become valuable for the interests of their fellow-men. The anonymity, dynamism and mobility of an open society maximize the disadvantages and risks of contingent or particular norms, and consequently the reasons which, from the point of view of a norm-giver, speak in favour of enacting substantial or universal norms acquire maximal importance.

Hence, it seems that in an open society we can indeed count on the workings of an 'invisible hand' which may see to it that an entrepreneur and norm-giver, as a rational utility-maximizer, decides and acts as if he pursued 'universalizable' interests and adopted a moral point of view. What is still uncertain, however, is how powerful this invisible hand is and what forces exist which possibly direct a self-interested actor and norm-giver in another direction.

VI. Power and Social Control

1. Cooperative and exploitative interests

For an entrepreneur, there is no strategy of discrimination which would generally allow him to avoid the disadvantages and risks of particular norms – at least not if he lives in an open society. However, the fact that in an open society an entrepreneur as a norm-giver has independent reasons to enact universalistic norms does not mean that those reasons always have more weight than other, potentially countervailing reasons. Surely, they will be decisive whenever there is no specific incentive to speculate with gains from the implementation of particular norms. But so far, not much has been said about the advantages an entrepreneur may draw from a limited scope of his entrepreneurial ethics. We must now abandon our exclusive focus on the risks of particular norms in favour of a broader perspective which takes into account their possible utility for a norm-giver.

In principle, the incentive for a norm-giver to prefer a particular and contingent norm over a universal and substantial norm is that he may profit if the norm-addressees do not comply with the norm when dealing with those who are excluded from its scope. An aristocrat will profit if other members of the aristocracy only behave virtuously towards aristocrats while exploiting and oppressing non-aristocrats to the aristocracy's advantage. The main incentive for an entrepreneur to promote 'regional' entrepreneurial ethics, thereby excluding certain people from the set of norm-beneficiaries, is the potential profit he can make if the members of his enterprise, in pursuing the enterprise's ends, are willing to lie and cheat, to deceive and take advantage of outsiders. An entrepreneur with a particularistic entrepreneurial ethics is able to pursue ends that can be reached only by disregarding the interests of other individuals or enterprises, and to choose means for pursuing his ends which can only be employed at a cost for those others – even going so far as to set up an enterprise with the only purpose of making a profit through theft, robbery, blackmail, intimidation, or subjection.[9]

[9] Note that even the principle of universalization does not exclude competition and therefore *limited* conflicts of interest between an enterprise and certain outsiders. It may well be in the interest of *all* those involved that in certain areas competition, and with it the partial superordination of each side's own respective interests, should be allowed – but only within the framework of certain 'rules of the game' compliance with which gua-

In other words: the enactment of particular norms, i. e. the exclusion of certain persons from the protective shield of those norms, will be potentially profitable for an entrepreneur whenever he has *no cooperative interests* regarding those persons. And the limitation of cooperative interests may not only arise from natural or social confines. It can also derive from the fact that, from the very beginning, certain people are not relevant as possible partners of cooperation, but only as possible objects of exploitation. If in some field a norm-giver's exploitative interests dominate his cooperative interests, he will have a reason for endorsing certain kinds of particularistic norms – without running the risk that with a strategy of discrimination he will harm his own cooperative interests.

Such an entrepreneurial strategy in pursuit of exploitative interests can come as an *open* or as a *hidden* strategy. It may aim at immediate subjugation and exploitation through the unveiled employment of power resources, including the use of physical force and coercion. But it may also consist in an attempt to exploit opportunities for the unobserved or non-imputable violation of norms. Hence, the prospects of gain from such strategies will depend either on an entrepreneur's *power*, i. e. his ability to win an open confrontation against other individuals or collectives, or on the *risk of discovery* of an entrepreneur's hidden malevolent strategy. Let us first look at strategies based on an entrepreneur's superior position of power.

2. INEQUALITY OF POWER

In contrast to single individuals, cooperative enterprises can differ substantially in their power. This applies especially to their ability to reach their goals by coercion and force. After all, the modern state with its monopoly of physical coercion is a cooperative enterprise just as the two-person grocery store. But once a self-interested actor possesses the means to impose his will on other individuals or collectives, he will not hesitate to make use of this power. Superior power of coercion enables an actor to oppress persons and groups with less power. And it may be more profitable to use one's resources for exploitative rather than for productive purposes, or to subject others and establish a rule of coercion instead of relying on the voluntary exchange of goods and services – whether with respect to other classes and strata within one's own society or with respect to other people or nations.

Entrepreneurs occupying a position of superior power thus have strong incentives to pursue a non-cooperative strategy towards less powerful actors. The more powerful an enterprise is, the less it depends on cooperative relationships with others. Instead, it can press such relationships into the form of non-cooperative, power-based relations of dependency and oppression. Only if an entrepreneur depends on cooperative relationships the loss of opportunities for cooperation implied by a particularistic entrepreneurial ethics will be a relevant inconvenience to him. A powerful entrepreneur, in contrast, will not have any dominant reason why he should prefer a universalistic entrepreneurial ethics, demanding that his partners and collaborators generally give equal consideration to the interests of outsiders. On the contrary, he will instruct them to make use of the enterprise's power resources without any consideration of such interests. Regardless of

rantees that the interests of others are basically taken into account. Here, however, I am speaking of entrepreneurial strategies which do not accept *any* 'rules of the game'.

whether an actor is a dispositional or a situational utility-maximizer: as a basically self-interested decision-maker he will use whatever power he has in order to satisfy his desires and impose his will as effectively as possible – and that means, if his superior power position allows it, also against the will and opposition of other individuals or groups. A rational utility-maximizer can be discouraged from behaving in such a way only by a countervailing power which increases the risks implied by non-cooperative strategies beyond some critical threshold and thus forces him to adopt a cooperative attitude.

What must be clear, however, is that the problems emanating from the unequal distribution of power among social groups cannot simply be solved by giving a monopoly of power to one single dominating enterprise, namely, to the state. Because what is true for others is also true for dispositional utility-maximizers acting as agents of coercive state powers: where there is power there is also a temptation to abuse it, and with absolute power the abuse can be absolute too. If the cooperative enterprise called 'state' possesses the effective monopoly of power in the sense that it has the ability to impose its will *ad libitum*, then dispositional utility-maximizers working as members of that 'enterprise' will not hesitate to exercise the power at their disposition in order to advance their personal interests. In this respect, the state with its apparatus of power and coercion is just one more enterprise among others which, because of their great power, are particularly dangerous.

3. Neutralized power relations

The inequality in the power of different enterprises can thus neither be compensated by conceding a monopoly of power to an agency which then dominates absolutely, nor by actually levelling out the power differences existing between enterprises. Thus, the only way left to reduce decisively the incentives of powerful entrepreneurs to pursue non-cooperative strategies seems to be the *neutralization* of the power differentials actually existing in a society. This means that it must be made impossible for the powerful to use their power for the subjugation of the weak. Neutralized power relations in this sense, by the way, are also a necessary condition for the stability of open societies, since if the actors who occupy superior power positions cannot effectively be discouraged from using their positions to their own advantage, the background conditions necessary for an open society cannot be maintained.

It is, in principle, *possible* that power relations can be neutralized despite the unavoidable existence of power differences. A relatively powerful enterprise can be prevented from actually exploiting its superior position in a bilateral relationship with a weaker enterprise, either by another enterprise with even greater power or by a collective action of enterprises which, taken individually, each possess less power. With the help of the solidarity and cooperation of other members of society, a relatively powerless enterprise can be protected from hostile interventions by more powerful enterprises. This presupposes, however, that the most powerful enterprise in society – which, as a rule, will be the state – must not be powerful enough to be able to impose itself even against the total collective power of all other members of society. Even, and above all, the power of the dominant enterprise in a society must be neutralized by a countervailing power if the domination of the majority by a minority is to be avoided.

The power structures in society are therefore very complex phenomena. They not only depend on the relative strengths of factually existing resources. They also depend on whether and to what extent the members of a society are willing and able to pool their respective powers in order to jointly prevent an abuse of power. Thus, the potential joint power of relatively weak cooperative enterprises may be considerably greater than the individual power of one single relatively powerful enterprise. But if the former are unable to pool their powers 'in solidarity' beyond their enterprise's borders, then their actually existing power over the latter will regularly be insufficient in any particular case of conflict. This reminds us of a point of central importance, which is that effective dominion, besides the dominator's own resources of power, can also rest on the fact that those subjected to it are unable to act collectively. For the effective power of a powerful enterprise it is decisive whether other enterprises and individuals pool their resources in order to defend their common interests against that enterprise.

The question under what conditions the neutralization of power relations can evolve from a mere *possibility* to a *reality* will be discussed later. At this point we can conclude that an entrepreneur can expect definitely positive payoffs from an openly non-cooperative strategy only if his enterprise occupies a relatively superior position of power *and* if he has the ability to exercise that power effectively over other enterprises and individuals. If all this is the case, then he can indeed expect that the gains from such a strategy will more than compensate the disadvantages and risks accompanying the enactment of particularistic norms.

If, on the contrary, an open society manages to ensure the neutralization of power relations, such that neither relatively weaker enterprises nor individuals are threatened by the power resources of stronger enterprises, then an openly non-cooperative strategy will not pay, i. e. powerful entrepreneurs will be unable to implement such a strategy successfully. When power relations are neutralized, even for a relatively powerful entrepreneur – and even for *the* most powerful entrepreneur – the only expedient choice, at least with respect to his visible relationships with other enterprises and individuals, will be a cooperative strategy. Therefore, under conditions of neutralized power relations, the relevance of cooperative interests will generally rise: when power is more and more devalued as a means of acquisition, *power* interests will be more and more replaced by *market* interests.

4. SOCIAL CONTROL

But not only with an *openly* non-cooperative strategy may an entrepreneur reap benefits from particularistic entrepreneurial ethics. Benefits can also arise from *hidden* attempts to pursue the ends of an enterprise without paying attention to the interests of others. Especially in this case, it may even be the only purpose of an enterprise to secretly pursue a 'mafia strategy', and to make 'profits' exclusively through robbery, fraud and blackmail. Even when power relations are neutralized, the incentives for a non-cooperative strategy and the pursuit of exploitative interests will not necessarily fall below a critical level for all entrepreneurs. Just as individuals, entrepreneurs too may be tempted to take advantage of 'golden opportunities' for the undiscovered or non-imputable violation of norms.

The strength of this incentive depends essentially on the *risks* accompanying such a strategy. If the likelihood of discovery is high and entrepreneurs must expect severe punishments and sanctions if caught, then a non-cooperative strategy will not pay. How great those risks are depends on the amount of *social control* existing in society, i. e. on the efforts spent on preventing or discovering the violation of norms and on catching and sanctioning offenders.

Again, just as with the neutralization of power relations, it seems that in principle it is *possible* to establish monitoring and sanctioning mechanisms capable of ensuring a sufficiently high level of risk for 'defecting' entrepreneurs. Such mechanisms can operate as an *informal* system if certain enterprises or individuals interested in such a system either fulfil the corresponding functions and tasks individually or pool their forces *ad hoc* in particular situations. Or they can be organized as a *formal* system, with the creation of a specialized enterprise which, by way of a concentration of resources, is provided with the necessary instruments of power and can operate as a central monitoring and sanctioning agency.

But along with the question whether the neutralization of power relations can be converted from an end into a fact, so too the question whether a sufficiently effective system of social control can grow from a mere possibility to a social reality will be shelved for the moment. Right now, we need to know more about the consequences that will ensue *if* such a system of social control exists. To this effect, I will first attempt to give a provisional summary of the results from the previous sections. We have seen that the reasons for a cooperative strategy may be dominant for an entrepreneur under three conditions:

1. We are dealing with an open society providing freedom of association and good expectations of gains from a cooperative entrepreneurial strategy.
2. We have neutralized power relations such that powerful entrepreneurs cannot choose an openly non-cooperative strategy.
3. There is an effective system of social control, raising the risks of a secretly non-cooperative strategy to a discouragingly high level.

If the social framework provides enough liberty for self-determined, voluntary cooperation, if it guarantees protection from the arbitrary exercise of power, and if by the instruments of social control violations of the 'rules of the game' are monitored and sanctioned, then the incentives to run enterprises with the purpose of profiting either openly or secretly from non-cooperative strategies will decrease. If the cooperative interests of an entrepreneur are neither limited by local confines nor entirely or partially dominated by his interests in power and exploitation, then as a norm-giver he neither has a reason to include in the scope of norms only a particular group of persons by *positive* discrimination, nor to exclude certain persons by *negative* discrimination. On the contrary, he then has good reason *not* to endorse any particularistic norms. The moral point of view of the impartial consideration of everybody's interests in this case coincides with his own interest-directed perspective.

But if an entrepreneur has reason to *demand* of his partners and collaborators that they respect norms of unlimited scope and, as their guarantor, invest in their enforcement, then his partners and collaborators also have reason to *comply* with norms of unlimited scope. In other words: the members of the respective enterprise, norm-givers and norm-addressees alike, will have reason to adopt a moral point of view and in their decisions and actions to fulfil the principle of universalizability. In an open society with neutralized power relations and effective social control, the individual interests of norm-givers and norm-addressees in cooperative enterprises may indeed harmonize with the interests of all other members of society – even if their decisions and actions are not based on the *conscious consideration* of these interests.

Under these conditions, norm-generating situations in cooperative enterprises may be more than just sources of particularistic norms. A dispositional utility-maximizer who, as a member of an enterprise, commits himself to universalistic norms will act according to the prescriptions of these norms even outside of his enterprise – regardless of whether or not it pays for him. Even if normative commitment is rewarded only within a cooperative enterprise, one could expect a 'spill-over' of norm-complying behaviour. And if the members of cooperative enterprises produce such a 'moral surplus' which reaches beyond the boundaries of the respective enterprise, then there may be a way to satisfy the 'moral demand' of a society as a whole.

VII. Moral Identity

1. PERSONAL NORMS AND PERSONAL NORMATIVE ORDERS

In ordinary usage, the concept of virtue generally means more than merely the fact that someone is honest, adopts a moral point of view and is reliably committed to certain norms. In addition, a virtuous person is expected to be someone with a 'moral identity'. But what does this mean? By moral identity, I understand the phenomenon that persons are committed not only to an additive collection of isolated norms in the sense of a *catalogue of rules*, but that their personal norms belong to a coherent *normative order* which, besides specific rules of conduct, also contains certain general fundamental principles as 'basic norms'.

There are seveal reasons why from an ethical point of view the development of such a moral identity is desirable, i. e. why the commitment of a norm-addressee to a normative order containing specific norms of conduct as well as general principles is preferable to a commitment to a mere catalogue of rules.

First, there are limits to the human capacities of absorption and differentiation. The number of rules individuals can reliably take into account in their actions is narrowly restricted. Consequently, if a mere catalogue of rules is to be effective, it must be a rather modest one. If morality consisted exclusively of a collection of specific norms of conduct, norm-addressees would either be quickly overwhelmed by their quantity, or relevant situations would be left unregulated.

Second, it is impossible to stipulate exhaustively in advance norms and rules for all relevant situations. Unpredictable empirical constellations can always arise. A rigid catalogue of specific rules will lead to inadequate obligations or prohibitions whenever relevant conditions change. It will also contain gaps which become visible when new problems arise that were not taken into account in the elaboration of the catalogue.

Third, it is not even desirable to stipulate in advance specifically targeted norms for all relevant situations. In some situations, a choice of action under consideration of the special circumstances of the particular case will lead to a morally better result than the application of an already existing rule.

Of course, the typical disadvantages of a mere catalogue of rules do not imply that one should always refrain from stipulating norms with a precise and specific content. They provide the means of making behaviour predictable in those areas where this is morally desirable above all else. But if one were to rely exclusively on such rules, one would have to accept that in many situations actions will be chosen in accordance with inadequate norms or that they will be left to everyone's arbitrary choice. If the problem of such 'open' situations is to be solved in an ethically satisfactory way, then besides precise rules of conduct there must also be some norms providing 'normative guidance' in situations which do not fall under any of those rules.

Such 'superior' norms may be generalized, abstract principles which, although they already include certain normative contents, must first be specified before concrete prescriptions can be derived from them. An example of an abstract principle of this kind is the norm 'Love thy fellow-men'. From this norm, by way of specification, we can derive the norms 'Thou shalt not kill' and 'Thou shalt assist the needy'. But 'basic norms' can also be principles which do not themselves contain any behavioural instruction, but only criteria and guidelines for the determination of the content of concrete behavioural norms. Such a principle is, for instance, the 'Golden Rule' which says 'Do as you would be done by'. The application of this principle can yield a norm with the specific content that one should not steal or cheat.

General and abstract principles, if included in a normative order, make it possible to regulate *all* situations with similar characteristics. Hence, if one wishes to extend the normatively regulated sphere of behaviour beyond a given catalogue of specific rules, one can look for a generalization of those rules in a principle which contains the essential reasons for those prescriptions. While a simple catalogue of rules merely fulfils the task of prescribing adequate modes of conduct for certain *standard situations*, a normative order including general principles can fulfil this task even for *similar* or *previously unknown* situations.

Of persons with a moral identity, it can therefore not only be expected that under certain circumstances they will reliably perform certain actions. It can also be expected of them that, in addition, they accept certain general "guidelines of moral reflection"[10]. A moral identity generally expands a person's sphere of behaviour that is subject to normative regulation. Besides, it strengthens the consistency of a person's norm-directed actions. If the norms and rules someone complies with are systematically connected within a normative order, then the logical relations between them also acquire a guiding function. Therefore, only persons with a moral identity can be influenced in their actions by 'moral justification' and 'moral arguments', in the sense of a reasoned reference to 'higher-level' norms and principles.

[10] Kliemt 1985, 257.

2. MORAL IDENTITY AND GLOBAL SOCIAL ORDER

But how closely will a dispositional utility-maximizer come to approximate these ethical ideals if the empirical basis of his morality and virtue is nothing but his membership in a cooperative enterprise? The importance of the question whether he can be expected to acquire a 'moral identity' can be seen if we consider it in analogy to the corresponding considerations with respect to the scope of norms. In this context, the problem was that a dispositional utility-maximizer has good reason to develop a commitment to norms only if he belongs to a cooperative enterprise. It therefore seemed reasonable to fear that the scope of such norms will basically be restricted to the members of the respective enterprise.

Now, a very similar fear arises with respect to the *content* of the norms a dispositional utility-maximizer would commit himself to as a member of some enterprise. Even if such norms are of unlimited scope, it is still open whether they will protect *all* individual and collective goods that are relevant to people outside of the enterprise. Thus, another possible obstacle for a universalistic morality with an impact on a society as a whole may be that the virtue of a dispositional utility-maximizer might be limited, if not in its scope, then at least in its content, to the *internal* needs and problems of the respective cooperative enterprise.

And again, scepticism does not seem unwarranted. Because the content of the norms a dispositional utility-maximizer as a member of an enterprise will commit himself to again depends only on the interests and desires of the norm-givers who are relevant to him, i. e. on the interests and desires of entrepreneurs. *Their* interests are decisive for the content of the norms a dispositional utility-maximizer as a member of an enterprise will accept. In order to determine whether his personal norms will include the protection of all individual and collective goods that are important for the maintenance of a global social order, we must therefore investigate whether it can be in the interest of an entrepreneur to enact norms which include the protection of all those goods.

But if we look at the problem from the point of view of the entrepreneurs, it does not seem very plausible that, as self-interested actors, they may have reasons to enact norms whose content is unrestricted in this sense. To be sure, it is plausible that certain norm-contents are equally relevant to social relations within and without a cooperative enterprise. One need only think of the prohibitions to kill, injure, lie or steal. In such cases, the entrepreneur will in any case stipulate a norm-content which – provided the scope of the norms is unlimited – will not only be directed towards his enterprise-specific 'problems of order', but will benefit outsiders too.

However, there will just as surely be norms which are relevant only within particular enterprises and whose content will be conditioned by their respective peculiarities, because it is their purpose to protect enterprise-*specific* interests. In this category, there are, for instance, all the duties which are linked to the production of a certain good or the provision of a certain service. And, undoubtedly, there will also be norms protecting interests which are *not* specific to an enterprise but are relevant to all members of a social group, such as norms stipulating duties for the production of collective goods for that group, for instance to protect the environment, to pay taxes, to vote, to serve in the army, or to display public courage and political commitment.

Of course, with a view towards a theory of social order, norms affecting the interests of all members of society are of particular importance. But it is not obvious why an entrepreneur should be willing to incorporate all of these norms into his entrepreneurial ethics. After all, the solution to the problems and tasks internal to the enterprise do not depend on the members of the enterprise complying with all norms of this kind. Someone who never goes to vote or who dodges military service may still be a reliable accountant or a diligent worker. And even if a restricted content of his entrepreneurial ethics is of no special advantage to an entrepreneur, it still seems that there is no reason for him to demand more of his partners and collaborators than that they comply with norms and rules the content of which is specifically geared towards the needs and interests of the enterprise.

At this point, from an empirical, explanatory perspective, the 'ethical phenomenon' of people's moral identity becomes important. The reason for this is that the restriction of the normative content of entrepreneurial ethics to enterprise-specific interests would seem to be an irrefutable consequence if an entrepreneurial ethics consisted in nothing but a *catalogue of rules*. If this were the case, it would indeed be incomprehensible why an entrepreneur should include rules which protect interests not related to the enterprise. Rather, one should expect him to lay down as precisely and exhaustively as possible those obligations and tasks which derive from the respective purpose of his enterprise and from its specific organizational structure. Thus, on the one hand this catalogue would certainly contain rules which are totally irrelevant to society as a whole and, on the other, it would *not* contain numerous norms which are important, if not essential, to the social order outside of the enterprise.

Another outcome can only be expected if it is in an entrepreneur's self-interest to demand more than a commitment to a collection of isolated rules. And again, we must look at the situation from another angle in order to assess the situation of the entrepreneur correctly. As long as the question is only which goods and interests should be protected by the norms of entrepreneurial ethics, we will not be able to discover a reason why a self-interested entrepeneur should extend the content of norms beyond the protection of enterprise-specific goods. Only if we ask whether it might be in the interest of an entrepreneur to require his partners and collaborators to have a *moral identity* will we have identified an aspect that makes another choice feasible. Just as with the distinction between norms of limited and unlimited scope, the problem again is to describe the relevant options in such a way that they acquire relevance from the point of view of a self-interested actor. What the concept of a substantial norm did in the former case, the concept of moral identity does here: regardless of which goods and interests are protected by the norms of entrepreneurial ethics, it makes a relevant difference for an entrepreneur whether or not his partners and collaborators have a moral identity.

Thus, we must now consider two questions: on the one hand, whether it is rational for an entrepreneur to require the members of his enterprise to have a moral identity, i. e. to be committed to more than just a catalogue of rules; and on the other, what consequences that would have for the normative content of entrepreneurial ethics. The answers to these questions will determine whether a gap between the norms of entrepreneurial ethics and the morality of a global social order is really unavoidable.

3. MORAL IDENTITY FROM THE ENTREPRENEUR'S POINT OF VIEW

The first question is easily answered. Every entrepreneur must have a fundamental interest in his partners and collaborators being guided not only by a catalogue of rules which are each specifically designed to satisfy a particular entrepreneurial purpose, but rather by a normative order which also contains general, abstract principles. And this applies equally to non-specific enterprises – such as, for instance, a friendship – and to enterprises producing highly specialized products – such as an industrial plant. After all, an entrepreneur faces the same problems which already made a catalogue of rules seem unattractive from a moral point of view:

First, he knows that his partners' and collaborators' capacities of absorption and differentiation are limited. Thus, he must be careful not to overwhelm them in a quantitative sense, with too large a catalogue of enterprise-specific rules and prescriptions. Therefore, if he relied exclusively on such a catalogue, he would have to expect that situations which are relevant to his entrepreneurial purposes would be left without normative regulation.

Second, he must be aware of the fact that it is impossible for him as a norm-giver to foresee all relevant empirical situations which from the point of view of the enterprise's interests would need to be regulated. Enterprise-specific norms simply cannot cover all possible contingencies. Therefore, if there is nothing but a catalogue of rules, this will in some situations lead to inadequate or nonsensical prescriptions, and in others to a lack of prescriptions altogether, i. e. to normative gaps that will be noticed only when new problems and challenges arise.

Third, he must keep in mind that in practically all cooperative enterprises sometimes situations and problems arise with respect to which it is to the advantage of the enterprise if its members decide *ad hoc*, according to the particular circumstances of the case, instead of 'stubbornly' applying a given norm or rule. In such situations, the 'bureaucratic' regulation of decisions and activities would not only be difficult to enforce, but undesirable.

To be sure, an entrepreneur will not wish and does not need to do entirely without some catalogue of precise rules stipulating enterprise-specific obligations and tasks. He will insist that in certain areas of his enterprise the members' behaviour will be predetermined and predictable to the highest possible degree. However, from his point of view it will be no less important that in situations for which there are, or can be, no pre-established rules of conduct the members will not decide arbitrarily, but that even in such cases they have some 'normative orientation'. An entrepreneur thus has good reasons to complement a catalogue of rules with general, abstract principles, in order to cover those cases and situations which cannot and should not be covered by the specific prescriptions of the catalogue.

Hence, it seems plausible that an entrepreneur will want more from his partners and collaborators than merely their commitment to a collection of particular prescriptions. He must also be interested in their being committed to a more encompassing normative order. For an entrepreneur too, it must matter whether he is dealing with persons whose behaviour can be influenced by 'normative arguments' and conclusions drawn from normative principles, and who do not immediately 'fall back' on their individual self-interest whenever in some situation no specific rule of conduct exists. As a norm-giver, an entrepreneur has good reasons to demand from his partners and collaborators not only personal integrity, but also a moral identity.

But the normative *orders* persons with a moral identity are committed to may themselves have very different contents. In that sense too, one must perhaps expect substantial limitations which reduce the value of a person's moral identity concerning its contribution to the global social morality. So, what basic principles can we expect to be incorporated into the normative order of entrepreneurial ethics, from the point of view of an entrepreneur's interests?

4. THE PRINCIPLES OF INTERPERSONAL RESPECT AND SOCIAL FAIRNESS

In order to answer this question, it is helpful to distinguish between 'norms of interaction' and 'norms of fairness'. If the norms contained in entrepreneurial ethics have a restricted content, this may be due to the fact that one of these two basic classes of norms plays *no role at all.*

'Norms of interaction' are norms which are relevant, above all, when people are in direct contact with each other, and which directly benefit a particular individual when complied with. Norms of interaction protect individual goods, they express 'consideration' and 'respect' for the individual interests of others: 'Don't lie', 'Don't steal', 'Keep your promises'. 'Norms of fairness', in contrast, are norms which benefit some collectivity of individuals jointly when complied with. Norms of fairness promote the provision of public goods and the protection of group interests. They demand of their subjects a 'fair' contribution to the fulfilment of a common task: 'Protect the environment', 'Pay taxes', 'Vote'. Both kinds of norms are necessary for any social order and social morality. But what role do these two classes of norms play in the interests of an entrepreneur?

Let us first consider norms of interaction. Besides all other aspects of an organization of collective action, in an enterprise there are personal relationships between those involved, through which they can directly benefit or harm each other , i. e. because of which their individual goods can be affected by the other members' conduct. Thus, for two reasons it must be in the interest of an entrepreneur to protect individual goods within his enterprise: on the one hand, because his own individual goods could suffer; and on the other, because an organization can function effectively only if its members also mutually respect their personal interests and do not kill, hurt, cheat or rob each other.

Now, concerning norms of fairness, it is obvious that the success of a cooperative enterprise depends on its members being 'fair' partners to each other, willing to make an adequate contribution to the fulfilment of common tasks. It is the purpose of a cooperative enterprise to organize the joint action of a group of people in order to reach a certain end. Such an undertaking can be successful only if each individual fulfils its obligations, takes on a 'fair' part of the burdens and contributes to its full capacity. But the demand to contribute 'fairly' to the pursuit of collective ends, to assist adequately with common tasks and duties, and to refrain from shirking is precisely what norms of fairness are about.

Hence, among the norms of entrepreneurial ethics, and therefore also among the norms a dispositional utility-maximizer as a member of an enterprise will commit himself to, there will be norms of interaction as well as norms of fairness. Thus, both basic classes of norms which are essential to the social morality of a global social order will be represented. Besides, the fact that norms of fairness are indispensable to entrepreneurial ethics shows that cooperative enterprises have a special status as norm-generating and morality-generating situations, because not in all potentially norm-generating situations do norms of fairness play an important role. In a regular commercial exchange between two persons, for example, unlike norms of interaction, norms of fairness are almost entirely irrelevant. Cooperative enterprises, however, are bound to be situations generating norms of fairness because it is their very purpose to pool individual forces for the sake of collective action.

But will the content of the norms of interaction and of fairness included in entrepreneurial ethics go beyond the confines of the respective enterprise? After all, the collective goods for a society as a whole will not be the same as the collective goods for a cooperative enterprise. On the other hand, we already saw that an entrepreneur will not be satisfied with a mere catalogue of rules. It must be in his interest that the norms of interaction and of fairness effective in his enterprise belong to a genuine normative order which serves to extend the normative regulation of conduct from 'standard situations' to similar new situations. Entrepreneurs will therefore incorporate into their entrepreneurial ethics not only norms of interaction and of fairness with a specific content, but also *universalization* of those norms in the form of certain fundamental principles. The question thus is what the content of these universalized principles will be.

An entrepreneur must choose the universalization of norms of interaction and of fairness in such a way that, on the one hand, the extension of the normative regulation will be as *broad* as possible, in order to prevent situations arising which do not even fall under the basic principles of the normative orde. On the other hand, he must be careful to design this extension of normative regulations in a *consistent* way, compatible with his interests. That means that he must see to it that, in applying a normative principle, equal consideration will be given only to those situations which are similar in respects that are relevant to him. Both objectives can be reached by including into the universalized principles of the normative order the reasons for the specific behavioural prescriptions contained in that order. The decisive question, therefore, is what reasons *generally* underlie the prescriptions of norms of interaction and of fairness. Once these are known, it becomes possible to formulate basic principles in order to cover all cases which are not covered by the specific norms, but which are similar in relevant respects.

Concerning norms of interaction, the 'universalizable' principle is that an actor should consider and respect the individual goods of others just as much as he wishes others to consider and respect his own individual goods. That principle demands that a norm-addressee respect the individual goods of another person if and only if it is worthwhile for him to do so in reciprocation for the respect of the same goods on his side, i. e. if it is generally in the interest of an actor to pay the price of complying with the norm in exchange for other people complying with it too. I will call this principle the *principle of interpersonal respect*, in the sense that it *generally* prescribes to 'respect' other people's individual goods to the extent that such 'respect' is also expected from and practiced by them.

The universalization of norms of interaction to a fundamental principle of interpersonal respect permits a *consistent* extension of the sphere of regulated behaviour because its application ensures that cases that are similar in some relevant aspect are treated equally; and it permits a *maximal* extension of the sphere of regulated behaviour because all cases that are similar in some relevant aspect are treated equally. For all norm-givers it is advantageous and gives them better protection if their partners are committed not only to isolated norms of interaction, specifically designed for the sake of particular individual goods, but also to such a universalized principle of interpersonal respect, i. e. if their partners *generally* respect the norm-giver's interests. All actors will thus prefer – and, if they are in a position to do so, will make it a prerequisite for entering into cooperative relationships with them – that their partners are committed to a broad principle of interpersonal respect and not only to a collection of isolated, unconnected norms of interaction.

In turn, the 'universalizable' principle underlying norms of fairness is that an actor ought to contribute to the provision of a collective good if and only if the individual costs of his contribution are more than compensated by the individual benefit he gains, directly or indirectly, from that good, that is, if the advantages he can draw from the fairness of others are greater than the sacrifice his own fairness means for him. Such a general *principle of social fairness* demands of its addressees that they *generally* contribute a 'fair' share to the realization of common ends and interests and to the fulfilment of common tasks and obligations.

Again, the universalization of norms of fairness to a fundamental principle of social fairness permits a consistent and maximal extension of the sphere of regulated behaviour because all cases that are similar in some relevant respect are treated equally. And again, it is advantageous for all those participating in some context of collective action if their partners not only comply with norms of fairness concerning only certain collective goods, but also with a general principle of fairness. In the case of collective goods, it will be even more difficult than in that of individual goods to know in advance exactly which of these goods may become relevant in a context of collective action and exactly which contributions are necessary in order to ensure their provision. Hence, in the case of norms of fairness, just as in the case of norms of interaction, all norm-givers will prefer their partners to be committed to a universal, non-specific principle of fairness which ensures that they will *generally* contribute to the provision of all collective goods relevant to the respective group.

In this context, it must be noted that both in the case of norms of interaction and in the case of norms of fairness, the starting point is always the desire of the norm-giver that his interests be respected and taken into account to the highest possible degree. Insofar, the formulation of specific rules regulating the protection of particular goods is only a means of realizing that general interest. But the interests of a norm-giver will be optimally protected only if the norm-addressees, besides specific rules of conduct, also accept the general principle of interest protection.

From all this it follows that an entrepreneur who has an interest in the moral identity of his partners and collaborators and who demands their commitment to a normative order will choose the principles of interpersonal respect and social fairness as fundamental principles of this normative order. As universalizations of specific norms of interaction and of fairness, they permit the consistent extension of the normative control of conduct, beyond the realm of standard situations, to situations with similar features. And they permit that extension in a way which ensures that no situation of this kind will be left out, because the principles of interpersonal respect and of social fairness themselves contain the relevant features in a general form.

Together with an unlimited scope of the norms in an entrepreneurial ethics, which prohibits restricting the application of the principles of interpersonal respect and of social fairness to some specific group of norm-beneficiaries, the incorporation of these principles into the entrepreneurial ethics ensures that its norms are unrestricted also from the point of view of their content. They not only protect individual and collective goods which are relevant to particular enterprises, but also individual and collective goods that are important for the stable existence of a global social order in general. Persons committed to a general principle of social fairness will contribute their 'fair' share to the provision and protection of public goods. Likewise, persons who accept a general principle of interpersonal respect will respect the interests of all those affected by their actions, regardless of whether they are members in the same cooperative enterprise or whether they are only, by chance, partners of interaction in the context of anonymous social relationships.

VIII. The Dispositional Utility-Maximizer as a 'Moral Person'

Under the influence of universalized principles of respect and of fairness, the gulf between norms that are relevant only within some enterprise and 'genuinely' moral norms relevant to the social group as a whole is bridged. It is not bridged because an entrepreneur has an immediate interest in demanding of his partners and collaborators the commitment to norms which are based on an impartial consideration of everybody's interest. Rather, it is bridged because an entrepreneur's interest in the moral identity of his partners will, once again, be led by an 'invisible hand' to a result that is advantageous to all members of society. An entrepreneur aspiring to protect his own interests to the greatest possible extent will demand of the members of his enterprise behaviours and behavioural dispositions which also automatically protect the interests of others and, in that sense, are 'moral'.

If dispositional utility-maximizers, as members of a cooperative enterprise, may have good reasons to commit themselves to the principles of interpersonal respect and social fairness, then we can conclude that from the point of view of individual utility-maximization, the personal acceptance of moral norms may indeed be rational – even if these norms have unlimited scope and an unrestricted content. Moral norms which are in the common interest of the members of a social group may be incorporated into a personal normative order because they can be derived from the fundamental principles of this normative order, i. e. from the principles of respect and of fairness.

The last obstacle to transforming a dispositional utility-maximizer from a member of some cooperative enterprise into a 'social being' has thus been removed. If the necessary preconditions inside and outside of the enterprise obtain, dispositional utility-maximizers will become persons with integrity and a moral identity – persons who in all their actions are committed to norms which take everone's interests into equal consideration. And this will not be due to some mysterious metamorphosis of their egoism, but to the fact that moral behavioural dispositions and character traits will be sufficiently rewarded to make their generation worthwhile, even from the standpoint of rational utility-maximization. The development of such persons is thus entirely due to the tangible interests of entrepreneurs who stand to gain if the members of their respective enterprise are persons who are authentically committed to the moral principles of interpersonal respect and social fairness.

If one takes into account the point of view of norm-*givers*, this result is much less surprising than it may seem from the point of view of a self-interested norm-*addressee*. The idea that others have an interest in an actor's integrity, moral identity and moral point of view is far less implausible than the idea that a self-interested actor himself should want to have such characteristics. In a world inhabited by such actors, it can only be the desires and interests of others which may motivate an actor to adopt a 'moral attitude'.

In any case, one can say without reservation that the personality which dispositional utility-maximizers develop as a result of such a process represents moral virtue in the strictest sense: such persons regularly comply with moral norms, even when this is not motivated by fear of punishment or expectations of gain. They are honest, take into account in their actions the interests of all those affected and actively promote the ends of their social community. Their 'fairness' and 'respect' towards the needs and desires of others has nothing to do with a rigid compliance with petty regulations and prescriptions. For such persons, 'being' and 'appearing' do not fall apart. They do not live according to double standards, not practising what they preach. They adopt a 'genuine' moral attitude, not some hidden way of situational utility-maximization. Under such conditions, we can say that dispositional utility-maximizers have evolved into *moral* persons.

But even concerning the promotion of his own interests, compared to a *homo oeconomicus* such a *'homo sapiens'* is better equipped. He can be just as flexible, versatile and adaptable as *homo oeconomicus*; but he is not *too* flexible, versatile and adaptable, as happens to *homo oeconomicus* when, in his exclusive concern for his advantage, he trips over his own prudence. When it is in the interest of a *homo sapiens*, he can just as well be inflexible, one-track minded and 'stubborn'. Unlike *homo oeconomicus*, he evades the 'paradox of hedonism' and promotes his interests precisely through his ability to avoid pursuing his personal advantage in each and every situation. *Homo sapiens* develops a social character and genuine altruism because there are conditions under which such a social character and genuine altruism are rewarded – but he does not 'exaggerate', giving up his interests without any calculation. He is willing to make sacrifices, but not blindly. A *homo sapiens* needs no pathos, ideology or faith in order to act 'morally' and 'virtuously'. He is a good, reliable partner for cooperative relationships, and a useful member of communities which trust their members to commit themselves fully to a common cause – but at the same time, he will not lose sight of his own interests and, on the whole, will behave in the way that is best for himself in the long run.

For him, a common cause must be linked to his own cause, his individual interests must be part of the common interests he contributes to promoting. In other words, a *homo sapiens*, while not practicing a narrow and myopic egoism, knows very well that there will be no compensation for him in this world should he generally refrain from looking after his own interests and pursuing his own ends.

Thus, in the eyes of some, such a *homo sapiens* will have at least *one* bad trait: it is often said that morality is such a valuable good because moral persons respect the interests of others for purely altruistic reasons. A *homo sapiens*, however, is moral and virtuous only if *in the end* morality and virtue serve his own interests too. He remains a rational *utility*-maximizer who in everything he does attempts to increase his individual utility, at least in the final balance. Of course, he does not do this in the way of a situational utility-maximizer who at all times 'restlessly' seeks his own personal advantage. He acquires the 'character' which in the long run is best for him, his virtue and morality are rooted in his individual interest – which explains why we will hardly find a saint or hero among his kind. This is a conclusion which is well corroborated by empirical evidence. For the social theorist, this should make *homo sapiens* all the more attractive. And if the development of morality can be explained by self-interest and the facts of human nature, the empirical scientist should feel much more comfortable than if such an explanation would have to depend on pure reason, objective norms or intelligible beings – or on 'society' as a holistic entity which shapes people according to its needs.

Besides, should human nature actually resemble the model of the dispositional utility-maximizer and *homo sapiens*, this would be relevant to moral theory too. In this case, the model could perhaps not only explain why people do *in fact* act in a certain way, but also elucidate how people *ought* to act. Such a moral theory would, of course, have no room for saints and heroes, but neither would it have room for fanatics and zealots. It can hardly count as a disadvantage if moral demands leave adequate room for the pursuit of people's self-interest. More than one historical catastrophe would probably have been avoided if people had not 'heroically' sacrificed their 'egoistic' interests for the sake of some actual or imagined interests of their respective collectivity.

CHAPTER 5

THE MARKET OF VIRTUE

I. Morality, Public-Spiritedness and the Workings of the Invisible Hand

If the arguments developed in the previous chapters are sound, then under certain circumstances there will be moral persons in a society – persons, that is, who comply with social norms even if they are not threatened by negative sanctions should they violate these norms and even if they cannot expect immediate rewards from complying with them. These are persons who do not only dissemble virtue. To the extent that the norms they comply with are of unlimited scope, they have genuinely adopted a moral point of view, and they are guided by universalized principles of respect and fairness. Such persons will exist, on the one hand, because under certain conditions it is in the interest of dispositional utility-maximizers to make use of their capacity to commit themselves to norms and, on the other, because it is in the interest of the norm-givers who are relevant for them that the norms they comply with are of unlimited scope and are universalized in the form of general principles of respect and fairness.

If norm-givers enforce such a commitment to universalistic principles in the norm-addressees, this is directly advantageous for the interests of others too. Moral persons produce a 'moral surplus' which also automatically benefits the other members of society. Persons guided in their actions by universalistic principles of interpersonal respect and social fairness respect the individual goods of others even if these are not members of the same cooperative enterprise, and they contribute fairly to the realization of common interests even if they are the interests of the members of a large, anonymous group.

The fact that an entrepreneur, as an 'active' norm-giver, unintentionally promotes the interests of others does not bring him any immediate gain. The set of persons who respect *his* personal goods and act fairly towards *him* is not thereby enlarged. But as a 'passive' norm-beneficiary, he profits from other active norm-givers who likewise demand of their partners and collaborators a commitment to norms and principles of unlimited scope. With respect to other norm-givers, he can assume the role of a norm-beneficiary who has received a 'gift', just like all those others who have benefited, free of cost, from his own efforts as a norm-giver.

In such circumstances, persons known as being members of cooperative enterprises will be much sought after as partners of cooperation. It will be assumed that as members in a cooperative enterprise they will have reasons to commit themselves to universalistic principles of interpersonal respect and social fairness – a disposition that can be expected to effect their actions in other social spheres. In this case, apparently, the unfavourable conditions of information in large, anonymous social groups will no longer necessarily constitute an insurmountable barrier; because the information that someone is a member of a cooperative enterprise with a 'good reputation' is easier to come by than information about the reputation of an individual as such and about his past behaviour in different kinds of situations.

All this seems to suggest that for the individual members of society there is a chance that the stability of a global social order will be ensured by an 'invisible hand', without their purposeful contribution, i. e. without this being the conscious objective of their own actions or those of other people involved. Even if norm-givers care only about their own interests, they would promote an end that is beyond their actual intentions, because for the sake of their own self-interest they would demand of their partners virtues which foster the conservation of a social order as a whole. The fact that an individual norm-giver can directly influence only a relatively small group of people would then not necessarily imply that he must fear the actions of all others and protect himself against them. Concerning these other people, the best option would simply seem to be to do *nothing*.

But even in this case, the efficacy of an invisible hand depends on the existence of an *institution*, namely the institution of a special *market* in which that hand can perform its beneficial workings. After all, the 'moral demand' of a social order has not already been satisfied when in a society there are *some* enterprises which pursue a cooperative strategy. The stability of social and moral norms rather depends on the fact that the society is made up of a *sufficient number* of moral persons. But that will be the case only if the cooperative enterprises existing in the society create a sufficiently large *market of virtue*, including an effective demand for virtuous persons as suitable partners and collaborators. Only if such a market is firmly established will the supply of persons with moral integrity not only ensure the continued operation of cooperative enterprises, but also satisfy the demand for that 'good' in the society at large. And only if this is the case will each individual have reason to believe that a substantial number of others are dispositionally committed to social norms and that, therefore, he can expect a certain degree of protection for his own interests.

The greatest advantage of such a market of virtue would be that it makes the production of public goods possible even under *prima facie* unfavourable conditions. The commitment of moral persons to a principle of social fairness makes the 'spontaneous', informal provision of public goods feasible in groups with a large membership: either directly, if such persons make a voluntary contribution to the production of the public good in question, or indirectly, if they make a voluntary contribution to a public good which – as, for example, an organization – is itself the precondition for the production of other public goods. A market of virtue could make it possible that the members of a large, anonymous social group practise morality and public-spiritedness and are thus able to produce outcomes which are in the common interest.

But if one takes a closer look at the conditions for the stable existence of a market of virtue, there seems to be a serious problem. It is a necessary condition for the operation of such a market that the majority of enterprises adopt a cooperative strategy and thus create a correspondingly high demand for moral persons. But that, in turn, presupposes the satisfaction of three other conditions already mentioned earlier: *first*, we must have an open society with freedom of association – the kind of society that offers good expectations of gain for a cooperative entrepreneurial strategy. *Second*, power relations must be neutralized, in order for powerful groups and enterprises to be unable to oppress the less powerful members of society. *Third*, there must be an effective system of social control, raising the risks of secretly deviating from a norm to a sufficiently high level. Only if the social framework guarantees some free space for self-determined cooperation as well as protection from arbitrary exercise of power and secret violations of norms will the incentives to run an enterprise with an openly or secretly non-cooperative strategy become weaker. And only in that case, entrepreneurs will have a reason to seek partners and collaborators who are committed to universalistic principles of interpersonal respect and social fairness.

So far, however, I have not answered the question as to the factors which determine whether or not these three conditions for a well-functioning market of virtue are satisfied. Knowledge of these factors might raise doubts about the feasibility of a market of virtue. There seems to be a certain circularity in this reasoning.

In the previous chapter I argued that neutralized power relations and a system of social control can theoretically be ensured by informal means: through the association of the members of a society for the purpose of defeating possible abuses of power and preventing or sanctioning norm-violating behaviours by individuals or groups. In modern societies, however, these tasks are performed mainly by the legal institutions of the state. Their monopoly of power is intended to prevent powerful individuals or collectivities in a society from using their positions of power for the oppression of those with less power, and their centralized means of sanctioning and coercion are intended to be an effective deterrent to norm-violating behaviour. Certain structures of these institutions – what is known as the 'rule of law' – are meant to prevent that they themselves will, in turn, be abused and turned against the members of society. To this end, in modern liberal constitutional states they are embedded in a system of separation of powers and mutal controls.[1]

But such legal institutions do not fall from heaven, nor are they supplied to a society by external agencies. For the members of a society, they are public goods which must be produced, maintained and protected by themselves. Although they are to relieve the citizens from the burdens of informally ensuring neutralized power relations and social control, in the last instance they remain rooted in the willingness of citizens to assume voluntarily the costs and burdens necessary for maintaining these institutions. In a liberal society, this includes, above all, the control of the administrative and legal institutions themselves, to ensure that they do not exercise power beyond the limits of their competence. Even, and above all, the power of the dominating agency in a society must be neutralized by a countervailing power if an abuse of power is to be prevented. The problems deriving from the unequal power of individuals and groups do not simply disappear because of the state's monopoly of power. On the contrary, this monopoly of power itself gives rise to a need for a basic and permanent counterweight. If necessary, citizens must be able to defend their common interests against abuses by the powers that be.

Hence, without civic virtues, without the citizens' ability to contribute voluntarily to the provision of public goods, the administrative and legal institutions even of a liberal society cannot be kept intact. They are not independent of the morality existing in a

[1] On the question whether the sovereign in a state can be legally constrained at all, cf. Garzón Valdés 1982; Kliemt 1978.

society; rather, they themselves depend on the moral conduct and public-spiritedness of its members. If citizens do not adopt an 'internal point of view' towards the norms of their social order, and if they have no 'intrinsic' motivation to respect and protect that order's constitution, neutralized power relations and an effective system of social control within the framework of a *Rechtsstaat* cannot be maintained for long.

But, according to the previous considerations, we can only expect the existence of a sufficient number of persons with moral integrity if the society *already has* a well-functioning market of virtue. Therefore, it seems that what has been presented as essential *prerequisites* for a market of virtue – i. e., neutralized power relations and an effective system of social control – will themselves only become *possible* if there is a market of virtue. And, what's more, an open society with freedom of association seems itself to depend on the existence of the rule of law and the corresponding institutions, and therefore on the provision of that public good by morally motivated citizens. But just as neutralized power relations and an effective system of social control, an open society is itself one of the necessary foundations and prerequisites for a well-functioning market of virtue, since only in an open society is there a possibility that power interests may generally be trumped by cooperative interests.

Thus, it seems that we cannot expect that the necessary framework for a market of virtue will be supplied by certain legal and administrative institutions; rather, such institutions themselves seem to depend on the existence of a market of virtue. So, how should such necessary institutions for the creation and maintenance of a market of virtue be able to arise if they, in turn, depend on an already existing market of virtue? A sufficient number of persons with moral integrity is needed for the provision of the collective goods of administrative and legal institutions 'tamed' by the rule of law; but a sufficient number of persons with moral integrity, again, seems to presuppose that such collective goods are already available.

In fact, however, there is no circular reasoning at all. Closer inspection even reveals, in some sense, quite the contrary: this apparent circularity can be an indication of the particularly high measure of *stability* and *resilience* of a market of virtue and, thus, also of its supporting institutions. In order to show how this is possible it is useful to distinguish between a situation where a well-functioning market of virtue already exists and a situation where such a market does not yet exist and where the question, therefore, is how it can come about. In other words, it is convenient to discuss the questions of the *existence* and the *generation* of a market of virtue separately.

II. Is the Existence of a Market of Virtue Possible?

If one assumes that a functioning market of virtue already exists, then it turns out to be no weakness of such a market, nor of its theoretical explanation, that it depends on social conditions which it must produce itself. On the contrary, that is precisely what its special resilience is based on. Once it exists, a well-functioning market of virtue is a *self-preserving* and *self-enhancing* system – a system containing the very mechanisms which guarantee its own conservation.

This can easily be seen: if a well-functioning market of virtue exists, it produces, *ex hypothesi*, such a great number of moral persons that the provision of public goods is basically ensured. Now, from the citizens' point of view, the institutions of a liberal constitutional state under the rule of law are necessarily among the central public goods of a society. Therefore, the moral persons who develop in the context of a market of virtue will see to it that the corresponding legal institutions are established and protected; but by doing so, at the same time they also see to it that the necessary framework for a market of virtue is maintained and stabilized – even if *this* result may not be their immediate intention. As a further consequence, they thus ensure that there will always be persons with moral integrity who work for the provision of public goods. In this sense, therefore, a market of virtue is self-*preserving*, taking care of the conservation of its own foundations in an indirect way, through the moral persons it produces and their efforts in favour of the institutions of the rule of law.

Moreover, it becomes evident that a market of virtue can produce a self-enhancing effect if one starts from the plausible assumption that even for a basically well-functioning market of virtue, the framework offers room for improvement most of the time – among other reasons, because the institutions guaranteeing an open society, a system of social control, and the neutralization of power relations can generally be improved. But the improvement of the quality of a collective good is itself a collective good. Hence, persons who voluntarily contribute a 'fair' share to the *provision* of a collective good will also voluntarily contribute a 'fair' share to the *improvement* of a collective good. The moral persons produced by a market of virtue will not look at the deficiencies of their social and legal order in resignation. They will attempt to overcome them.

But the improvement of the stability, functioning and reliability of these institutions means, at the same time, an improvement of the framework for a market of virtue. More stable, effective and reliable legal institutions result in greater stability of the structures of an open society, a more effective system of social control and better protection against abuses of power. If the framework for a market of virtue is improved, this will lead to the existence of a greater number of moral persons. And the more members of a society actively work for the provision of public goods, the more successful they will be, *ceteris paribus*, which means that the framework and thereby the 'moral productivity' of the market of virtue will be further improved – with the consequence that the percentage of persons with moral integrity will rise still more, and so on. A positive, self-perpetuating and self-enhancing cycle may thus evolve which, *in principle*, leads both to an ever higher quality of public and legal institutions and an ever increasing efficiency of the market of virtue.

The fact that the institutions of the rule of law and the market of virtue are both elements of a practically closed and 'autonomous' system is a great advantage for their stability and resilience. Once they are firmly established, because of their 'internal' mechanisms they are no longer dependent on favourable external factors but can reproduce themselves, above all by being able to produce the supply to meet the 'moral demand' that is necessary for their own conservation. And this theoretical result is perfectly compatible with empirical findings. Wherever a liberal constitutional system manages to survive for some time, its stability and resilience usually tend to increase.

On the other hand, however, this 'systemic nature' may contain specific dangers for the institutions of the rule of law and the market of virtue, because most of the time these institutions *depend* on their internal capacity for reproduction. Usually, they cannot count on external support. This entails certain risks, because the system of a state under the rule of law and a market of virtue, although it is a self-reproducing system, is not a self-*regulating* system. A self-regulating system has mechanisms which keep the system in a stable state and perform corrections if deviations from that state are imminent. The institutions of the rule of law and the market of virtue do not have such mechanisms, or only to a very limited extent.

Just as for a single cooperative enterprise, one of the main dangers for these institutions is that, precisely because of the self-enhancing tendency to produce moral persons, the exercise of social control will be weakened and its role underestimated. Where norm-complying behaviour is widespread, the obvious need for such control disappears. But even if, in favourable circumstances, a society contains a high percentage of persons with moral integrity, a certain degree of social control which permanently reduces the incentives for the individual or collective violation of norms remains an important factor for the stability of that state of affairs. An effective system of social control not only operates as a deterrent with regard to case-by-case calculations of benefits and costs. It also contributes decisively to the fact that it 'pays' for norm-addressees to develop and keep a dispositional commitment to norms. If such a system of control is neglected for some time, this inevitably leads to an erosion of the 'level of morality' – with the consequence that there will not only be an increase in violations of norms, but there will also be fewer moral persons.

And just as in a single cooperative enterprise, in a society as a whole, too, one must expect that there will be 'cycles'. A period of 'strictness' and 'severity' will be followed by a period of leniency, until too many members of society take advantage of it and behave in opportunistic, non-cooperative ways and the reins will be tightened once more. But there is also the danger that during a period of leniency the social institutions and the market of virtue suffer so much damage that their efficiency falls below a critical threshold. This may lead to the breakdown of the entire system. A creeping erosion may turn into a sudden collapse. Not always will there be clearly visible indicators making it possible to reverse the process in time. By the time a latently predominant opportunism causes obvious effects in a society, it may be too late. Too many individuals and groups may already pursue a non-cooperative, egoistic strategy, and administrative and legal institutions may already be too subverted and corrupted for the fatal tendency to be halted. When the symptoms of the disease become apparent, the virus may already be resistent.

Once a certain threshold has been crossed in the course of such a process of decadence, the institutions of a liberal constitutional state and the market of virtue, practically as a mirror-image of their mechanism for self-preservation and self-enhancement, also reveal a mechanism of self-*destruction*. If the number of persons with moral integrity in a society decreases, there will also be fewer public goods, and public and legal institutions will therefore suffer. This, in turn, will reduce the 'moral productivity' of the market of virtue, with the consequence that still fewer people will feel committed to principles of respect and fairness, and the provisions of public goods will become even more difficult. All this means that the positive, ascending spiral may also become a negative, descending one. But even then, there is something like the 'edge' of a 'precipice' where the slide down a slippery slope will turn into a free fall. If, for example, because of transgressions committed by powerful groups or agencies, the neutralization of power relations no longer seems possible, then even for the remaining persons with moral integrity a commitment, with its incalculable risks, no longer makes sense. In this case, the balance of power will be abruptly destroyed in favour of those who hold resources of state or non-state power. The doors will then be wide open for the usurpation of power by despots and autocrats.

Despite these dangers and risks, the chances of survival of a liberal legal and political order, and thus of a market of virtue, are, on the whole, quite good. This is partly due to the fact that a 'dangerously' high degree of morality will usually not arise among the members of a society. A market of virtue most of the time reaches its 'saturation point' long before the measure at which social vigilance would decline. Even with a well-functioning market of virtue, individual and collective violations of norms in private and public life will be frequent, and the need for social control will therefore remain obvious. Thus, some degree of 'immorality' is, in fact, useful for the protection of morality – an insight already formulated, though under different premises, by Emile Durkheim.

III. Is the Emergence of a Market of Virtue Possible?

Even if I may have succeeded in dispelling the initial 'suspicion of circularity' concerning the *existence* of a market of virtue, that same doubt returns even more forcefully regarding the question of how a market of virtue may *emerge*. If a market of virtue already exists, it can reproduce itself, because through the production of moral persons it indirectly produces its own prerequisites. But it is precisely the fact that this is a closed circle which raises the question how it may be possible that such a circle emerges in the first place, out of a state where a market of virtue does not yet exist. Should it be possible that according to our theoretical premises a market of virtue in a liberal society could well exist, but cannot emerge?

After all, seen in historical perspective, it is an undeniable fact that the emergence of the institutions of a liberal society is a very unlikely phenomenon. Only a very small percentage of human beings has ever experienced anything better than a repressive and autocratic system of political dominion. Against this background, it would not even be a serious setback for the explanatory power of our theory if, according to its premises, a market of virtue, and hence a liberal society, could *not* emerge under 'normal' conditions and rather requires extraordinary empirical circumstances which actually existed perhaps only in one single historical situation.

And in fact, according to the theory I have elaborated here, the normal course of affairs does not lead to a liberal society and the rule of law. In most cases, it will result in a state that is not a public good, but a public bad and an instrument of oppression – just as it has been, and still is, the case in historical reality. After all, the development of a society does not start with an amorphous and anonymous mass society in which 'free' individuals can associate with others and dissociate from them *ad libitum*. At the beginning, there is not the dynamism and mobility of an open society, but life in small communities with clear demarcations against other groups and the rigid, static arrangements of a closed society where individuals spend their entire life basically within the very same communities whose members they have been from birth, and where the barriers between clans or tribes are insurmountable.

Where such conditions hold, a state with a monopoly on coercion will not arise by way of a voluntary transference of power, based on the model of a 'social contract', but by way of usurpation and subjection. The reason for this is that even if for their internal organization collectivities and communities take advantage of the capacity for 'genuinely' moral action, under the conditions of archaic, traditional societies a particularistic morality will develop, which only regards the promotion of the interests of one's own group as obligatory and virtuous. The normal course of affairs will be the development of rival 'gangs of thugs' attempting to exploit the labour of as many 'peaceful' producers as possible. The emergence of an oligarchy or of despotism will not come as a result of the voluntary establishment of a central political power. Rather, the creation of such a central power itself will already be the result of a fight for power and dominion. Dictatorship and coercion, and the oppression and exploitation of subjects will be part of the usual nature of a state. As we learn from the facts of history, "ever since the emergence of large states it has been the normal fate of humanity in almost all areas of civilizations on the globe to live under a despotic regime [...] The normal idea of the state in the pre-industrial era was, one can say, that of conquest and exploitation. States were based to a large extent on forced labour, and characterized by an endemic lack of rights of the oppressed populations."[2]

Hence, we cannot expect open and peaceful societies to develop out of a 'state of nature'. Instead, we must expect closed societies with static social structures, and the oppression of the great majority of the population by a more or less unscrupulous ruling class. The arrangements in such societies will not by themselves lead to a modification of these structures, but rather cement them even more. After all, such social orders too have a self-preserving and self-enhancing 'systemic character'. By no means do they induce the internal developments by which they can be overcome. Rather, the ruling classes have good reasons to consolidate the closed nature of their society in order to keep their power. And the more closed a society is, the fewer opportunities there are for the oppressed classes and strata to free themselves by their own efforts.

All this means that a number of favourable *external* factors must coincide if the emergence of a market of virtue is to be even conceivable – but in any case, it is not generally impossible that such a constellation may arise. It is not generally impossible because although the preconditions for a market of virtue *can* be reproduced by an already existing market of virtue itself, they *must not* always be produced that way. The evolution towards an open society with freedom of association, neutralized power relations, and an effective system of social control does not *necessarily* depend on the existence of moral persons. At least the important first steps on the way towards such a process may also be induced by other intervening factors.

[2] Albert 1990, 253 ff.

IV. The European Miracle

Max Weber is probably the social scientist who emphasized more than any other the extraordinary, unique development in Europe which led to the 'rational capitalism' of occidental modern society. In the present context, of course, neither Weber's theory nor the historical facts can be presented in detail. But what is important in Weber's theory for our purpose is the fundamental observation that European social history has been presented with a unique combination of factors which was able to induce a social development towards non-despotic political systems. This observation can help us describe this extraordinary empirical constellation at least in a general way and to explain plausibly why such a constellation can initiate the development towards a society with a liberal political system.

The historical constellation was based on the fact that – not least because of its particular natural conditions – Europe consisted for a long time of a system of small states in competition with each other and yet connected by close contacts and exchange. Unlike the large empires, for instance in Asia, European states were constantly exposed to the competition of other states in their immediate neighbourhood. Because of their more or less equal powers, however, none of them was able to gain a permanent position of hegemony. Besides, that plurality of states and political systems was accompanied by a cultural unity which made it possible for individuals to become fully integrated citizens in another state. Most European states were approximately on the same level of development, which meant that their citizens were able to leave their own state without too much effort and prohibitively high personal costs.

That permanent 'threat of emigration' considerably reduced the options of political rulers. In order to hold their own in the interstate competition regarding economic power and military force, they could no longer simply disregard the interests of their subjects. Since, for demographic, economic, or military reasons they wished to prevent the loss of citizens, they were obliged to adapt the social conditions within their states to their subjects' interests. They had to offer attractive living conditions and could not establish a pure system of oppression if they did not wish to lose their citizens' consent, and hence the citizens themselves. If a ruler depends on voluntary support from his own population, he cannot treat his subjects merely as objects of exploitation. Fear of a loss of capital and manpower thus led to constraints on the arbitrary exercise of power.[3] Rulers were obliged to concede a relatively high degree of freedom of movement as well as certain personal rights. At the same time, their interest in a steady inflow of taxes led to an interest in a flourishing and stable market.[4]

Although this particular European constellation did not directly lead to the establishment of liberal institutions in the different states, it initiated a path of development at the *end* of which stood the creation of such institutions, and thus of the fundamental

3 "The potential 'exit' of propertied men was an implicit rein on arbitrary power. [...] Similar opportunities were not open to subjects sealed, as it were, whithin vast land empires." (Jones 1981, 118). About the unique European trajectory in general, cf. also Albert 1986, 1990, 1994; North 1981, 1990; North/Thomas 1973.

4 "Arbitrary behavior such as confiscations could only harm revenues from this source and princes learned the trading benefits of subduing the waywardness of their subjects, and grudgingly of themselves too." (Jones 1981, 103)

framework for a market of virtue. Because of the pressures of interstate competition and the subjects' exit options, rulers felt obliged to concede certain rights and freedoms, and since this necessarily implied a constraint on arbitrary power, they also produced relatively neutralized power relations. And in order to strengthen the economic basis of their power they provided a free sphere for economic activities. At least to some extent, there evolved the situation of an open society in which citizens could pursue their economic interests and entrepreneurial objectives in a more or less undisturbed way – secured by a system of social control that was provided by the existing state apparatus. Besides, because of the small geographical extensions and the balance of power between the political units, there already existed a high degree of individual mobility. A 'bourgeois' class could thus develop whose interests of accumulation and cooperation were relatively well protected.

Once the aristocracy in Europe had begun to concede certain freedoms and rights to the *bourgeoisie*, they had opened a Pandora's box. The emerging bourgeois class possessed a considerable latent power potential which, if realized, meant there was a good chance that the interests of this class could be successfully imposed – if necessary, even by a 'bourgeois revolution'. For autocratic rulers, it is always risky to 'liberalize' the conditions of a closed society and concede freedoms to members of underprivileged classes because the use of such freedoms may lead to the development of precisely those personal qualities which will enable them to defend their interests against the rulers.

The class interest of the *bourgeoisie* had to be, above all, to further improve and extend the social conditions which were favourable especially for the attainment of their economic ends. What is decisive in this context is the fact that the bourgeois class generally prefers peaceful cooperation and the exchange of goods and services under a stable political framework to the use of force against weaker people.[5] As Weber observed, the specific occidental form of capitalism is not oriented towards possible gains from political power, but towards the 'profitability' of the enterprise, i. e. the rationally calculable gain of a continuous flow of profits from peaceful market activities. This is what distinguished Western bourgeois capitalism from all other types of politically imposed, speculative capitalism "oriented towards the acquisition by force, and especially the acquisition by way of booty: short-term booty by war, or chronic fiscal booty (exploitation of subjects)".[6] The political objective of the *bourgeoisie* therefore is not merely the inversion of power relations, but a general discrediting of force and coercion as means to economic ends. Basically, the *bourgeoisie* will want market interests to be protected over power interests. This has several implications:

First, the bourgeois class will be interested in the ever closer approximation of social conditions to the ideal type of an open society, i. e. in eliminating existing barriers to trade and industry, and in promoting unimpeded cooperation and association. The bourgeois entrepreneur will prefer the market with its exchange relations based on economic functionality to the personal economic relations found in traditional social communities. Those interested in the market will want to see the static nature of traditional structures replaced by social dynamism and mobility, in order to be able to employ eco-

[5] "Trade raised a class with international connections, rising political influence, and probably a greater interest in peaceful intercourse than in the hazardous sweets of trade war." (Jones 1981, 124)
[6] Weber 1920a, 7.

nomic resources where they can be used most efficiently and promise their owners a maximum of profits.

Second, the members of the bourgeois class will desire a neutralization of power relations, in order to gain the highest possible degree of security for their freedom and property. Any kind of arbitrariness in the use of public or private power is poison to the economic interest of the *bourgeoisie*. Instead of liberties and privileges conceded in an 'act of grace' by a well-meaning ruler, it needs the predictability and calculability of a social order in which the public exercise of power is subjected to general and effective normative constraints.

Third, the *bourgeoisie* needs a reliable peaceful order within the state, because the market, as the stage for its economic activities, does not tolerate acquisitions based on force and coercion. The bourgeois must have the security that transfers of goods and services conforming to market rules are protected by an effective system of social control and that he does not have to fear expropriation by force.

But the social framework which is favourable for the interests of the bourgeois class is, *at the same time*, also favourable for a market of virtue. Of course, the representatives of the *bourgeoisie* will begin to fight for an open society with neutralized power relations and an effective system of social control primarily with a view to their own economic purposes; but in doing so, they will expand not only the economic market, but also the market of virtue, and will bring more and more people under its influence.

In this way, a process is triggered at the end of which there may be not only a well-functioning market of virtue, but also a liberal society with the corresponding political and legal institutions. The more members of a society must struggle to become successful providers of 'moral qualities' because they can no longer participate in cooperative relationships on the basis of former privileges or of their membership in traditional social communities, the more of them will have to give up their commitment to the particularistic group morality typical of closed societies and to accept norms which transcend such narrow confines. Through this 'process of individualization' they also become persons interested in a liberal order under the rule of law. As 'normal' citizens without a special position of power or the permanent membership in some protective community, they must have a primary interest in the protection of individual rights and the limitation of state power. Those members of society who are drawn into this transformation process will, as moral persons, also contribute to the imposition and conservation of such a social order.

The analysis of the 'European miracle' thus confirms the hypothesis that it is possible in principle, but can happen in fact only under extraordinary empirical circumstances, that the preconditions for a market of virtue will be 'provided' externally. Normally, in closed societies we will have unequal power relations, such that the powerful have no reason and the subjects no chance to induce change. It was a historical coincidence that rulers in Europe neutralized power relations and 'opened' their societies to such an extent that they unintentionally set in motion a process which subsequently escaped their control.

V. The Vision of Liberalism and Its Critics

The starting point of the present investigation was the question whether it is possible to defend the vision of liberalism to the effect that enlightenment, prosperity, freedom and morality are in harmony with each other, or – more precisely – that a secular social order with an efficient economy, a 'tamed' political power, and citizens who prove to possess personal virtue, is compatible with, or will even be promoted by, the rational pursuit of individual interests.

According to the vision of liberalism, self-interest, rationality and the desire for peaceful cooperation give rise to a social order in which people live and work together to the benefit of all, without the need of suppressing or distorting the nature of man by political dominion and coercion. In such a 'liberal' society, economic prosperity would be ensured by the 'miracle of the market' which induces people to use their resources in an efficient way. Besides, the rulers' interest in a well-functioning economy and the influence of a self-confident *bourgeoisie* is thought to guarantee the moderate and prudent exercise of political powers. Finally, through the mild force of the *doux commerce* which educates individuals, as participants in the market, to be honest and reliable partners, individual morality and virtue are expected to flourish.

In the Introduction, I have offered a rough sketch of how, around the end of the 18th century, this vision had already suffered a considerable loss of attractiveness. Especially the assumption that a social order in which the forces of self-interest remain unconstrained will contribute not only to economic efficiency, but also to the promotion of the virtue of citizens and the morality of rulers soon seemed implausible. A liberal and capitalist society was looked upon with increasing scepticism, and the social relations accompanying it were severely criticized. Instead of regarding individual interests in the context of a liberal social order as useful impulses, henceforth the capitalist market, above all, was considered a source of economic, political and moral evils. The 'miracle of the market' became the 'Moloch of the market', supposedly leading to the breakdown of social communities and human ties and permitting nothing but 'alienated' economic relations between people. The vision of liberalism according to which the pursuit of self-interest will lead to beneficial effects for the individual and for society alike was displaced by a 'self-destruction thesis', asserting that a society dominated by individual interests undermines its own foundations and will in the end fail in economic, political and moral terms.

Recently, the critique of liberalism has been represented primarily by two movements whose main contentions are, briefly, the following:

1. On the one hand, there is so-called *communitarianism*, claiming that both liberal theory and liberal practice over-emphasize 'individualism' at the expense of the relevance of 'communities'. Communitarians have offered three main arguments:

According to a *philosophical argument*, the liberal model of man assumes an 'atomized' and 'isolated' self capable of choosing ends and values independently of any social ties. This assumption, however, is thought to ignore the fact that a firm 'embeddedness' in social relationships is a necessary prerequisite for the development of a personal identity. Integration into a community is important not only for instrumental reasons. It also achieves irreplaceable 'internal goods' for a person, which are linked to participation in a common practice as such.

The *ethical argument* of communitarianism is that the 'unencumbered' individual in the concept of liberalism is incapable of reaching binding decisions about values and norms. Without 'constitutive attachments', they say, moral and social orientations are necessarily characterized by arbitrariness and relativism. Communitarians consider it impossible to provide a rational foundation and an effective motivation for the compliance with moral and social norms based exclusively on individual interests. In the communitarian view, the criteria *as well as* the incentives for moral behaviour can arise only from an individual's roots in a social community.

The *sociological argument*, finally, repeats the thesis that a liberal, interest-dominated society necessarily tends to undermine its own foundation. In the long run, this argument continues, such a society cannot ensure the degree of commitment and participation on the part of its citizens which would be needed for the preservation of the political and economic institutions of a liberal society. The promotion of the individualist ethos of utility, the uncontrolled dynamics of the economic process, and an ever increasing mobility are believed to lead to the destruction of 'naturally developed' communities and social ties and thus of the indispensable basis for the development of moral virtues. But without such virtues, elementary community interests will lose out against individual interests.

2. In turn, the immanent critique of the vision of liberalism is based on the instruments and results of the economic-theory tradition itself, and especially on insights into the gulf between individual and collective rationality. This gulf is said to endanger all three promises of the liberal vision. It endangers, *first* of all, the viability of the market, because, although the existence of competition is in the common interest of economic actors, it is a rational strategy for the individual to circumvent it, if possible. As a result, 'distributional coalitions' emerge which impose their particular interests without any regard for the common good. What inevitably follows is the 'sclerosis' of market mechanisms and economic stagnation. *Second*, in a liberal democracy the state has a tendency to become part of the problem. On the one hand, in order to stay in power government members make deals with influential groups instead of opposing particular interests. On the other, citizens and voters, to the extent that they behave as rational opportunists, are unable to promote their common interests. *Third*, the market cannot educate individuals to behave morally. Not only are the cooperative tendencies effective in an economic market usually too weak, but the anonymous relationships in a market also offer destructive incentives, inducing people to behave in an unsocial and non-cooperative way. The economic market, conceived as a sequence of transactions between more or less isolated individuals, cannot 'produce' morality and virtue. Rather, the proper operation of the market itself presupposes the existence of morality and virtue.

In summary, then, the arguments of the critics of liberalism amount to a sweeping rejection of the features characteristic of modern liberal society. They are directed against anonymity and mobility, laicism and secularism, the predominance of individualism and subjectivism, as well as against the absence of ideologies and a lack of belief in objective values. At the centre of this critique is the complaint about a fundamental 'moral deficit' as the key problem of liberal society, and about the allegedly inevitable lack of individuals for whom the realization of common interests is an effective motive to act. From the Introduction, it is also known what the critics of liberal society propose as a therapy against the 'crisis of morality'. Since their diagnosis states that the problem is caused by the free play of forces, what is needed is a planned intervention: a moral and ideological rearmament, a conscious battle against the 'pragmatic acceptance of the world', and the systematic production and distribution of morality.

Against this background, and in view of the dangers for internal and external freedom regularly implied by attempts to improve the morality of people by indoctrination or through the intervention of social institutions, the basic question of the present investigation was: is it possible to defend the vision of liberalism against the claim that a moral 'restauration' of society is needed, or do we have to resign ourselves to the insight that human nature, to the extent that it is characterized by self-interest and the pursuit of personal benefits, needs to be constrained by coercion, ideology, or religion?

At the beginning of this book, I proposed a revised version of the economic model of behaviour, the model of a *dispositional utility-maximizer*. It is a model which departs substantially from the classical *homo oeconomicus*, but it is still useful as an adequate model of interest-based action in the sense of the vision of liberalism. The core of an 'economic model of man', according to which human action is guided by the rational orientation towards one's self-interest, remains unaffected in this new model. Since a dispositional utility-maximizer acts in a norm-committed way only when such a strategy realizes his subjective utility better than a case-by-case calculation, he generally pursues his interests no less consistently than a *homo oeconomicus*. A world populated by such actors can claim to correspond to the liberal vision of a secular and interest-dominated society just as a world of *homines oeconomici* – although what matters then is no longer merely rational decision-making, but the question which features and characteristics it is in a person's interest to have. But while on the basis of the economic model of *behaviour* the gulf between individual and collective rationality appears to be unbridgeable in view of the circumstances existing in modern mass societies, on the basis of the model of a dispositional utility-maximizer it becomes plausible that even in such circumstances it may be in an individual's long-term interest to acquire moral dispositions and virtues.

So, what can we say in terms of a final résumé of the results we obtained with the model of a dispositional utility-maximizer, regarding the vision of liberalism?

VI. The Vision of Liberalism and the Market of Virtue

To begin with, in two central points the critics of liberalism are right: *first*, for the stable existence of a liberal society it is indeed of decisive importance that its members display some degree of unselfish, moral action. There is not always an invisible hand which reliably converts actions intended exclusively for the gain of personal advantages into public goods. Without persons who voluntarily fulfil their political, legal, and moral obligations and, because of an 'intrinsic' motivation, accept a fair share of the burdens of the realization and protection of common interests, a stable social order in the interests of the citizens is *inconceivable* – not even, or particularly not, the order of a liberal society which offers ample space for the pursuit of individual interests. The social, economic, and legal institutions of such a society, supposed to guarantee and protect that space, can themselves survive only if individuals do not use, or rather abuse, them the whole time only to further their own interests. In that sense, *virtue* is an indispensable 'cohesive' for a liberal social order.

Second, there is indeed hardly any doubt that the basic 'moral demand' of a liberal society will not be sufficiently satisfied by an *economic* market. The 'doux commerce' thesis that trade and exchange by themselves can produce sufficient incentives because citizens, as participants in the market, will realize that it is to their own good to acquire character traits such as loyalty and honesty, is untenable. On the contrary, it can hardly be denied that in many cases competitive, impersonal and profit-oriented relations on the economic market foster opportunistic strategies and are not suitable to further morality and virtues. Trade and exchange may produce a demand for honesty, trustworthiness and reliability. But the transitoriness and anonymity of the exchange-relations in a large economic market, the mobility of the participants and the replaceability of the respective partners constantly produce opportunities and incentives to cheat and deceive and to disregard the interests of others. The network of mutual social control that is woven by the contacts on a market is too widemeshed to make conformity with moral rules congruent with rationally calculated self-interest in each case.[7] Because of the fleetingness and anonymity of exchange relationships, the mobility of market participants, and the substitutibility of partners, 'golden opportunities' for a riskfree enrichment at the expense of others abound. Trade and exchange can function in a reliable and stable way only if the partners already possess a certain degree of morality and virtue.

But even *if* the economic market did motivate participants to commit themselves to social norms, it could still do close to nothing to further the implementation of those norms which are of central importance to the existence of a social order, namely, that of norms of fairness demanding fair contributions to the production of public goods. As a rule, in exchange relationships only the *individual* goods of the participants are at stake. In the case of exchange partners, one will therefore primarily expect compliance with the principle of interpersonal respect. A principle of fairness only becomes important when, in a context of collective action, we are dealing with the production of *public* goods. Such a context is not entailed in the exchange transactions in a market. It exists only in cooperative enterprises. This underlines the special status of cooperative enterprises as indispensable 'factories' of morality and virtue.

With this, the decisive aspect of the overall result of our investigation into the vision of liberalism has been touched on: it is of central importance that exchange relations on the market and competition between individuals are not the only salient features of a liberal social and economic order – even if its critics often convey such a distorted image successfully. The conspicuousness of activities in the economic market should not mislead us into overlooking or underestimating another significant feature of liberal societies. On the contrary, this feature must come to the centre of our attention when we

[7] That is one of the reasons why entrepreneurs abandon the market scenario and integrate economic relationships in enterprises. Cf. Baurmann/Kliemt 1995.

are looking for factors which might induce the production of morality and public-spiritedness in such societies.

In this respect, it is of utmost importance that in a modern liberal society not only the economic market is liberated from impediments and barriers of all kinds and citizens are free to engage in economic activities. Rather, what counts even more is that such a 'liberation' can also be seen in regard to self-chosen joint cooperation and to voluntary association.[8] The citizens of a liberal society not only enjoy the freedom to indulge in individual economic enterprises and have the fundamental rights to self-determination and the possession of personal property. They also have the right to unite freely with other people and to form associations according to their own discretion and estimation: whether it be the founding of a firm to increase private material welfare, or the forming of a union to promote common political or economic interests, the opening of a club to follow immaterial aims, or the coming together in a community to enjoy the 'internal goods' of a communal relationship as such. And a liberal society not only allows for the formation of joint enterprises and communities, but also protects them from intrusion and destruction. It ensures that people have the corresponding *rights*, by providing institutions which offer special protection and effective tools for certain forms of cooperation. Freedom of market *and* freedom of association are thus the essence of the liberal society.

Historically, the freedom to choose autonomously the form of desired association and the partners with whom one wants to associate is as much a genuine product of the liberal society as is the universal spread of market-relations. Full implementation of freedom of association presupposes that the barriers and privileges of traditional societies break down, that 'personal' bonds which exist on the basis of birth, social position, geographical location, race or class become increasingly insignificant for the formation of cooperative relations and communities. People must become free and mobile enough to choose the social context of their lives from the point of view of where and how they could best employ their abilities and could best realize their aims. The constantly bemoaned anonymity and mobility of the modern mass society which do indeed undermine 'grown' personal and social relationships are essential to utilizing to the full the potential advantages of human cooperation and organization. Everyone can search for partners who are most suitable for his projects and is no longer dependent on those who by chance belong to his family, kin, tribe, local community or class. Such a substantial freedom to enter into cooperative relationships with others is one of the most important advantages of a liberal over a traditional, closed society.

Therefore, the voluntary cooperation between partners in joint enterprises is just as much an essential element of liberal society as is the peaceful struggle between competitors on the economic market. And if a liberal society approaches the institutions of an open society in which the citizens' freedom of cooperation and association is effectively protected against arbitrary power, then the necessary conditions for a well-functioning market of virtue will be satisfied too. In such a framework, there is a stable demand for persons with moral integrity who are suitable partners of cooperation. With its invisible hand, a market of virtue will produce moral persons without any need for the

8 "Liberalism is best understood as a theory of relationship, which has voluntary association at its center and which understands voluntariness as the right of rupture or withdrawal." (Walzer 1990, 21)

intervention of public agencies or planned production. Such persons will commit themselves to the principles of interpersonal respect and social fairness, and they will voluntarily contribute to the provision of the public goods necessary for the survival of social order – even if a liberal society is an interest-dominated society the members of which, when it comes down to it, only care about their own personal profit.

The vision of liberalism is thus given a new basis. Because under this presupposition there will be compelling reasons for many individuals *particularly* in a liberal society to acquire moral virtues and personal integrity even from the point of view of pure self-interest. In this case, however, the decisive question for individuals is not whether they will obey the precepts of morality in a *particular case,* but whether they will develop a moral *personality:* whether they want to be persons who in all situations are guided by considerations of expediency and always are on the lookout for their personal advantage, or persons who are reliably committed to certain moral principles and norms and therefore able to act contrary to their immediate personal avantages. *This* alternative itself can be judged solely on the grounds of a purely interest-based consideration. In the long run, it can be much more useful for a self-interested person to be endowed with a moral disposition than to act continuously according to the principles of utility maximization. So the rational pursuit of individual interest would still be the basis for the emergence and maintenance of morality and virtues. And that would mean that the core of the vision of liberalism can be upheld.

As long as a liberal society guarantees conditions favourable to the free and effective cooperation of its citizens, and thus approaches the situation of an open society with neutralized power relations and an effective system of social control, such a society will have a market of virtue, and hence provide sufficient incentives for many of its members to acquire and conserve moral commitments. As long as a market of virtue is functioning efficiently, it will, by *its* invisible hand, take care of that measure of morality that society as a whole needs for its proper existence. Accordingly, a liberal, competitive market-society by no means only encourages an egoistic, 'amoral' calculus, though it does motivate people to the 'pragmatic acceptance of the world' and to recognize their individual interests. A breeding ground for morality can evolve in such a society entirely irrespective of the activities of professional 'moral entrepreneurs' such as moral philosophers, priests, and teachers, or the purposive interventions on the side of morality-producing institutions. Morality will be effective in an interest-dominated society because it is in the interest of people to request moral conduct from others *and* because under certain conditions it is in the interest of those other people to practice the requested conduct. The most important factor for the 'moral productivity' of a liberal society is the *freedom* it guarantees and promotes: the freedom of a commitment to cooperative relationships is the decisive basis for the development of persons with a 'social character' – persons with moral integrity who can be expected to respect social norms voluntarily and to work for the society and its constitution and institutions.

If, in a liberal society, the gulf between individual and collective rationality can be bridged by a market of virtue, then the objections against the vision of liberalism which are based on that gulf lose much of their weight. If a liberal society can solve the main problem, i. e. that of satisfying the basic 'moral demand' every social order develops, then we neither need to fear an inevitable 'erosion of democracy' which would make it impossible for an elected government to impose the general interest against group interests, nor is it inevitable that market mechanisms will be replaced by political distributional struggles.[9] Citizens in a democratic society *need* not conform to the caricature the economic theory of politics has drawn: if they feel committed to a principle of social fairness, they *will* vote, they *will* inform themselves about political programmes and actors, they *will* refrain from reelecting politicians who favour particular interests with their decisions, and they *will* give their votes to those parties which, in their view, best promote the common good. Under such conditions, it does not seem impossible from the outset that in a democracy those who govern fight against the paralization of market mechanisms and protect competition, instead of ruining it by ever more prerogatives, privileges and subventions.

And this refutes not only the arguments of an immanent critique of liberalism, but also communitarian reservations against liberalism and liberal society.

First, liberalism does not need to start from a model of man that conceives of individuals as 'unemcumbered' and 'isolated' selves generally capable of existing without social ties and the 'embeddedness' in communities. On the contrary: since a liberal society protects the freedom of cooperation and association of its citizens to a much higher degree than any other social formation, it enables individuals to satisfy their need for participation in social communities without impediments.[10] It is true, of course, that modern liberal society destroys traditional communities, since its mobility and dynamism does not permit the existence of fixed boundaries between different groups and does not guarantee the preservation of *particular* groups. But in their stead, it enables individuals to become members of social groups by personal choice. It permits them to found communities with partners they can determine according to their own wishes, *and* it permits them to leave a group or community if it ceases to meet their expectations. Especially if one emphasizes the great value of community bonds for individuals, as communitarians do, it must be regarded as a great disadvantage if individuals are unable to free themselves of such bonds even if they turn out to work against their own interests. At least in this respect, the basic freedom of choice offered by liberal societies

[9] Even Mancur Olson, at the end of his *Rise and Decline of Nations*, concedes that despite strong incentives for opportunistic politics favouring special interests, the hope for "intelligent and resolute public policies" is not entirely illusory: "May we not then reasonably expect, if special interests are (as I have claimed) harmful to economic growth, full employment, coherent government, equal opportunity, and social mobility, that students of the matter will become increasingly aware of this as time goes on? And that the awareness eventually will spread to larger and larger proportions of the population? And that this wider awareness will greatly limit the losses from the special interests? That is what I expect, at least when I am searching for a happy ending." (Olson 1982, 237) Such an expectation, however, *especially* against the background of Olson's own theory, is equivalent to the expectation that people's behaviour will to a great extent be determined by 'moral' motives and an orientation towards the common good.

[10] This had already been noted by Alexis de Tocqueville with respect to the "individualist" conditions in North America: "Americans of all ages, all conditions, and all dispositions constantly form associations. They have not only commercial and manufacturing companies, in which all take part, but associations of a thousand other kinds, religious, moral, serious, futile, general or restricted, enormous or diminutive. The Americans make associations to give entertainments, to found seminaries, to build inns, to construct churches, to diffuse books, to send missionaries to the antipodes; in this manner they found hospitals, prisons, and schools. If it is proposed to inculcate some truth or to foster some feeling by the encouragement of a great example, they form a society." (Tocqueville 1835, 106)

seems to fit much better to the model of man advocated by communitarians than social orders in which individuals are 'condemned' to be members of certain groups and communities.

It is also not true that liberalism, or a model of man as a basically self-interested actor, must deny that human beings can draw 'internal goods' from a common practice. On the contrary: in elaborating the model of a dispositional utility-maximizer, I have tried to account for such a non-instrumental, expressive aspect of human needs and to integrate it into a model of interest-based action. However, even here it seems that a liberal society which leaves it to the individuals to decide under what conditions, in what form and with whom they want to satisfy their need for authentic interpersonal relationships is better suited to promote the 'internal goods' of common action than a society which does not give individuals any choice.

Second, neither liberal theory nor liberal practice lead to relativism and arbitrariness in decisions regarding norms and values. If the members of a liberal society act according to their individual interests, they certainly do have a fundament on which to base rational decisions about social and moral norms. This applies to a 'minimal' morality concerning the protection of elementary individual and collective goods[11] as well as to norms outside of that minimal morality, which – for instance, as norms to a democratic legislative procedure – can ensure the enactment of rules in case of conflicts of interest or when bargaining costs are prohibitively high. In all these cases, there is no threat of 'relativism' or 'nihilism'. This applies especially to the institutions of a liberal society themselves: as a citizen, a self-interested person who opts for the constitution of a liberal society has no reason to regard this decision as unjustified or arbitrary.

But individual interests are not only appropriate *guidelines* in regard to the content of social norms. Even in modern mass society they can also be a sufficient *motivational base* for norm-addressees to comply with these norms and for norm-givers actively to enforce them – provided norm-givers and norm-addressees are able to commit themselves to norms and live under the conditions of an open society with a well-functioning market of virtue. And that means that the *third*, 'sociological' argument of communitarianism, according to which a liberal society with its 'ethos of utility' is unable to satisfy its vital 'moral demand', is refuted too. Even in such a society citizens may be sufficiently 'intrinsically' motivated to engage in the measure of political activity and participation necessary to preserve their social institutions.

All in all, then, one can reasonably hope that the political and intellectual freedom citizens of a liberal society enjoy do not need to be restricted in favour of the restoration of traditional social structures and ideological indoctrination. If a liberal society has a functioning market of virtue, then even as a basically secular and interest-dominated society it can solve the 'problem of social order'. The epoch-making achievement of taming political power is compatible with the assumption – perhaps *only* with this assumption? – that the members of a society are oriented towards the pursuit of their own interests. There is no need to turn the clock back in the process of enlightenment, if what is meant by this process is that people are no longer guided in their actions by

[11] On the concept and the foundation of such a minimal morality, cf. Hoerster 1981.

metaphysical speculations or religious beliefs, but by knowledge of the empirical world, including their own nature and their interests.

VII. The Myth of Community

The familiar and widespread criticism of the anonymity and mobility of modern mass-society and of the exaggerated individualism and materialism of its culture frequently draws it apparent plausibility from an underlying assumption which one can refer to as the 'myth of community'. [12] We come across this myth as much in everyday wisdom and common sense as in varying scientific theories. At the core of this myth lies the assertion that a persisting and reliable moral conduct can only be expected of people who are integrated in comparatively small, transparent and stable social groups. The intensive and continuous personal relationships in such groups are claimed to be the ideal basis for mutual respect and solidarity. Permanent and easily comprehensible arrangements create emotional bonds between group members and foster the transmission of immaterial value-judgments to the next generation. Where deep-rooted social roles and conventions leave little room for conflicts and distributive struggles, the competition for scarce resources is thought to be unable to divide people. It is the familiar picture of traditional social relationships in which people help each other and commit themselves to the common cause without permanently looking to their personal benefit – and its counterpart of the 'cold' and impersonal atmosphere in a metropolis where even neighbours remain strangers to each other, where unsettled people move restlessly from one place to another, where personal intimacy and close community is rare, precarious and always at a risk, and where in this jungle people are only concerned with their own survival and personal material welfare.

Now, there is a kernel of truth in this myth. As I have argued, in a large-scale society a solid basis for moral conduct can only develop if this society is not an amorphous, unstructured mass, but has some built-in elements of small-group relations in the form of associations and common enterprises. It is also true that within the close-knit personal relationships of a small and closed group, mutual loyality and solidarity among the members is guaranteed in a high degree. The more intensive and durable the contact to certain persons, the better the chance to find out about their personality, their character and moral integrity, and also the higher the risk for a deviator to be identified and

[12] "The idol of this epoch is community. As if in compensation for the toughness and insipidness of our life, in this idea all sweetness has been condensed to mawkishness, all delicacy to weakness, all softness to indignity. In its manifestations – the phantoms of overly tormented hearts – what had been buried under awful rudeness reemerges. The immense cooling of human relations as a result of mechanical, commercial, political abstractions causes an immense counter-movement, in the ideal of an ardent community overwhelming all its supporters. Calculation and brutal profit-making is opposed, in the counter-image, by the bliss of unconsciously giving oneself away; the distrustful division into armoured states, by the worldwide association of people for the establishment of eternal peace. The law of distance has thus become invalid, loneliness has lost its charm. But the tendency to destroy all forms and boundaries promotes the aspiration to assimilate all differences. When the right to distance between people is ideologically abandoned for the ideal of the joint absorption into an all-encompassing organic compound, man himself is in danger." (Plessner 1924, 26)

excluded. Under these circumstances one can be almost certain that one gets an equivalent return for one's own investment in moral conduct.

But what will be the *scope* of the kind of morality fostered in the limits of such a group? According to the degree of unflexibility of group-membership and depending on the isolation and immobility among the existing groups, the incentives for the members of such tightly knitted groups will increase to establish within their groups a *particularistic* group-morality the benefits of which are limited exclusively to group-members. Small social groups with stable structures and little mobility are typical of traditional societies in which persons are bound together almost inseparably by various ties – like family, kin, tribe, race, place or occupation. Under these conditions there is no reason for the members of the respective groups to demand from their partners a form of morality which would also take the interests of outsiders into consideration. Quite the contrary: if a number of people form a homogenous 'interest group' with a more or less unsurmountable demarcation between itself and the outside world, why should they not increase the benefits of their own group by trying to exploit, cheat, deceit, oppress or tyrannize outsiders and 'strangers'? The morality of such a closed community would therefore tend to be an 'in-group morality' with an 'immoral', hostile attitude towards non-members, a morality which will restrict altruism and unselfishness to the dealings with the other members of the same group.

Hence, the morality of traditional communities will not be a *universalistic* morality which impartially takes care of the interests of *all* persons affected. When seen in this way, there seems to be no reason to glorify the 'moral conditions' in static and local social communities. Personal willingness to make sacrifices for the common cause can here be accompanied by strict group egoism. And above all, such a morality cannot satisfy the special 'moral demand' of a liberal social order under the conditions of large modern societies. The myth of community offers a distorted, overly idyllic picture.

It is an important result of our investigation that, in fact, precisely those attributes of modern mass-society which, like its mobility and anonymity, are regularly condemned by communitarians are in reality *the* indispensable empirical fundamentals for the establishment of a non-particularistic morality. This means especially that it is the *decline* of the traditional form of local and tightly forged communities which is an essential precondition for overcoming group egoism. The much more instable and fragile associations and communities which are typical of mobile and anonymous liberal societies are the cradle of moral universalism. In such a society, the lack of static social relations leads to a more or less frequent change of reference groups and partners of interaction and cooperation. For the small-scale associations and communities which exist in such circumstances, it is characteristic that they possess *no* impermeable borders to their outer world. They are 'porous', their members fluctuate and move from one group to another. There are hardly any bonds which tie people inseparably together. In such a society, borders and demarcations are *temporary* and cannot be relied on.

Therefore, when searching for a suitable partner for a cooperative enterprise in an anonymous, mobile, changing society one will not look out for persons who are moral only in regard to a *particular* circle of people, but for persons who *in general* have a moral attitude: persons, that is, who take a moral point of view, in the sense of being impersonal and impartial towards the interests of others. Only in such a society, which is the exact counterpart to the social life in a traditional community, will there be a reasonable interest in a universalistic morality. Every kind of group-egoistic morality would be judged as too risky for the members of the respective group themselves. Thus, the special kind of communities in mobile and dynamic liberal societies also produce a demand for a special kind of persons as suitable partners. The required moral qualification is no longer an unconditional loyality to a certain class of people, but a general adherence to the precepts of moral respect and fairness.

Societies with a great number of members, with prosaic and impersonal relations between people, with frequent fluctuation between social groups and communities, are often seen as destructive powers which erode and undermine traditional social structures and personal bonds. According to this opinion, the pursuit of individual interests in the framework of our modern societies is the source of cultural, political and moral evil. But societies of this sort also bring about the phenomenon that people who are strangers and at first have little in common come into contact and establish relationships. They encourage cooperation and association regardless of natural, social or cultural differences. And only under such circumstances do individuals committed to a universalistic morality become relevant to the interests of others. The destruction of traditional structures and relationships in modern mass society is therefore an indispensable prerequisite for an *empirical establishment* of a kind of morality conforming to our modern ideas about ethics, and of the kind that is necessary for the conservation of a liberal society.

This result disenchants the myth of community. After all, it is impossible to overcome the mobility of modern society without erecting more or less impermeable demarcations between social groups. And it is impossible to overcome the anonymity of social relations without restricting the set of potential partners of cooperation. Those who want a society without mobility and anonymity must also accept the conditions of a closed society in which cooperative interests remain purely local and their restriction creates an incentive to give preference to power interests beyond those confines. And this insight corresponds perfectly to historical experience. The stable internal morality of firmly established communities has always been compatible with hostility towards outsiders and the brutal subjection of those who do not belong to the community.

What needs explanation, therefore, is not primarily the exclusion and discrimination of others on the basis of a particular morality, but rather the inclusion and equal treatment conceded to others on the basis of a universalistic morality. In the natural course of human affairs, the starting point has been the confined and isolated community with a morality which benefits only its own members. Divisions are not created but are pre-existing and need to be eliminated. The unlimited scope of social relations and moral norms is an 'artificial' and fragile product of the historical development towards an open society.

This result is quite the contrary of what is widely believed to be true. According to this opinion, the source of all cultural, political, and moral evils is the orientation towards individual interests, combined with the conditions of modern society. But unless the social and natural barriers of traditional societies fall, unless indissoluble 'personal' bonds between individuals are abolished, and unless people become 'mobile' and can choose their own place of residence and way of life, there cannot be a market of virtue which produces a demand for people with moral integrity and a moral identity, people who commit themselves to the universal principles of interpersonal respect and social fairness. And only then will there be a sound basis for a social order in which ideological enlightenment, political freedom, economic prosperity and individual morality are all conceivable at the same time – that is, in which the old vision of liberalism may yet become reality.

BIBLIOGRAPHY

Albert, Hans (1977), Individuelles Handeln und soziale Steuerung – Die ökonomische Tradition und ihr Erkenntnisprogramm, in: H. Lenk (ed.), Handlungstheorien interdisziplinär IV, Munich, 177-225.

– (1986), Freiheit und Ordnung. Zwei Abhandlungen zum Problem einer offenen Gesellschaft, Tübingen.

– (1990), Die Verfassung der Freiheit. Bedingungen der Möglichkeit sozialer Ordnung, in O. Marquard (Hrsg.), Einheit und Vielheit. XIV. Deutscher Kongreß für Philosophie, Hamburg, 253-276.

– (1994), Das Ideal der Freiheit und das Problem der sozialen Ordnung, Freiburg i. Br.

Alchian, Armen A. / Harold Demsetz (1972), Production, Information Costs and Economic Organization, in: American Economic Review, 777-795.

– / S. Woodward (1987), Reflections on the Theory of the Firm, in: Zeitschrift für die gesamte Staatswissenschaft, 110-136.

– / – (1988), The Firm Is Dead: Long Live the Firm. A Review of Oliver E. Williamson's 'The Economic Institutions of Capitalism', in: Journal of Economic Literature, 65-79.

Arrow, Kenneth J. (1971), Essays in the Theory of Risk-Bearing, Chicago.

– (1985), Applied Economics, Cambridge, Mass. and London.

Axelrod, Robert (1984), The Evolution of Cooperation, New York.

– (1986), An Evolutionary Approach to Norms, in: American Political Science Review, 1095-1111.

Barber, Benjamin (1983), The Logic and Limits of Trust, New Brunswick.

Baurmann, Michael (1987), Zweckrationalität und Strafrecht. Argumente für ein tatbezogenes Massnahmerecht, Opladen.

– / Hartmut Kliemt (1995), Zur Ökonomie der Tugend, in: P. Weise (ed.), Ökonomie und Gesellschaft. Jahrbuch 11, 13-44.

Becker, Gary S. (1976), The Economic Approach to Human Behavior, Chicago.

Behrens, P. (1986), Die ökonomischen Grundlagen des Rechts. Politische Ökonomie als rationale Jurisprudenz, Tübingen.

Bellah, Robert N. / Richard Madsen / William M. Sullivan / Ann Swidler / Steven M. Tipton (1985), Habits of the Heart. Individualism and Commitment in American Life, Berkeley.

– / – / – / – / – (1991), The Good Society, New York.

Blau, Peter M. (1967), Exchange and Power in Social Life, New York.

Bohnen, Alfred (1975), Individualismus und Gesellschaftstheorie, Tübingen.

Briefs, G. (1920), Untergang des Abendlandes; Christentum und Sozialismus, Freiburg i. Br.

Brennan, Geoffrey / James M. Buchanan (1985), The Reason of Rules. Constitutional Political Economy, Cambridge, Mass.

Breyer, Friedrich / Peter Bernholz (1993/94), Grundlagen der politischen Ökonomie, Vol 1: Theorie der Wirtschaftssysteme, Vol. 2: Ökonomische Theorie der Politik, 3rd ed. Tübingen.

Buchanan, James M. (1975), The Limits of Liberty. Between Anarchy and Leviathan, Chicago and London.

– (1990), The Domain of Constitutional Economics, in: Constitutional Political Economy, 1-18.

– / Gordon Tullock (1962), The Calculus of Consent, Ann Arbor.

– / Robert D. Tollison / Gordon Tullock (1980) (eds.), Toward a Theory of the Rent-Seeking Society, College Station.

Coase, Richard H. (1960), The Problem of Social Cost, in: Jourmal of Law and Economics, 1-44.

Coleman, James S. (1987), Norms as Social Capital, in: G. Radnitzky / H. Bouillon (eds.), Ordnungstheorie und Ordnungspolitik, Berlin, 133-155.

– (1990), Foundations of Social Theory, Cambridge, Mass. and London.

Dahrendorf, Ralf (1968), Homo Sociologicus. Versuch zur Geschichte, Bedeutung und Kritik der Kategorie der sozialen Rolle, in: id., Pfade aus Utopia, Munich, 128-194.

Downs, Anthony (1957), An Economic Theory of Democracy, New York.

Durkheim, Émile (1893), The Division of Labor in Society, New York 1964.

Eisenhardt, K. M. (1989), Agency Theory: An Assessment and Review, in: Academy of Management Review, 57-74.

Ekman, P. (1985), Telling Lies. Clues to Deceit in the Marketplace, Politics, and Marriage, New York.

Elster, Jon (1979), Ulysses and the Sirens. Studies in Rationality and Irrationality, Cambridge et al. and Paris.

Elster, Jon (1982), Rationality, in: G. Floistad (ed.), Contemporary Philosophy. A New Survey. Vol. 2: Philosophy of Science, The Hague, 111-131.

– (1983), Sour Grapes, Cambridge et al. and Paris.

– (1986), Introduction, in: id. (ed.), Rational Choice, Oxford, 1-33.

– (1988), Economic Order and Social Norms, in: Zeitschrift für die gesamte Staatswissenschaft, 357-366.

– (1989), The Cement of Society, Cambridge.

Esser, Hartmut (1990), 'Habits', 'Frames' and 'Rational Choice'. Die Reichweite der Theorie der rationalen Wahl, in: Zeitschrift für Soziologie, 231-247.

– (1991a), Alltagshandeln und Verstehen. Zum Verhältnis von erklärender und verstehender Soziologie am Beispiel von Alfred Schütz und 'Rational Choice' Tübingen.

– (1991b), Die Rationalität des Alltagshandelns. Alfred Schütz und 'Rational Choice', in: id. and K. G. Troitzsch (eds.), Modellierung sozialer Prozesse, Bonn, 235-281.

Etzioni, Amitai (1988), The Moral Dimension. Toward a New Economics, New York and London.

Frank, Robert H. (1987), If Homo Economicus Could Choose His Own Utility Function, Would He Want One with a Conscience?, in: American Economic Review, 593-604.

– (1988), Passions Within Reason. The Strategic Role of the Emotions, New York and London.

Frey, Bruno S. (1980), Ökonomie als Verhaltenswissenschaft, in: Jahrbuch für Sozialwissenschaft 31, 21-35.

– (1988), Ein ipsatives Modell menschlichen Verhaltens. Ein Beitrag zur Ökonomie und Psychologie, in: Analyse & Kritik, 181-205.

– (1992), Tertium datur: Pricing, Regulating and Intrinsic Motivation, in: Kyklos, 161-184.

– (1993a), Motivation as a Limit to Pricing, in: Journal of Economic Psychology, 635-664.

– (1993b), Shirking or Work Morale?, in: European Economic Review, 1523-1532.

– / Iris Bohnet (1994), Die Ökonomie zwischen extrinsischer und intrinsischer Motivation, in: Homo Oeconomicus (Munich), 1-19.

Furubotn, Eirik G. / Svetozar Pejovich (1974) (eds.), The Economics of Property Rights, Cambridge, Mass.

Gambetta, Diego (1988) (ed.), Trust: Making and Breaking Cooperative Relations, Oxford.

Gauthier, David (1986), Morals by Agreement, Oxford.

Garzón Valdés, Ernesto (1982), Die gesetzliche Begrenzung des staatlichen Souveräns, in: Archiv für Rechts- und Sozialphilosophie LXVIII: 4, 431-447.

Granovetter, Mark (1985), Economic Action and Social Structure: The Problem of Embeddedness, in: American Journal of Sociology, 481-510.

Güth, Werner / Hartmut Kliemt (1993), Menschliche Kooperation basierend auf Vorleistungen und Vertrauen, in: Jahrbuch für Politische Ökonomie 12, Tübingen, 145-173.

– / – (1994), Competition or Co-operation: On the Evolutionary Economics of Trust, Exploitation and Moral Attitudes, in: Metroeconomica, 155-187.

Hardin, Russell (1971), Collective Action as an Agreeable *n*-Prisoners' Dilemma, in: Behavioral Science, 472-481.

– (1982), Collective Action, Baltimore.

– (1991), Trusting Persons, Trusting Institutions, in R. Zeckhauser (ed.), The Strategy of Choice, Cambridge, Mass., 185-209.

– (1992), The Street-Level Epistemology of Trust, in: Analyse & Kritik 14:2, 152-176.

Harsanyi, John C. (1986), Advances in Understanding Rational Behavior, in: J. Elster (ed.), Rational Choice, Oxford, 82-107.

Hart, H. L. A. (1961), The Concept of Law, Oxford.

Hayek, Friedrich A. von (1973), Law, Legislation and Liberty. Vol. 1. Rules and Order, London.

Hegselmann, Rainer / Werner Raub / Th. Voss (1986), Zur Entstehung der Moral aus natürlichen Neigungen. Eine spieltheoretische Spekulation, in: Analyse & Kritik, 150-177.

Hill, W. / R. Fehlbaum / P. U. Ulrich (1992), Organisationslehre, Parts 1 and 2, 4th ed. Bern and Stuttgart.

Hirsch, Fred (1976), The Social Limits to Growth, Cambridge, Mass.

Hirschman, Albert O. (1977), The Passions and the Interests. Political Arguments for Capitalism before its Triumph, Princeton.

– (1981), Morality and the Social Sciences: A Durable Tension, in: id., Essays in Trespassing: Economics to Politics and Beyond, New York, 294-306.

– (1982), Rival Views of Market Society, in: Journal of Economic Literature 20 (Dec.) 1463-1484.

Hirshleifer, Jack (1987), On the Emotions as Guarantors of Threats and Premises, in: J. Dupré (ed.), The Latest on the Best: Essays in Evolution and Optimality, Cambridge, Mass., 307-326.

Hobbes, Thomas (1651), Leviathan, ed. C. B. Macpherson, Harmondsworth 1985.

Hoerster, Norbert (1977), Utilitaristische Ethik und Verallgemeinerung, 2nd ed. Freiburg and Munich.

– (1981), Zur Begründung einer Minimalmoral, in: Ethik. Akten des 5. Internationalen Wittgenstein-Symposiums, Vienna, 131-133.

– (1982), Rechtsethik ohne Metaphysik, in: Juristenzeitung, 265-272; 714-716.

– (1983), Moralbegründung ohne Metaphysik, in: Erkenntnis, 225-238.

Hogarth, Robin M. / Melvin H. Reder (eds.) (1987), Rational Choice. The Contrast Between Economics and Psychology, Chicago.

Humboldt, Wilhelm von (1792), The Limits of State Action, ed. J. W. Burrow, Indianapolis 1993.

Hume, David (1739), A Treatise of Human Nature, ed. E. C. Mossner, Harmondsworth 1984.

– (1777), An Enquiry Concerning the Principles of Morals, reprinted from the posthumous edition of 1777, ed. by L. A. Selby-Bigge, 3rd ed. with text revised and notes by P. H. Nidditch, Oxford 1975.

Jasay, Antony de (1989), Social Contract, Free Ride. A Study of the Public Goods Problem, Oxford.

Jones, E. L. (1981), The European Miracle. Environments, Economics, and Geopolitics in the History of Europe and Asia, Cambridge.

Kahneman, D. / P. Slovic / A. Tversky (1982), Judgement under Uncertainty: Heuristics and Biases, Cambridge, Mass.

Kieser, A. / H. Kubicek (1992), Organisation, 3rd ed. Berlin and New York.

Kirchgässner, Gebhard (1991), Homo Oeconomicus. Das ökonomische Modell individuellen Verhaltens und seine Anwendung in den Wirtschafts- und Sozialwissenschaften, Tübingen.

Kliemt, Hartmut (1978), Can There be Any Constitutional Limits to Constitutional Powers?, in: Munich Social Science Review, 106-129.

– (1980), Zustimmungstheorien der Staatsrechtfertigung, Freiburg and Munich.

– (1984), Nicht-explanative Funktionen eines 'Homo oeconomicus' und Beschränkungen seiner explanativen Rolle, in M. J. Holler (ed.), Homo oeconomicus II, Munich, 7-49.

Kliemt, Hartmut (1985), Moralische Institutionen. Empiristische Theorien ihrer Evolution, Freiburg and Munich.

– (1987), The Reason of Rules and the Rule of Reason, in: Crítica (Mexico-City), 43-86.

– (1990a), Papers on Buchanan and Related Subjects, Munich.

– (1990b), The Costs of Organizing Social Cooperation, in: M. Hechter et al. (eds.), Social Institutions. Their Emergence, Maintenance and Effects, New York, 61-79.

– (1991), Der Homo oeconomicus in der Klemme, in H. Esser / K. G. Troitzsch (eds.), Modellierung sozialer Prozesse, Bonn, 179-203.

– (1993a), Constitutional Commitments, in: Ph. Herder-Dorneich et al. (eds.), Jahrbuch für Politische Ökonomie 12, Tübingen, 145-173.

– (1993b), Ökonomische Analyse der Moral, in: B.-T. Ramb / M. Tietzel (eds.), Ökonomische Verhaltenstheorie, Munich, 281-310.

– / Ruth Zimmerling (1993), Quo vadis Homo oeconomicus?, in Homo oeconomicus (Munich) X, 1-44 and 167-195.

Koslowski, Peter (1988), Prinzipien der Ethischen Ökonomie. Grundlegung der Wirtschaftsethik und der auf die Ökonomie bezogenen Ethik, Tübingen.

Kreps, D. M. / P. Milgrom / J. Roberts / R. Wilson (1982), Rational Cooperation in the Finitely Repeated Prisoners' Dilemma, in: Journal of Economic Theory, 245-252.

– / R. Wilson (1982), Reputation and Imperfect Information, in: Journal of Economic Theory, 253-279.

Kutschera, Franz von (1973), Einführung in die Logik der Normen, Werte und Entscheidungen, Freiburg and Munich.

– (1982), Grundlagen der Ethik, Berlin and New York.

Lindenberg, Siegwart (1989), Social Production Functions, Deficits, and Social Revolutions, in: Rationality and Society, 51-77.

– (1990), Homo Socio-Oeconomicus: The Emergence of a General Model of Man in the Social Sciences, in: Zeitschrift für die gesamte Staatswissenschaft, 727-748.

– (1993), Framing, Empirical Evidence, and Applications, in: Jahrbuch für politische Ökonomie 12, 11-38.

– / Bruno Frey (1993), Alternatives, Frames, and Relative Prices: A Broader View of Rational Choice Theory, in: Acta Sociologica, 191-205.

Luce, D. R./Howard Raiffa (1957), Games and Decisions, New York.

MacCormick, Neil (1981), H. L. A. Hart, London.

MacDonald, G. (1984), New Directions in the Economic Theory of Agency, in: Canadian Journal of Economics, 415-440.

MacIntyre, Alasdair (1984), Is Patriotism a Virtue?, The Lindley Lecture, University of Kansas.

– (1985) After Virtue. A Study in Moral Theory (1981), 2nd ed. London.

– (1988), Whose Justice? Which Rationality?, London.

– (1990), Three Rival Versions of Moral Enquiry, Notre Dame.

Mackie, John L. (1977), Ethics. Inventing Right and Wrong, Harmondsworth.

– (1982), Morality and the Retributive Emotions, in: Criminal Justice Ethics, 3-10.

Mandeville, Bernard (1714), The Fable of the Bees: or, Private Vices Publick Benefits, ed. F. B. Kaye, 2 vols., Indianapolis 1988.

Margolis, Howard (1981), A New Model of Rational Choice, in: Ethics, 265-283.

– (1982), Selfishness, Altruism, and Rationality: A Theory of Social Choice, Cambridge.

Mayntz, Renate (1982), Soziologie der öffentlichen Verwaltung, 2nd ed. Heidelberg.

McKenzie, R. B. (1977), The Economic Dimension of Ethical Behavior, in: Ethics, 208-221.

– (1987), The Fairness of Markets. A Search for Justice in a Free Society, Lexington and Toronto.

– / Gordon Tullock (1978), The New World of Economics – Explorations into the Human Experience, Homewood.

Milgrom, P. / J. Roberts (1982), Predation, Reputation, and Entry Deterrence, in: Journal of Economic Theory, 280-312.

– / – (1992), Economics, Organization and Management, Englewood Cliffs.

Mill, John St. (1859), On Liberty, ed. C. V. Shields, New York 1956.

Mueller, Dennis C. (1979), Public Choice, Cambridge, Mass.

– (1986), Rational Egoism versus Adaptive Egoism as Fundamental Postulate for a Descriptive Theory of Human Behavior, in: Public Choice, 3-23.

– (1991), Public Choice II, Cambridge, Mass.

– (1992), On the Foundations of Social Science Research, in: Analyse & Kritik, 195-220.

Myers, M. L. (1983), The Soul of Modern Economic Man. Ideas of Self-Interest, Chicago and London.

North, Douglass C. (1981), Structure and Change in Economic History, New York.

– (1990), Institutions, Institutional Change and Economic Performance, Cambridge.

North, Douglass C. / R. P. Thomas (1973), The Rise of the Western World. A New Economic History, Cambridge.

Olson, Mancur (1965), The Logic of Collective Action. Public Goods and the Theory of Groups, Cambridge, Mass.

– (1982), The Rise and Decline of Nations: Economic Growth, Stagflation and Social Rigidities, New Haven and London.

– (1991), Umfassende Ökonomie, Tübingen.

Opp, Karl-Dieter (1979), Das 'ökonomische Programm' in der Soziologie, in: H. Albert / K. H. Stapf (eds.), Theorie und Erfahrung – Beiträge zur Grundlagenproblematik der Sozialwissenschaften, Stuttgart, 313-349.

– (1983), Die Entstehung sozialer Normen. Ein Integrationsversuch soziologischer, sozialpsychologischer und ökonomischer Erklärungen, Tübingen.

– (1986), Das Modell des Homo Sociologicus. Eine Explikation und eine Konfrontierung mit dem utilitaristischen Verhaltensmodell, in: Analyse & Kritik, 1-27.

Parfit, Derek (1984), Reasons and Persons, Oxford.

Plessner, Helmuth (1924), Grenzen der Gemeinschaft. Eine Kritik des sozialen Radikalismus, Bonn.

Popitz, Heinrich (1992), Phänomene der Macht, 2nd ed. Tübingen.

Posner, Richard A. (1977), Economic Analysis of Law, Boston and Toronto.

Pratt, J. W. / R. J. Zeckhauser (1991) (eds.), Principals and Agents. The Structure of Business, 2nd ed. Boston.

Raphael, D. D. (1969), The British Moralists. 1650-1800, Oxford.

Raub, W. (1990), A General Game-Theoretic Model of Preference Adaptations in Problematic Social Situations, in: Rationality and Society, 67-93.

– / Th. Voss (1981), Individuelles Handeln und gesellschaftliche Folgen, Neuwied and Berlin.

– / J. Weesie (1990), Reputation and Efficiency in Social Interactions: An Example of Network Effects, in: American Journal of Sociology, 626-654.

Rawls, John (1985), Justice as Fairness: Political, Not Metaphysical, in: Philosophy & Public Affairs 14, 223-252.

Rowe, Nicholas (1989), Rules and Institutions, Ann Arbor.

Sandel, Michael J. (1982), Liberalism and the Limits of Justice, Cambridge.

Schelling, Thomas C. (1960), The Strategy of Conflict, New York.

– (1984), Choice and Consequence. Perspectives of an Errant Economist, Cambridge, Mass. and London.

Schneider, Louis (1967), The Scottish Moralists. On Human Nature and Society, Chicago and London.

Schumpeter, Joseph A. (1942), Capitalism, Socialism, and Democracy, 2nd ed. New York 1947.

Schüßler, Rudolf (1990), Kooperation unter Egoisten: Vier Dilemmata, Munich.

Sen, Amartya (1986), Behavior and the Concept of Preference, in: J. Elster (ed.), Rational Choice, Oxford, 60-81.

Shoemaker, Paul J. H. (1982), The Expected Utility Model: Its Variants, Purposes, Evidence and Limitations, in: Journal of Economic Literature, 529-563.

Simon, Herbert A. (1982), Models of Bounded Rationality, Cambridge, Mass.

Singer, Peter (1979), Practical Ethics, Cambridge.

Singer, M. (1961), Generalization in Ethics. An Essay in the Logic of Ethics, with the Rudiments of a System of Moral Philosophy, London.

Sommer, V. (1993), Lob der Lüge. Täuschung und Selbstbetrug bei Tier und Mensch, 2nd ed., Munich.

Strawson, Peter F. (1974), Freedom and Resentment, in: id., 'Freedom and Resentment' and other essays, London, 1-25 (first published in: Proceedings of the British Academy 48 [1962], 187-211).

Taylor, Charles (1979), Hegel and Modern Society, Cambridge.

– (1985), The Nature and Scope of Distributive Justice, in: id., Philosophical Papers, Vol. 2: Philosophy and the Human Science, Cambridge, 289-317.

– (1989a), Sources of the Self. The Making of the Modern Identity, Cambridge.

– (1989b), Cross-Purposes: The Liberal-Communitarian Debate, in: N. L. Rosenblum (ed.), Liberalism and the Moral Life, Cambridge, Mass., 159-182.

Taylor, Michael (1993), Cooperation, Norms, and Moral Motivation, in: Analyse & Kritik, 70-86.

Thaler, Richard H. (1992), The Winner's Curse. Paradoxes and Anomalies of Economic Life, New York.

– / H. M. Shefrin (1981), An Economic Theory of Self-Control, in: Journal of Political Economy, 392-421.

Tocqueville, Alexis de (1835), Democracy in America, New York 1966.

Tullock, Gordon (1970), Private Wants. Public Means, New York.

Tversky, Amos / Daniel Kahnemann (1986), The Framing of Decisions and the Psychology of Choice, in: J. Elster (ed.), Rational Choice, Oxford, 123-141.

Vanberg, Viktor (1975), Die zwei Soziologien. Individualismus und Kollektivismus in der Sozialtheorie, Tübingen.

– (1988a), Morality and Economics. De Moribus Est Disputandum, Bowling Green.

– (1988b), Rules and Choice in Economics and Sociology, in: Jahrbuch für Neue Politische Ökonomie 7, Tübingen, 146-167.

– (1993a), Rational Choice, Rule-Following and Institution. An Evolutionary Perspective, in: U. Mäki et al. (eds.), Rationality, Institutions and Economic Methodology, London and New York, 171-200.

– (1993b), Rational Choice vs. Adaptive Rule-Following: on the Behavioral Foundations of the Social Sciences, in: Jahrbuch für Neue Politische Ökonomie 12, Tübingen, 93-110.

– / Roger D. Congleton (1992), Rationality, Morality, and Exit, in: American Political Science Review, 418-431.

Walzer, Michael (1983), Spheres of Justice, New York.

– (1990), The Communitarian Critique of Liberalism, in: Political Theory 18:1 (February), 6-23.

Weber, Max (1920a), Gesammelte Aufsätze zur Religionssoziologie I, Tübingen 1988.

– (1920b), Gesammelte Politische Schriften, Tübingen 1971.

– (1921), Economy and Society, 2 vols., New York 1968.

– (1922), Gesammelte Aufsätze zur Wissenschaftslehre, Tübingen 1985.

Weede, Erich (1989), Der ökonomische Erklärungsansatz in der Soziologie, in: Analyse & Kritik, 23-51.

– (1990), Wirtschaft, Staat und Gesellschaft. Zur Soziologie der kapitalistischen Marktwirtschaft und der Demokratie, Tübingen.

Weizsäcker, Carl Ch. von (1971), Notes on the Endogenous Change of Tastes, in: Journal of Economic Theory, 345-372.

– (1984), The Influence of Property Rights on Tastes, in: Zeitschrift für die gesamte Staatswissenschaft, 90-95.

Willgerodt, H. (1968), Grenzmoral und Wirtschaftsordnung, in: J. Broermann / Ph. Herder-Dorneich (eds.), Soziale Verantwortung. Festschrift für Goetz Briefs zum 80. Geburtstag, Berlin, 141-171.

Williamson, Oliver E. (1983), Credible Commitments: Using Hostages to Support Exchange, in: The American Economic Review, 519-532.

– (1985), The Economic Institutions of Capitalism, New York.

Wilson, R. (1985), Reputations in games and markets, in: A. E. Roth (ed.), Game-theoretic models of bargaining, Cambridge, 27-62.

Wright, Georg Henrik von (1963), The Varieties of Goodness, London.

Zintl, Reinhard (1989), Der Homo Oeconomicus: Ausnahmeerscheinung in jeder Situation oder Jedermann in Ausnahmesituationen?, in: Analyse & Kritik, 52-69.

INDEX OF NAMES

[Italicized numbers refer to references in footnotes only.]

Law and Philosophy Library

1. E. Bulygin, J.-L. Gardies and I. Niiniluoto (eds.): *Man, Law and Modern Forms of Life.* With an Introduction by M.D. Bayles. 1985 ISBN 90-277-1869-5
2. W. Sadurski: *Giving Desert Its Due.* Social Justice and Legal Theory. 1985 ISBN 90-277-1941-1
3. N. MacCormick and O. Weinberger: *An Institutional Theory of Law.* New Approaches to Legal Positivism. 1986 ISBN 90-277-2079-7
4. A. Aarnio: *The Rational as Reasonable.* A Treatise on Legal Justification. 1987 ISBN 90-277-2276-5
5. M.D. Bayles: *Principles of Law.* A Normative Analysis. 1987 ISBN 90-277-2412-1; Pb: 90-277-2413-X
6. A. Soeteman: *Logic in Law.* Remarks on Logic and Rationality in Normative Reasoning, Especially in Law. 1989 ISBN 0-7923-0042-4
7. C.T. Sistare: *Responsibility and Criminal Liability.* 1989 ISBN 0-7923-0396-2
8. A. Peczenik: *On Law and Reason.* 1989 ISBN 0-7923-0444-6
9. W. Sadurski: *Moral Pluralism and Legal Neutrality.* 1990 ISBN 0-7923-0565-5
10. M.D. Bayles: *Procedural Justice.* Allocating to Individuals. 1990 ISBN 0-7923-0567-1
11. P. Nerhot (ed.): *Law, Interpretation and Reality.* Essays in Epistemology, Hermeneutics and Jurisprudence. 1990 ISBN 0-7923-0593-0
12. A.W. Norrie: *Law, Ideology and Punishment.* Retrieval and Critique of the Liberal Ideal of Criminal Justice. 1991 ISBN 0-7923-1013-6
13. P. Nerhot (ed.): *Legal Knowledge and Analogy.* Fragments of Legal Epistemology, Hermeneutics and Linguistics. 1991 ISBN 0-7923-1065-9
14. O. Weinberger: *Law, Institution and Legal Politics.* Fundamental Problems of Legal Theory and Social Philosophy. 1991 ISBN 0-7923-1143-4
15. J. Wróblewski: *The Judicial Application of Law.* Edited by Z. Bańkowski and N. MacCormick. 1992 ISBN 0-7923-1569-3
16. T. Wilhelmsson: *Critical Studies in Private Law.* A Treatise on Need-Rational Principles in Modern Law. 1992 ISBN 0-7923-1659-2
17. M.D. Bayles: *Hart's Legal Philosophy.* An Examination. 1992 ISBN 0-7923-1981-8
18. D.W.P. Ruiter: *Institutional Legal Facts.* Legal Powers and their Effects. 1993 ISBN 0-7923-2441-2
19. J. Schonsheck: *On Criminalization.* An Essay in the Philosophy of the Criminal Law. 1994 ISBN 0-7923-2663-6
20. R.P. Malloy and J. Evensky (eds.): *Adam Smith and the Philosophy of Law and Economics.* 1994 ISBN 0-7923-2796-9
21. Z. Bańkowski, I. White and U. Hahn (eds.): *Informatics and the Foundations of Legal Reasoning.* 1995 ISBN 0-7923-3455-8

Law and Philosophy Library

22. E. Lagerspetz: *The Opposite Mirrors*. An Essay on the Conventionalist Theory of Institutions. 1995 ISBN 0-7923-3325-X
23. M. van Hees: *Rights and Decisions*. Formal Models of Law and Liberalism. 1995 ISBN 0-7923-3754-9
24. B. Anderson: *"Discovery" in Legal Decision-Making*. 1996 ISBN 0-7923-3981-9
25. S. Urbina: *Reason, Democracy, Society*. A Study on the Basis of Legal Thinking. 1996 ISBN 0-7923-4262-3
26. E. Attwooll: *The Tapestry of the Law*. Scotland, Legal Culture and Legal Theory. 1997 ISBN 0-7923-4310-7
27. J.C. Hage: *Reasoning with Rules*. An Essay on Legal Reasoning and Its Underlying Logic. 1997 ISBN 0-7923-4325-5
28. R.A. Hillman: *The Richness of Contract Law*. An Analysis and Critique of Contemporary Theories of Contract Law. 1997 ISBN 0-7923-4336-0; 0-7923-5063-4 (Pb)
29. C. Wellman: *An Approach to Rights*. Studies in the Philosophy of Law and Morals. 1997 ISBN 0-7923-4467-7
30. B. van Roermund: *Law, Narrative and Reality*. An Essay in Intercepting Politics. 1997 ISBN 0-7923-4621-1
31. I. Ward: *Kantianism, Postmodernism and Critical Legal Thought*. 1997 ISBN 0-7923-4745-5
32. H. Prakken: *Logical Tools for Modelling Legal Argument*. A Study of Defeasible Reasoning in Law. 1997 ISBN 0-7923-4776-5
33. T. May: *Autonomy, Authority and Moral Responsibility*. 1998 ISBN 0-7923-4851-6
34. M. Atienza and J.R. Manero: *A Theory of Legal Sentences*. 1998 ISBN 0-7923-4856-7
35. E.A. Christodoulidis: *Law and Reflexive Politics*. 1998 ISBN 0-7923-4954-7
36. L.M.M. Royakkers: *Extending Deontic Logic for the Formalisation of Legal Rules*. 1998 ISBN 0-7923-4982-2
37. J.J. Moreso: *Legal Indeterminacy and Constitutional Interpretation*. 1998 ISBN 0-7923-5156-8
38. W. Sadurski: *Freedom of Speech and Its Limits*. 1999 ISBN 0-7923-5523-7
39. J. Wolenski (ed.): *Kazimierz Opalek Selected Papers in Legal Philosophy*. 1999 ISBN 0-7923-5732-9
40. H.P. Visser 't Hooft: *Justice to Future Generations and the Environment*. 1999 ISBN 0-7923-5756-6
41. L.J. Wintgens (ed.): *The Law in Philosophical Perspectives*. My Philosophy of Law. 1999 ISBN 0-7923-5796-5
42. A.R. Lodder: *DiaLaw*. On Legal Justification and Dialogical Models of Argumentation. 1999 ISBN 0-7923-5830-9
43. C. Redondo: *Reasons for Action and the Law*. 1999 ISBN 0-7923-5912-7

Law and Philosophy Library

44. M. Friedman, L. May, K. Parsons and J. Stiff (eds.): *Rights and Reason*. Essays in Honor of Carl Wellman. 2000 ISBN 0-7923-6198-9
45. G.C. Christie: *The Notion of an Ideal Audience in Legal Argument*. 2000 ISBN 0-7923-6283-7
46. R.S. Summers: *Essays in Legal Theory*. 2000 ISBN 0-7923-6367-1
47. M. van Hees: *Legal Reductionism and Freedom*. 2000 ISBN 0-7923-6491-0
48. R. Gargarella: *The Scepter of Reason*. Public Discussion and Political Radicalism in the Origins of Constitutionalism. 2000 ISBN 0-7923-6508-9
49. M. Iglesias Vila: *Facing Judicial Discretion*. Legal Knowledge and Right Answers Revisited. 2001 ISBN 0-7923-6778-2
50. M. Kiikeri: *Comparative Legal Reasoning and European Law*. 2001 ISBN 0-7923-6884-3
51. A.J. Menéndez: *Justifying Taxes*. Some Elements for a General Theory of Democratic Tax Law. 2001 ISBN 0-7923-7052-X
52. W.E. Conklin: *The Invisible Origins of Legal Positivism*. A Re-Reading of a Tradition. 2001 ISBN 0-7923-7101-1
53. Z. Bańkowski: *Living Lawfully*. Love in Law and Law in Love. 2001 ISBN 0-7923-7180-1
54. A.N. Shytov: *Conscience and Love in Making Judicial Decisions*. 2001 ISBN 1-4020-0168-1
55. D.W.P. Ruiter: *Legal Institutions*. 2001 ISBN 1-4020-0186-X

Volumes 1–55 were published by Kluwer Academic Publishers.

56. G. den Hartogh: *Mutual Expectations*. A Conventionalist Theory of Law. 2002 ISBN 90-411-1796-2
57. W.L. Robison (ed.): *The Legal Essays of Michael Bayles*. 2002 ISBN 90-411-1835-7
58. U. Bindreiter: *Why Grundnorm?* A Treatise on the Implications of Kelsen's Doctrine. 2002 ISBN 90-411-1867-5
59. S. Urbina: *Legal Method and the Rule of Law*. 2002 ISBN 90-411-1870-5
60. M. Baurmann: *The Market of Virtue*. Morality and Commitment in a Liberal Society. 2002 ISBN 90-411-1874-8

KLUWER LAW INTERNATIONAL – THE HAGUE / LONDON / NEW YORK